PROFESSORS ON THE PARASHAH

STUDIES ON THE WEEKLY TORAH READING

PROFESSORS
ON THE
PARASHAH

STUDIES ON THE WEEKLY TORAH READING

Edited by Leib Moscovitz

Bar-Ilan University

URIM PUBLICATIONS
Jerusalem • New York

Professors on the Parashah: Studies on the Weekly Torah Reading
Edited by Leib Moscovitz
Copyright © 2005 by Bar-Ilan University, Ramat-Gan

Professors on the Parasha is volume 3 in a series. The first two volumes were published by Bar-Ilan University as *A Divinely Given Torah in Our Day and Age,* Vol. 1 (1998), edited by Joshua Schwartz, and *A Divinely Given Torah in Our Day and Age,* Vol. 2 (2002), edited by Aryeh A. Frimer.

Urim Publications, P.O. Box 52287, Jerusalem 91521 Israel

Bar-Ilan University
Ramat Gan, Israel 52900
www.biu.ac.il

Lambda Publishers Inc.
3709 13th Avenue Brooklyn, New York 11218 U.S.A.
Tel: 718-972-5449 Fax: 718-972-6307 mh@ejudaica.com

www.UrimPublications.com

ACKNOWLEDGEMENTS

The Bar-Ilan *Parashat Ha-Shavua* series is a joint project of Bar-Ilan's Faculty of Jewish Studies, the Paul and Helene Shulman Center for Basic Jewish Studies, and the Office of the Campus Rabbi. Our sincere thanks are due to the many colleagues whose devoted efforts ensure the regular Internet posting of the *Parashat Ha-Shavua* studies from which this collection is drawn.

We are particularly grateful to various people who have played a key role in helping make this volume a reality: the President of Bar-Ilan University, Prof. Moshe Kaveh, who initiated publication of this volume; Prof. Joshua Schwartz, Dean of the Faculty of Jewish Studies, for his unceasing assistance and encouragement, Mr. Yitzchak Kerner, Director of the Faculty, who has supported the *Parashat Ha-Shavua* Series from its inception, and Prof. Daniel Sperber, for his encouragement of the series from the outset; Rabbi Shlomo Sheffer, the Campus Rabbi; Dr. Meir Raffeld, Director of the Paul and Helene Shulman Center for Basic Jewish Studies, and his assistant administrator, Mr. Naftali Stern; Dr. Isaac B. Gottlieb and Rachel Hacohen, the English and Hebrew editors of the *Parashat Ha-Shavua* Studies, respectively; Rachel Rowen, translator; Dr. Shlomo Sela of the Computer Center; Mr. David Weinberg of Beyad Halashon Advocacy & Communications, for his help and support in producing this volume; and Tzvi Mauer of Urim Publications, for his devoted and professional work in publishing this book.

Our profound thanks to them all.

CONTENTS

Sefer Bereshit – The Book of Genesis

Sefer Vayikra – The Book of Leviticus

Sefer Devarim – The Book of Deuteronomy

Preface by the President of Bar-Ilan University

THIS UNIQUE VOLUME of collected Torah studies is a sterling example of Bar-Ilan University scholarship at its best. Combining extensive knowledge of Torah and traditional Jewish sources with excellence in the sciences and humanities, Bar-Ilan University faculty strive to synthesize the sacred and the material, the spiritual and the scientific. Their studies on the Torah, distributed weekly by the University to thousands of readers from Israel and throughout the world, constitute a singular product of scholarship and faith. Indeed, Bar-Ilan University is the premier house of Torah scholarship in the modern age.

This year Bar-Ilan University celebrates its jubilee. The University's importance to the State of Israel and to the entire Jewish people is greater now than ever before. In these times of strife and division, Bar-Ilan presents a rare model of cooperation and mutual respect between religious and nonreligious Jews, of aspiration for academic excellence and true quest for Jewish identity in the modern world.

Evidently, our message is being embraced by increasing numbers of Israelis. During the past decade Bar-Ilan University has doubled the size of its campus and its student body, and it is now the largest institution of higher education in Israel. The University's 75,000 alumni are the best proof of the importance of our unique combination of religious tradition with scholarship and progress.

The studies on which the present volume is based have been issued regularly for more than a decade, a laudable initiative of the Faculty of Jewish Studies and the Office of the Campus Rabbi under the auspices of the Shulman Center for Basic Jewish Studies. I thank our friends Paul and Helene Shulman of Luxembourg and Israel for their ongoing support for the work of the Center. I also thank Tzvi Mauer of Urim Publications for his wise counsel and cooperation in publication of this volume.

As President, I have been honored to support these undertakings through the President's Fund for Torah and Science.

I salute Prof. Leib Moscovitz of the Department of Talmud, who edited this collection, his colleagues on the editorial board, and all the faculty who contributed essays to this collection.

May this volume engender intensified Torah study for Jews everywhere.

Prof. Moshe Kaveh

Sefer Bereshit – The Book of Genesis

FAITH AND SCIENCE IN THE THIRD MILLENNIUM

Prof. Moshe Kaveh

President, Bar-Ilan University

Director, Resnick Institute for Advanced Technology in Physics

JUDAISM IS THE WORLD'S most ancient monotheistic religion. The development of monotheism was the greatest ideological revolution that the world has ever known. The transition from paganism to belief in a God "who is incorporeal and has no bodily form" was more revolutionary than the transition from classical to modern physics. God cannot be defined in terms of human reality, and therefore He stands above science, which describes the laws that govern reality. According to this approach, there cannot be a contradiction between science and belief in God, for science only describes physical reality, and therefore cannot describe God.

In addition, Judaism introduced two principles into the tenets of religion: God is the Creator of the Universe, and God extends His providence over the world. These principles were subsequently adopted by Christianity and Islam.

These two assumptions, which give God the specific functions of Creator and Sustainer of the world, were strongly attacked during the classical era of science in the eighteenth and nineteenth centuries, but they withstood these attacks and received further support in the twentieth century. What can we learn from the conflicts between science and religion?

If we define the laws of science as expressing the "will of God," there can be no contradiction between science and religion. Even though the laws of nature belong to the realm of science, every natural law that is confirmed by scientific criteria must be accepted by religion as a divine law coming from the Creator of the universe. Despite this, religious figures throughout the generations have been unwilling to accept certain laws of nature, as we shall see below. On the other hand, from time to time scientists have attacked religion, even though such contradictions cannot exist according to the fundamental assumptions of each discipline. Although the conceptual separation of science from religion should have led to co-existence between the two, history has proven their relationship to be far more complex.

Before moving on to the twentieth century, let us review the great conflicts between religion and science in previous centuries. Before the seventeenth century, aside from the two fundamental religious principles noted above, it was generally believed, particularly among Christian clerics, that man stood at the center of Creation. This approach placed the Earth in the center of the universe, and dictated that all the stars and planets revolve around it. Along came Copernicus, Kepler and Galileo, who stated that all the planets, including Earth, revolve around the sun.

Instead of accepting this scientific assertion as a new understanding of the laws of nature and an expression of the will of God, the Church viewed this approach as heretical. Because of the Church's hegemony, Galileo was imprisoned. Without doubt, this was the low point in the Church's confrontation with science. It was not until the end of the twentieth century that the Pope proclaimed the Church's desire to ask forgiveness of Galileo. Today every child knows that man is not at the center of the universe, nor is this an article of faith in any religion.

Let us consider the opposite case, in which science sought to dictate to religion. In the seventeenth century, when Newton calculated the orbits of the planets around the sun, it was not clear why the solar system should be stable. Most remarkably, Newton's answer was that "God watches the system" so that it remains stable.

Such an answer could only have been given by a scientist who believed that science had reached the "ultimate theory" and that the role of God was to fill in the gaps. This is undoubtedly a confusion of science and religion. Indeed, such a suggestion is surprising coming from a person of the caliber of Isaac Newton, who was considered the greatest scientist of the seventeenth century and one of the great scientists of all time.

What happens when a scientist believes he has attained the ultimate theory and that, unlike Newton, the gaps need not be filled in? This is precisely what happened to the great scientist Laplace. In the early nineteenth century, Laplace succeeded in applying Newton's law of universal gravitation to describe the orbits of the planets as mathematical equations. When Laplace showed his theory to Napoleon, the latter asked him, "Where is God in your equations?" To this Laplace gave the haughty answer for which he is famous: "There is no need for God in my equations."

Laplace lived in what is considered the century of determinism, when scientists attempted to deny the two fundamental tenets of monotheistic religion. The idea that the universe has a Creator underwent difficult times. Clearly, in the case of Laplace, one could argue that God created the world according to Laplace's equations, which describe the planetary orbits as we observe them. The difficulty lay in how to reconcile scientific determinism, which held that the laws of science unequivocally determine the future, with the belief that God intervenes in the world and can change the future. Many leaders of the world's three monotheistic religions maintained that one cannot adopt natural laws that contradict the tenets of faith, such as divine providence and free choice.

Furthermore, Judaism adopted the notion of Creation as a religious tenet, as expressed in the first verse of the Torah: "In the beginning God created heaven and earth." In the nineteenth century the universe was perceived as infinite, fixed and unchanging, and the notion of Creation, especially *ex nihilo*, seemed scientifically impossible. Most of the nineteenth-century attempts to reconcile these contradictions satisfied neither the philosophers nor the scientists nor the clergy.

Towards the mid-nineteenth century Charles Darwin developed his theory of evolution that weak animals become extinct and that strong ones survive through a process of natural selection. According to this theory, human origins go back to an evolutionary process taking billions of years, from the microbe through man. This theory evoked a direct attack from all religions. Not a single religion was willing to claim that these were divine laws. In other words, a situation emerged in which laws of nature required approval by the clergy.

Apparently, religious leaders also learned a lesson, for when in the twentieth century Penzias and Wilson showed that the universe was created in a Big Bang, they accepted this as proof of the biblical assertion that "In the beginning God created heaven and earth," i.e., that one could equate the Big Bang with God's laws and that the Big Bang equals Creation.

Despite the aggressive stand that science took towards religion in the nineteenth century, religion survived that period to witness the scientific revolution of the twentieth century, which proved once more (for whoever still needed such proof) that we are very far from having reached the ultimate scientific theory. The twentieth century appears to have made both camps somewhat more tolerant, as attested by the number of endowed chairs and centers for the study of religion and science in universities throughout the world. The twentieth century is characterized by greater humility than the classical science of previous centuries, which viewed itself as omnipotent and capable of predicting everything. Some religious leaders even claimed that science in the twentieth century had "repented" and returned to religious belief. Two surprising laws in our time took science from the level of the "divine" to that of the human.

According to the notions of modern physics, nothing is absolute and everything except the velocity of light, even time, is relative! This is Einstein's theory of relativity. Second, quantum theory holds that nothing is certain. The fundamental law is Heisenberg's uncertainty principle, which states that the location and the velocity of a particle cannot be predicted simultaneously.

These two theories are not intuitive, and the world they describe is not what we see or feel! The transition from a world of determinism to a world of probability, governed by quantum theory, actually elicited the unflattering remark from the greatest scientist of all time, Einstein, who said of probability: "God does not play dice with the universe."

If all this were not enough, "the messianic era" had almost arrived when science discovered Creation. The twentieth century came close to acknowledging that the universe had been created by the Big Bang – that moment when the universe was born. Since space and time are linked according to Einstein, the beginning of the universe geometrically also marks the beginning of the universe temporally. Before the existence of the universe, time did not exist. In other words, what we have here is creation *ex nihilo*. The creation of the universe, according to the theory of relativity, is also the creation of time. Thus *bereshit*, "in the beginning" of time, is a most accurate description for the inception of the universe.

The most brazen remark of the twentieth century belongs to Stephen Hawking of Cambridge University, who maintained in his book, *A Brief History of Time: From the Big Bang to Black Holes*, that if time did not exist before the Big Bang, there could be no cause for the creation of the universe, because nothing existed before the Creation. Therefore he asked, "Where is there a place for a Creator of the Universe?" This remark calls to mind the haughty words of Laplace in the nineteenth century. Science now recognized Creation yet still had its doubts whether God was its cause.

Clearly, if we ascribe to God characteristics which belong to the world of reality embodied by our universe, then these characteristics did not exist before the Big Bang, because then there did not exist any reality as we know it according to the laws of nature. But there is no such problem in Judaism, which defines God as abstract – He is not only "incorporeal," He even "has no bodily form." The notion of space cannot be ascribed to such a being, and therefore neither can time. God's Hebrew name attests that He "was," "is," and "will be," as we say in the liturgical poem, *Adon Olam*. In other words, He is independent of the notion of time.

In similar fashion, Maimonides explains the paradox between "God's knowledge," which covers the past, present, and future, and the idea of free choice. Therefore, God in Judaism is not tied to physical existence, the absence of which before the Big Bang or the presence of which thereafter could change the fact of His being. This is attested by the words of the wonderful poem, *Yigdal*: "Primal to all that was created / First, with no beginning to His beginning."

What has the present century to say about the idea of man having been created and there being a "God who extends His providence over him"? Our new understanding of creation has not solved the problem of faith. Science will never be able to prove religious tenets, and likewise religious tenets must not negate the laws of science.

Even though there is consensus among scientists that the world was created, there is still controversy over who created the world. The natural religious response is that God created the world. But there are scientists who maintain that one need not come to this conclusion, but that the world could have created itself spontaneously (by quantum fluctuations, for example).

Steven Weinberg, Nobel Laureate in physics, made the following atheistic statement: "The universe seems pointless." According to such a view, there is no divine providence. Weinberg's view is based on the uncertainty of the end of the universe. If gravitational forces turn out to be sufficiently strong to halt the expansion of the universe, then at some time in the future the universe will collapse to a geometric point! If gravitational forces turn out not to be strong enough, then the universe will continue to expand forever and will die for lack of "nuclear fuel," e.g., the sun and all the stars that provide light as a result of thermonuclear reactions will cease to do so in another few billion years. According to this theory, we will reach a universe that has burned up all its energy, a "dead universe." This is the pessimistic view of the future.

In contrast to this approach, there is an optimistic view that is known as the anthropic principle, from the Greek *anthropos*, meaning "man." According to this approach, the laws of the universe were established for the benefit and well-being of mankind: truly divine providence. This view maintains that the creation of man was accompanied by so many rare occurrences of such low probability that man could only have been created by miracle. The key remark is that of Freeman Dyson, who said, "It appears that the universe knew we were coming." In other words, the universe was planned in such a way as to make the creation of man possible.

According to the anthropic principle,[1] if the slightest changes had occurred in the parameters of the laws of the universe, such as the nuclear force or the gravitational force, or the radius of Earth's orbit around the

---

[1] Several articles and books have recently appeared on the anthropic principle, e.g., J. D. Barrow and F. J. Tipler, *The Anthropic Cosmological Principle* (Oxford 1986); C. Domb, "Religion and Science" (preprint); N. Aviezer, *BDD* 5; S. J. Gould, *Wonderful Life* (New York 1989).

sun, or in the chain of events that preceded the creation of man, such as the force of impact of the meteor which struck Earth (causing dinosaurs, but not mammals, to perish), a universe with human life would not have been possible. As the famous physicist Sir Fred Hoyle put it, "The universe was planned in a very intelligent way."

One of the surprising things about the anthropic principle is that scientists are now trying to predict new laws that will be consonant with this principle, namely laws of nature that make human existence possible. In 1990 Fred Hoyle hypothesized that the carbon nucleus must have an energy level of 7.7 million electron volts, for otherwise human life (which is made of carbon chains) would not have come about on earth.[2] Following Hoyle's hypothesis based on the anthropic principle, it was indeed experimentally shown that the nucleus of the carbon atom has precisely this energy level, known as the "resonance energy of carbon." Richard Feynman, Nobel Laureate and one of the greatest physicists of the twentieth century, remarked on this finding, "If one can make such successful predictions, it is a sign we are beginning to understand the universe."

Clearly the anthropic principle buttresses the religious approach that believes in divine providence. Opposing this is the atheistic approach, which maintains that an almost infinite number of universes may have been created, but none of them, save for ours, was able to survive. Not only does such a thesis come closer to mysticism than to science, its shortcoming lies in requiring almost infinite energy in order to create a single successful universe. The atheistic approach must go to all this effort simply to avoid acknowledging that there is a Creator who planned the most successful universe from the outset. Moreover, if we accept the approach that numerous universes were created, that does not negate the existence of a God who created them. This idea, incidentally, is reminiscent of the well-known midrashic statement that God created many worlds and destroyed them until He finally created our world.

The anthropic principle has been accepted by a large part of the scientific and clerical communities of the world, which points to the

---

[2] Cf. his research on nuclear reactions in very high temperature stars.

amazing affinity between religion and science, the former using the term "divine providence," and the latter speaking of the "anthropic principle." In this sense we can say that today numerous scientists either consciously or unconsciously accept the notion of "divine providence."

In conclusion, we see that the Jewish religion has entered the third millennium stronger than ever. Without doubt, we have reason to be proud. Scientific theories have come and gone, civilizations have arisen and fallen, views of the world have changed, but the Jewish faith has stood strong, ready to face the challenges ahead.

In every generation science will undoubtedly continue to seek the "ultimate theory." Since the laws of nature are expressions of the will of God, it is the role of scientists to try to discover them. These laws will also give invaluable depth to religious thought, as Maimonides wrote: "Knowledge of the divine cannot be attained except after [mastery of] the science of nature." In other words, understanding the laws of nature can lead to knowledge of God.

The converse is also the case; in the third millennium, science will need religion more than ever. The discovery of the genetic code, genetic engineering, cloning and the possibility of understanding the beginning and end of life have all raised moral questions, causing science to become overly haughty and consequently want to "play God." In this millennium, religion will have a major role to play in maintaining the delicate balance between the "omnipotence" and the morality of science.

Parashat Noah

SCIENCE AND THE FLOOD

Prof. Moshe Kaveh

President, Bar-Ilan University

Director, Resnick Institute for Advanced Technology in Physics

THE STORY OF THE FLOOD in *Parashat Noah* is one of the most dramatic in the annals of man. The massive destruction and calculated deliverance described in this narrative have sparked the imagination of novelists, poets and humanists, making the story of the flood and its hero, Noah, the most recounted story in human society throughout history.

Two hundred and seventeen cultures around the world have a flood story.[1] Many studies document stories of the flood in the region of Mesopotamia, including stories written on stone or papyrus.[2]

From the documents that have been recorded and survived, we see that in most of the stories the dove heralds the end of the flood, appearing with an olive branch in its mouth, which was eventually adopted universally as the symbol of peace.

For over a century the flood has also been the object of scientific research, including recent studies by scientists at the world's leading universities. These studies examine the flood in terms of chronology, geology and oceanography, biology and zoology, archaeology, as well as philosophy and theology. Thus we see that interest in the flood is not confined to esoteric fields; rather it encompasses a broad spectrum of

---

[1] See C. Sellier and D. Balsinger, *In Search of Noah's Ark* (Los Angeles 1976).

[2] Cf., for example, the documentation in W. G. Lambert and A. R. Millard, *Atra-hasis: The Babylonian Story of the Flood* (Oxford 1969).

disciplines. Everything, it turns out, can be a topic for research, even whether the zebra was on the second level of Noah's ark, next to the lions, or on the third level, next to the bears.

The Flood Waters

Generations of scientists have sought an explanation of the source of the vast quantity of water in the flood. Some have argued that the water resulted from subterranean volcanic shifting, and others believe that gases covered the earth's surface and turned into droplets of water. According to the latter theory, which today is considered more of a curiosity than a scientific claim, the gases blocked the ultraviolet radiation, causing Noah to live nine hundred years. Scholars today generally accept the hypothesis that most of the water came from glaciers melting. Both cite the Bible in support of water flowing from above and from below: "All the fountains of the great deep burst apart, and the floodgates of the sky broke open" (Gen. 7:11).

Early studies dated the flood to around 5,600 B.C.E., and a British archaeologist by the name of Leonard Wooley dated the flood to 2,800 B.C.E. Recently Gene Faulstich, from the Iowa Research Institute, proved the exact date of the flood to have been 2,345 B.C.E. Using methods from astronomy, he dated the onset of the flood precisely to the 14th of May in that year. The Sages also dealt with the timing of the flood. Rabbi Joshua said that it took place in the month of Iyyar (approximately May; see *Sanhedrin* 108a); thus Faulstich's findings match rabbinic teaching.

Noah's Ark

Attempts to find Noah's ark have almost become an obsession for more than a century. In 1887 two Persian princes reported that they had seen Noah's ark on one of the mountains of Ararat, and in 1916 two Russian pilots claimed to have seen it from the air. Since then dozens of similar reports have been published.[3] Since 2000, in the wake of the findings mentioned above, the flood has become accepted as definite scientific fact.

---

[3] See Bruce Feiler, *Walking the Bible* (New York 2001).

It should be noted that none of the expeditions in search of the ark on the mountains of Ararat have come up with anything. Recently it was suggested to use satellite imaging from outer space to locate the ark. There is currently a plan to send up a photo satellite, Okono 2, which is capable of photographing objects as small as one square meter, which researchers hope to use to discover the remains of Noah's ark.

Life in Noah's Ark

Finding Noah's ark is a fascinating archaeological challenge. But short of actually discovering the ark itself, the idea of the ark has aroused the curiosity of zoologists and biologists. They consider the ark the largest biological laboratory in the history of the universe. According to the Torah, Noah's ark was 300 cubits long, 50 cubits wide, and 30 cubits high. That makes it about half as large as the Titanic. One of the most widely researched questions is how the ark could have contained some two million kinds of animals. John Whitcomb surmises that Noah's ark hosted 3,700 mammals, 8,600 birds, and 6,300 reptiles, and in view of the size of the ark there was room for them all.

Another related question is how these animals were fed. How much food did Noah have to load on his ark in order to support all the living things in it? The question of garbage disposal has also been researched. According to zoologists from San Diego University, the animals in the ark must have produced about 800 tons of refuse. The stimulation for all this research is provided by this week's Torah reading.

The Scope of the Flood

Now we get to the motivation for writing this article, namely, the amazing recent story, announced by the world press, that "decisive proof of the flood" had been discovered. The plain text of the biblical narrative gives the clear impression that the flood encompassed the entire world: "All existence on earth was blotted out – man, cattle, creeping things, and birds of the sky; they were blotted out from the earth. Only Noah was left and those with him in the ark" (Gen. 7:23). However, scientific computations show that there is not enough water to cover the entire earth to the height of Mount Ararat. Moreover, there is no tradition of a flood story in the ancient civilizations of the Far East. Chinese civilization, which is well documented as far back as 7,000 years ago, makes no mention of any event resembling a flood. In the Ancient Near East, however, there are numerous flood stories, such as the Gilgamesh Epic from Mesopotamia.

Views of the flood as local in scope go back to the time of the Sages. According to R. Yohanan (*Zevahim* 113b), the torrential rains did not fall on the Land of Israel. Likewise, Rabbi Baruch Epstein writes in his *Torah Temimah*: "Regarding Babylonia receiving more rain than any other country in the world and being drowned by the flood, it should be noted that according to Tractate *Zevahim*, ibid., Babylon was called Shinar because all the creatures that perished in the flood were tossed (Heb. *nin'aru*) there. It is a deep valley, and therefore is also called *metzulah* ('the deep')." In the mind of the Sages, Babylonia constituted the entire world. This is evident in *Pirkei de-Rabbi Eliezer* (ed. Horev, ch. 10, s.v. *be-shishi*): "All the creatures lived in one place, and were afraid of the waters of the flood, with Nimrod as king over them, as it is written: 'The beginning of his kingdom was Babylon'" (Gen. 10:10).

Noah's Flood: The New Scientific Discoveries About the Event that Changed History (New York 1999), a book by geologists Dr. William Ryan and Dr. Walter Pitman from Columbia University, suggests a fascinating theory based on research indicating that Noah's flood was a local event that occurred after European icebergs began to melt towards the end of the Ice Age. The floods that resulted from this melting turned a fresh-water lake into a sea – the Black Sea. A study published in 1993 suggested that a local body of fresh water was flooded by salt water. The Bosphorus blocked the water from flowing out, but gradually a channel was formed, and about ninety days later the water broke through with great force. Analysis of various shells from the area indicates the existence of a subterranean division line that was formed thousands of years ago. Ryan and Pitman's study also showed that the melting of icebergs caused the level of the Mediterranean Sea to rise and water to flow through the Bosphorus Straits. Scientists calculated that water flowed through the Bosphorus so fast that the size of the lake increased at the rate of one and a half square kilometers a day.

Amazing Recent Discoveries by Robert Ballard

An expedition called Black Horizon set out in the year 2000 under the leadership of the well-known oceanographer Robert Ballard (famed for his discovery of the Titanic) to substantiate the above-mentioned flood theory based on remains of findings from the bottom of the Black Sea. About 20 kilometers offshore from Turkey, near the city of Sinop, the expedition discovered a well-preserved structure that was thousands of years old. This finding adds greatly to our knowledge about life in the ancient civilizations of this part of the world. It appears that from time to time the ancient dwellers of this area had to relocate due to floods.

An article in *National Geographic* describes the operations of a submarine robot that was lowered into the sea to photograph the area. The photos reveal a rectangular area, approximately 15 meters long and 4 meters wide, into which a structure of wood and mortar had apparently collapsed. The findings from this site – carved wooden pillars, tree branches and stone vessels – are well-preserved. There is broad consensus among scientists that this study, publicized worldwide in the press, is conclusive proof of the historicity of the flood.

The Flood in Rabbinic Literature

The comments of the Sages in the midrash did not focus on the physical aspects of the Deluge, but on its moral and religious repercussions. They did not think that Noah's deliverance from the flood bore religious meaning for later generations. The Sages thought that one should not declare a day of rejoicing in honor of Noah's having been saved when so many other lives were lost. But the covenant made between God and Noah at the cessation of the Flood was preserved for all time by the Sages in the benediction they formulated, "Blessed art Thou...who remembers the covenant," which is recited whenever one sees a rainbow after a storm.

Rather, the Sages thought we can learn important lessons from the causes of the Flood. In *Parashat Noah* (Gen. 6:11) we read: "The earth became corrupt before God; the earth was filled with lawlessness." The virtues necessary to maintain a proper society had been destroyed, and corruption and lawlessness reigned. Such a society was not worthy in God's eyes: "And the Lord regretted that He had made man on earth, and His heart was saddened" (Gen. 6:6). The sadness felt by God at having to drown the work of His hands did not give rise to a day of rejoicing, but to an everlasting covenant between Him and man. Even though "the devisings of man's mind are evil from his youth," God promised never again to destroy all His creatures.

The very rainbow that forms in the sunlight after a rainstorm reminds human beings that God remembers the covenant (as indicated by the formulation of the blessing, "Who remembers the covenant"). Moreover, the rainbow symbolizes both division into the various colors of the spectrum and the unity of the great light. Human beings, diverse as they are, must lead their lives as creatures made "in the image of God" (Gen. 9:6).

Parashat Lekh Lekha

"O That Ishmael Might Live by Your Favor!"

Dr. Yair Barkai
Jerusalem

Towards the end of this week's highly eventful reading God reveals Himself to Abraham once again, reinforcing the covenant between them. God informs Abraham that he is destined to become "the father of a multitude of nations," changes his name, reiterates the promises of progeny and inheriting the land, and commands Abraham to circumcise himself, his entire household and all his servants, home-born as well as those purchased from outsiders. Abraham does not respond to God's words, accepting them with silent consent.

In the second part of the revelation, God announces that Sarai's name is to be changed to Sarah, and adds: "I will bless her; indeed, I will give you a son by her. I will bless her so that she shall give rise to nations; rulers of peoples shall issue from her" (Gen. 17:16). Abraham threw himself on his face and laughed, and said to himself, "Can a child be born to a man a hundred years old, or can Sarah bear a child at ninety?" (17:17). And Abraham said to God, "O that Ishmael might live by Your favor!" (17:18).

Prima facie, the second part of Abraham's response is peculiar. When God brings him tidings of something that he has been longing for ever since his departure from Haran fourteen years before and Abraham responds with an embarrassed laugh, this is perfectly natural. But what was the meaning of Abraham's request to God about Ishmael? Did Sarah's giving birth to a son depend on whether Ishmael would live or die? Couldn't the two sons live together?

The commentators, who differ about this question, fall into two main groups. The first group holds that Abraham was indeed afraid that the tidings of Isaac's birth might presage the death of Ishmael. The second group, however, takes Abraham's response as an expression of modesty: "God, You have given me enough!"

Rashi writes: "If only *(hallevai)* Ishmael would live, although I am not worthy of such a reward." Thus, Rashi seems to adopt both of the above-mentioned interpretations: Abraham indeed feared Ishmael's imminent death, and out of his great sense of modesty, he did not feel worthy of another son after God had given him one son at Sarah's request.

Nahmanides seems to take a slightly different tack:

> Abraham said that if Ishmael lived, [Abraham] would want the blessing that God had just given him – having offspring through Sarah – since he had been promised at the outset that "none but your very own issue [in the singular] shall be your heir" (Gen. 15:4). This suggests that he would have only one heir. Abraham thought that that heir was Ishmael, but now that he had been told that Sarah would have a child and that this child would be his heir, he was afraid that Ishmael might die.

According to Nahmanides, Abraham's fears for Ishmael's life were genuine.

Abarbanel's interpretation is similar:

> When [Abraham] saw that God had destined him to have another son, and that this would happen through a miracle rather than by natural means, and, knowing that God does not perform miracles except in dire necessity, he concluded that this meant one of two things. Either the Holy One, blessed be He, knew that Ishmael would soon die and hence He was preparing another son in his place, or if he were not destined to die, it was not God's will that the covenant should be continued through him, with its promise of the land, closeness to God, and all the accompanying benefits; therefore He would give him another son to receive all of this.

Consequently Abraham took courage and said to God, "O that Ishmael might live by Your favor," as a query and request, as if to say: If only I knew whether Ishmael will live or is destined to die soon, which could be proven by Sarah having a son.

Abarbanel goes beyond Nahmanides in mentioning the issue of a miracle. Since Isaac's birth involved a miracle, and since God had already fulfilled His promise to give Abraham offspring, Abraham thought that God would not perform a miracle unnecessarily, and hence Ishmael was presumably likely to die soon. (Malbim, who often follows Abarbanel, interprets the text similarly.)

Yehuda Kiel, author of the *Da'at Mikra* commentary on Genesis, takes the same line: "'That he might live' and not die...and the blessings that his mother received would be fulfilled through him."

Another point is made in *Da'at Mikra*: God had promised Hagar that Ishmael would be fruitful and multiply, so how would these blessings be fulfilled if Ishmael were destined to die soon? It seems as if Abraham was reminding God of His blessings to Ishmael, and was requesting that these blessings keep Ishmael alive even after the birth of Isaac.

As indicated above, one group of commentators attributes Abraham's response to his great modesty, not to his fear that Ishmael might die. This idea finds expression in as early a text as *Genesis Rabbah* 47.3:

> Rabbi Judah said in the name of Rabbi Judan: [It is like] the king's favorite, who received an annual allowance. The king said to him, "I would like to double your allowance," and he answered, "Do not fill me with cold, refreshing water; rather, would that you not terminate what you have been giving me." Thus, "O that Ishmael might live."

This parable emphasizes the humble attitude of the king's favorite, who does not think himself worthy of the king's generosity. Yet it also conveys to the reader the sense of doubt and insecurity felt by the favored one, lest the increase lead to cancellation of the original allowance, a feeling that if one is too greedy, one loses everything; hence it is better to settle for a small amount that is secure than to place one's hopes on a large but doubtful bounty.

Thus the Midrash, like Rashi's commentary with which we began, reflects the combination of the two approaches adopted by commentators.

R. Joseph Bekhor Shor (12th century, France), writes: "It would have sufficed for me if Ishmael alone were to live...The Holy One, blessed be He, said to him: Both of them shall live, for Isaac will be born and Ishmael will live." Clearly, Bekhor Shor sees Abraham's response as a polite figure of speech: One son was enough for me, and now you offer me a second! "O that Ishmael might live by Your favor!" bears not the slightest implication that Ishmael might die.

Radak (Provence, 1160–1235) writes:

> In other words: What you have given me – Ishmael – is quite enough, for I am not worthy of this great kindness that you propose to give me. What You have given me suffices – that he may live – meaning a good life of blessing and fruitfulness...and through him may You fulfill what You said to me: "I will assign this land to your offspring" (12:7), for Ishmael is my offspring.

Radak, like Bekhor Shor, emphasizes Abraham's humility, yet his interpretation also reflects Abraham's fear regarding Ishmael's future.

In any event, it is clear that Abraham was concerned for Ishmael. Abraham's concern for Ishmael also finds expression further on, in chapter 21, where we read of the expulsion of Hagar and Ishmael and Abraham's response: "The matter distressed Abraham greatly, for it concerned a son of his" (Gen. 21:11).

Abraham acted on Hagar's request only after God intervened: "But God said to Abraham, 'Do not be distressed over the boy or your slave; whatever Sarah tells you, do as she says, for it is through Isaac that offspring shall be continued for you. As for the son of the slave-woman, I will make a nation of him, too, for he is your seed'" (Gen. 21:12–13). This time, too, Abraham's mind was not set at ease until God explicitly promised to fulfill the blessing about Ishmael, although here the Torah emphasizes that these blessings would be fulfilled because Ishmael was Abraham's son.

The Midrash (*Pirkei de-Rabbi Eliezer*, ch. 30, and cf. *Midrash ha-Gadol* on *Parashat Vayera*) stresses Abraham's compassion towards Ishmael. There we read that after having received Sarah's consent, Abraham went off twice to the Paran Desert to visit his son Ishmael. The first time Abraham found a woman in Ishmael's tent whose conduct did not reflect the hospitality that Ishmael had been taught to give in his father's home, and Abraham indicated his displeasure at this. On his second visit Abraham found another woman who received him graciously, and through her he indicated his pleasure and satisfaction.

The Midrash concludes with the lesson that Ishmael learned from his father's visits: "Ishmael knew that his father felt mercifully towards him." Abraham's great concern for his son Ishmael indeed bore fruit; for according to the Sages, Ishmael eventually repented,[1] and Abraham was rewarded by having both of his sons bury him when he died: "His sons Isaac and Ishmael buried him in the cave of Machpelah" (25:9). Likewise, Isaac maintained close relations with Ishmael throughout his life.

---

[1] Cf. *Megillah* 14a, *Bava Batra* 16b, and Rashi on Gen. 25:17.

Parashat Vayera

WHAT DID SARAH SEE?

Yonah Bar-Maoz
Department of Bible

"AND SARAH SAW THE SON whom Hagar the Egyptian had borne to Abraham making sport [*metzahek*]" (Gen. 21:9). This verse is the Torah's explanation of why Sarah demanded that Abraham banish Ishmael. However, Sarah's own words suggest another reason: "For the son of this slave woman shall not share in the inheritance with my son Isaac" (v. 10). In the Tosefta (*Sotah* 6:6) we find tannaitic disputes about this:

> R. Simeon b. Yohai said: R. Akiva used to offer four explanations, and mine follows from his. R. Akiva said that the "playing" or "making sport" refers to idolatry, as in "The people sat down to eat and to drink, and rose up to *make merry* [*letzahek*]" (Ex. 32:6). From this we learn that Sarah saw Ishmael building altars, hunting grasshoppers and offering sacrifices to pagan gods. R. Eliezer, son of R. Jose of Galilee, said the "sport" refers to illicit sexual relations, as in Gen. 39:17, where the same Hebrew verb occurs: "The Hebrew servant, whom you had brought to us, came in to me to *mock* me [*letzahek*]." In other words, Sarah saw Ishmael molesting and assaulting the women. R. Ishmael said "sport" refers to bloodshed, citing II Sam. 2:14–16, where a similar verb occurs: "And Abner said to Joab: Let the young men, I pray you, arise and *play* [*visahaku*] before us...Then they arose and were counted...Each one grasped his opponent's head and thrust his sword into his opponent's side, so they fell down together." From

this we learn that Sarah saw Ishmael taking his bow and arrow and shooting in Isaac's direction, as it is written, "As a madman who casts firebrands, arrows, and death, so is the man that deceives his neighbor" (Prov. 26:18–19).

But I say: Heaven forbid that such a person live in the house of so righteous a man! How could there be idolatry, sexual licentiousness and bloodshed in the home of [Abraham], of whom it is said, "For I have singled him out, that he may instruct his children..." (Gen. 18:19)? Therefore "sport" (*tzehok*) here can only refer to the matter of inheritance. For when Isaac was born to Abraham, everyone rejoiced, saying, "Abraham has a son, who will inherit the world and take a double portion!" So Ishmael laughed to himself, saying, "Do not be silly; I am the firstborn, and I shall take a double portion." Indeed, we may infer this from Sarah's response: "For the son of this slavewoman shall not inherit" (v. 10). My interpretation is more sound than that of R. Akiva.

R. Simeon b. Yohai's view appears closer to the plain sense of the text, since it relies on an explicit remark made by Sarah, in contrast to the other interpretations, which are based on the obscure verb *letzahek* (playing, making sport, etc.), which can be understood in a variety of ways. This approach, however, raises two questions. First, what claim could Ishmael make to the inheritance? It is clear from Genesis 16 that Hagar was and remained Sarah's maidservant. Thus we read: "Abraham said to Sarai, 'Your maid is in your hand; deal with her as you think right'" (v. 6). Hagar acknowledges, "I flee from my mistress Sarai" (v. 8), and in chapter 21, Sarah calls her a "slavewoman" (v. 10). Hence any property that might fall into the hands of Ishmael, the "son of the slavewoman," even by inheritance, belongs to Sarah and ultimately would be Isaac's.

Indeed, *Genesis Rabbah* 45:1 describes Hagar's status as a "usufructuary handmaid," a servant brought into the marriage as part of the dowry. *Ketubbot* 79b states that "the animals born by a usufructuary animal belong to the husband, and the children born by a usufructuary handmaid belong to the wife." If this is the case, it is difficult to understand why Sarah preferred to banish her servants ("cast out that slavewoman," v. 10), thereby setting them free, instead of having them remain subservient to her and leaving their property under her control, by virtue of the law that "whatever a servant acquires is acquired by his master" (*Pesaḥim* 88b).

Second, God's reaction is also difficult to understand: Why did Sarah receive such extensive backing from God, Who gave her *carte blanche* for whatever she wished to do ("Whatever Sarah tells you, do as she says" – Gen. 21:12)? This was a petty dispute over inheritance which could easily have been resolved in any human court according to standard legal practice.

Only the interpretation offered by R. Akiva and the other Sages can resolve these difficulties. Sarah understands that Isaac is endangered, whether spiritually, because of Ishmael's deviation from the way he was educated in Abraham's house, or physically, by a threat on Isaac's life. Both types of danger stem from the great difference in age between Isaac and Ishmael. Abraham was 86 years old when Ishmael was born (Gen. 16:16) and 100 years old when Isaac was born (Gen. 21:5). Thus little Isaac was likely to emulate his older brother, fourteen years his senior, since an older brother is often much admired by the younger brother. However, the age difference can also lead the older brother to feel frustrated, since the older brother had been considered the sole heir of his father's wealth for many years, and suddenly he is displaced by a younger brother whose claim to the inheritance has greater validity, as the son of the chief wife. How tempting it must have been for the older brother, a "wild ass of a man" (16:12) whose "hand shall be against every man, and every man's hand against him," (ibid.) to stage a little mishap for the tender young child!

Close examination of our text shows that Sarah considered Ishmael's connection to Abraham secondary. Ishmael was first and foremost "the son of Hagar." To be sure, "she bore him to Abraham," but she also impressed the culture of Egypt on her child. This culture was the product of the disgraceful behavior of Ham, ancestor of the ancient Egyptians, who knew no respect for his father. It was a culture of illicit sexual practices and bloodshed. The Egyptians had no qualms about stealing a man's wife, and hence the life of a man who had a beautiful wife was always in danger (cf. Gen. 12:10 ff.).

When Sarah addressed Abraham, she stressed the fact that Ishmael belonged to Hagar, "the son of the bondwoman," in contrast to other places where the Torah calls Ishmael the "son of Abraham." Apparently, God agreed with Sarah and severed the tie between Abraham and Ishmael. While Abraham found the entire affair troublesome, "for it concerned a son of his," God said to him, "Do not be distressed over the lad" (Gen. 21:11–12).

But if Sarah's main concern was Isaac's spiritual and physical welfare, why did Sarah dwell on the issue of inheritance? Knowing some of the legal practices current at the time of the patriarchs helps explain why she demanded that Abraham banish them. Articles 170 and 171 of the Code of Hammurabi govern issues of inheritance among brothers born to mothers of different status, mistress and maid. The father's behavior during his lifetime towards sons born to him by a maidservant determined whether or not they would inherit from him. If, during his life, the father treated them as sons in every respect, calling them "my sons," they would inherit equally with the sons of the mistress. If, however, the father did not treat the sons this way, they would not share the inheritance with their brothers, and they would be set free upon the father's death.

Thus, if Sarah wished to keep Isaac away from the pernicious influence of Hagar and Ishmael during Abraham's lifetime, she could not do so by selling them as slaves to some far-away place. Indeed, article 146 of the Code of Hammurabi discusses a case similar to that of Hagar's becoming haughty towards her mistress because she had born her master a son, and there we read that the mistress may not sell the maidservant. We may reasonably assume that this law also applied to the son of the maidservant. Hence Sarah could only eliminate Ishmael by banishing him. But since Abraham had treated Ishmael as his son from the child's birth, banishing him would be tantamount to giving Ishmael a reward: even though Ishmael had not adopted his father's spiritual values, upon his father's death he would be eligible to receive his inheritance, which was in part spiritual, and as a free man his property would not be subject to control by Isaac. However, if Abraham were to banish Ishmael, this would be tantamount to declaring him an illegitimate heir and would indicate his dissatisfaction with Ishmael's actions. This was apparently what led to God's directive, "regarding whatever Sarah says to you, listen to her, for your progeny shall be named in Isaac" (21:12), despite the fact that "As for the son of the slavewoman I will make a nation of him, too, because he is your seed" (Gen. 21:13).

Sarah's forethought prevented violent confrontation between Isaac and Ishmael. Ultimately Ishmael recognized his own spiritual inadequacy and Isaac's superiority. However, he also viewed Isaac as a brother, as we see from the account of their next meeting: "And Abraham expired, dying at a good ripe age, old and contented; and he was gathered to his kin. His sons Isaac and Ishmael buried him" (Gen. 25:8–9). On this *Genesis Rabbah* 62.3 remarks, "Here the son of the bondwoman paid homage to the son of the mistress."

Parashat Vayera

DON'T FEED THE ANGELS

Yonah Bar-Maoz
Department of Bible

WHO WERE THE THREE "men" who visited Abraham? While they are called "men" in chapter 18 – men who eat and drink and perhaps even wash their feet – later it becomes clear beyond a shadow of doubt that these are special beings. They bring tidings of a miraculous event that will take place exactly one year later, and, as if by telepathy, they know that Sarah overheard them and that she laughed, even though she did so at a distance. In chapter 19, even though they are called "angels," the Torah intimates[1] that these are the very same "men" whom we met in chapter 18, but now we become aware of the exceptional behavior of two of these "men." They rescue Lot and his family and destroy Sodom and Gomorrah, confirming our impression that these are not men of flesh and blood, but supernatural beings capable of miraculous deeds.

This raises a problem concerning the beginning of the story: if these "men" were really angels, why were they eating and drinking? This question arises not from a priori notions about the conduct of angels, but from the Bible itself. For in those biblical passages where angels are asked to eat and drink, they vigorously refuse even when their hosts insist; so in the story of Gideon (Judg. 6) and that of Manoah, the father of Samson (Judg. 13). In the latter story the Bible even explains why Manoah was so insistent about

---

[1] See Genesis 18:16: "The men set out from there and looked down toward Sodom. Abraham walked with them to see them off." Immediately after this, Abraham implores God to have mercy on the people of Sodom.

feeding the angel: "For Manoah did not know that he was an angel of the Lord" (Judg. 13:16).

The extraordinary behavior of the angels in Genesis 18 is explained with relative ease by the Midrash:[2] angels can do many miraculous things, including pretending to eat and drink. However, the explanation given by the Midrash did not satisfy later generations, who avoided the figurative language of the Midrash. Thus, Maimonides wrote that "angels are not corporeal, but separate forms,"[3] and elsewhere: "The angels are not bodies...This is also what Aristotle says...These separate intellects are also intermediaries between God...and the existents, and it is through their intermediation that the spheres are set in motion."[4] According to these suggestions, the "speech" of angels might refer to thought, but no sense can be made of claims that angels eat, drink, and wash their feet!

Maimonides, attempting to understand the Torah in light of the philosophical and scientific axioms current in his day, interpreted Genesis 18 in a way that evoked the wrath of other commentators who were less devoted to philosophy than he. Maimonides discussed Genesis 18 in two places. In his *Guide of the Perplexed* (2.42), he interpreted verse 1 as a heading summarizing the contents of the chapter, namely, God's revelation to Abraham, and the rest of the chapter describes the details of this revelation by mention of men-angels:[5]

> For in a vision of prophecy or in a dream of prophecy, the prophet sometimes sees God speaking to him...and sometimes an

---

[2] *Genesis Rabbah*, ch. 48: "R. Tanhuma said in the name of R. Eleazar and R. Avin in the name of R. Meir: The proverb says, 'When in Rome, do as the Romans.' In the upper spheres, where there is no eating, Moses became like them, as it is written: 'I stayed on the mountain forty days and forty nights [eating no bread and drinking no water]' (Deut. 9:9). In the lower realms, where people do eat, it is written: 'He waited on them under the tree as they ate' (Gen. 18:8). But were they really eating? They only appeared to be eating." See also *Bava Metzia* 86b.

[3] Maimonides, *Mishneh Torah, Hilkhot Yesodei ha-Torah* 2.3.

[4] Maimonides, *Guide* 2.6. Elsewhere Maimonides offers other suggestions, but this is not the place to discuss them.

[5] This was also the approach taken by Rashbam: "'The Lord appeared to him' – how so? In the form of three men who were angels." This interpretation is cited by R. Hezekiah ben Manoah.

angel speaking to him; this is quite similar to the story concerning Abraham, which first informs us generally, "And the Lord appeared unto him," and so on, and then it proceeds to explain how this happened.

This interpretation contrasts with Rashi's, who followed another opinion in the Midrash,[6] according to which our chapter contains two revelations. In the first, God revealed Himself to Abraham, and when He saw that Abraham was saddened at not having guests, He sent three angels in the form of men to visit him. In his excitement at receiving guests, Abraham asked God to wait for him: "If it please you, do not go on past your servant" (Gen. 18:3).

Maimonides' objection to viewing the chapter as containing two revelations is rooted both in the philosophical foundation of his approach and in his tendency to interpret the Bible according to its plain sense. According to Maimonides' analysis of prophecy (see *Guide* 2.45), the revelation of God in the daytime, when a person is fully awake, is the very acme of prophecy, for then mental awareness is almost absolute, and the faculties of imagination have no place to create false notions. This supreme level of prophecy was attained only by Moses, and hence his prophecy was superior to that of all the other prophets. Accordingly, he could not interpret our text as indicating that God appeared to Abraham while he was sitting at the entrance of the tent, undoubtedly awake, "as the day grew hot" (i.e., in broad daylight), watching for visitors to arrive. Nor could Maimonides accept an interpretation that presented God as revealing Himself briefly to a human in a revelation that was incomprehensible and lacked purpose and content, immediately after which, in an abrupt and illogical transition, that same person received another revelation (see Maimonides' explanation of transitions from one level of revelation to another in *Guide* 2.41).

Likewise, Maimonides could not accept the midrashic interpretation cited by Rashi that "receiving guests is more important than greeting the

---

[6] Cf. *Bava Metzia* 86b and *Midrash Tehillim* 18.29.

Divine Presence"[7] as an explanation of the plain sense of this verse, even if he was willing to accept its lofty moral message. For this interpretation does not fit the relationship between man and God mandated by the Halakhah. Thus, we read in the Mishnah (*Berakhot* 5.1): "Even if the king greets one [while praying], he may not return the greeting. And even if a snake is curled around his heel, he must not pause." Hence a person must not interrupt the intimate connection between himself and God when he is addressing God, and all the more so when God is addressing him!

The second place where Maimonides treats Genesis 18 is in his discussion of the twelve levels of prophecy. Here Maimonides briefly presented a revolutionary way of understanding our *Parashah* (see *Guide* 2.45): "The tenth degree [of prophecy] consists in the prophet's seeing a man who addresses him in a vision of prophecy, as with Abraham by the terebinths of Mamre, and as with Joshua in Jericho." Claiming that the men spoke with him in a prophetic vision means that the entire story took place in Abraham's prophetic imagination and did not exist in external physical reality.[8]

Nahmanides understood the implications of this interpretation and presented them outspokenly in his commentary on Gen. 18:1:

> The *Guide of the Perplexed* states that this passage is a general statement followed by its details: first Scripture says that God appeared to [Abraham] in a prophetic vision, but how did this vision occur? For he looked up in his vision, and "he saw three men standing near him...he said, 'if it please you...'" (Gen. 18:2–3). This is an account of what [Abraham] said in the prophetic vision to one of them, the senior of them. If what appeared to him in the vision was simply men eating flesh, how could Scripture say "the Lord appeared to him"? For here God did not appear to him either in a vision or in thought, and such things do not occur in any prophecy. According to what [Maimonides] says, Sarah did not knead cakes and Abraham did not prepare a calf, nor did

---

[7] *Shabbat* 127a.

[8] See the definition of a "vision" in *Guide* 2.41.

Sarah laugh, for it was all in a vision. If so, this dream came like most false dreams, and what was the use of showing him all this?...In [Maimonides'] opinion, this need not be said regarding Lot, because the angels did not come into his house and he did not bake for them cakes which they ate; rather, it was all a vision. But if [Maimonides] elevates Lot to the rank of receiving prophetic vision, how could the sinful, evil people of Sodom be prophets? For who told them that men had come to his house? If it was all a prophetic vision of Lot's, then all the passages, "the angels urged Lot on, saying, 'Up, take your wife'" (19:15), "Flee for your life!" (19:17), "Very well, I will grant you this favor too" (19:21), are all a vision, and Lot remained in Sodom...Such things contradict Scripture; they must not be heard, and certainly not believed!

In other words, Maimonides' interpretation flatly rules out the possibility that the angels drank and ate, or that Abraham ran to greet them and feed them. Further, nothing in Abraham's actions suggests that he was dealing with angels. Even when they brought him tidings of a miracle for Sarah, Abraham's behavior towards them did not change. Compare this with the behavior of other biblical heroes who tried to give food to angels, namely, Gideon and Manoah: once it became clear to them that they were dealing with angels, they acted accordingly. For these reasons, too, Maimonides had to claim that all the actions that Abraham performed occurred in a prophetic vision and were not actual events.

Nahmanides flatly rejected Maimonides' resolution of these problems, offering an alternative solution. Regarding the first difficulty he raised – what was the content of God's revelation – Nahmanides responds that we find revelation in the Bible without God's speech, as reward for a *mitzvah*:

This revelation of the Divine Presence to [Abraham] was in tribute to him, as happened with the Tabernacle: "When they came out they blessed the people; and the Presence of God appeared to all the people" (Lev. 9:23): they were rewarded for their endeavors in performing the commandments of the

Tabernacle by seeing the Divine Presence. In neither case is the Divine Presence revealed in order to enjoin them regarding a commandment, or to speak to them. Rather, it is the reward for a commandment that has already been performed, indicating God's approval of their deeds.

Nahmanides resolved the remaining difficulties by positing a new being, different from the angels. The men that Abraham saw were not angels, but they were not normal men either. Rather, they were special creatures:

> Wherever angels are referred to by the word "men," as in this passage, the story of Lot, and the verses, "a man wrestled with him" (Gen. 32:25), as well as "a man came upon him" (Gen. 37:15), according to our rabbis (*Tanhuma Vayeshev* 2), in all these cases there was a special Glory (*kavod*) created in the angels. This Glory was called by those who know the mysteries of the Torah a "garment" (*ha-malbush*), which can be perceived by human eyes in the purest of souls, such as the righteous and the sons of prophets. However, I cannot be more explicit.

The assumption that the narrative refers to special creatures created to honor Abraham solves the two difficulties that perplexed Maimonides. These creatures were created in a way that enabled them to eat and drink. Likewise, the fact that Abraham stood and fed them without sensing their special nature indicated no flaw in Abraham's prophetic receptivity, since they were created for this express purpose.

Parashat Hayyei Sarah

A Parting Kiss

Dr. Admiel Kosman
Department of Talmud

THIS WEEK'S READING opens with Abraham mourning for his wife Sarah. He eulogized her and grieved for her (Gen. 23:2), but he had to put aside his grief to see to her burial. Abraham's cessation from mourning is briefly reported: "Then Abraham rose from beside his dead and spoke to the Hittites" (23:3). Rabbi Abraham Seba, a 16th-century Spanish commentator, notes in his *Tzeror ha-Mor* that it might have sufficed for the Torah to say "rose from his dead [*me'al meto*]," without adding *penei* ("rose from *beside* his dead [*me'al penei meto*]"). This led Rabbi Seba to conclude:[1]

> Since it says of Abraham that after Sarah's death he "rose from beside his dead," we must carefully analyze the words of the text, "rose from *beside* [Heb. *penei* literally means "from over the face of"] his dead"...This tells us that it was a kiss of parting, as the Sages remarked concerning Joseph, of whom it is said: "and he wept over [Jacob] and kissed him" (Gen. 50:1). Hence we conclude that a person must kiss his dear departed, and so it is written here "from over the face of his dead."

---

[1] *Tzeror ha-Mor*, ed. Joseph al-Nakaveh, Jerusalem 1985 (first printed in Venice, 1522), *Parashat Hayye Sarah*, p. 99. See also his comments on *Parashat Vayehi*, p. 263: "'Joseph flung himself upon his father's face...and kissed him' – hence they said that this was a kiss of parting. Therefore, one must kiss the deceased when parting from him."

According to the Midrash as understood by Rabbi Seba, a parting kiss to the deceased is obligatory when paying one's last respects, as indicated by the description of Joseph's final parting from his father.[2] This is rather strange, since the currently accepted view does not require parting from the dead with a kiss, but rather forbids this. For example, Rabbi Abraham Danzig, author of *Hayyei Adam*, writes:[3] "One should not kiss one's children who have died...for it is a great danger."[4]

The Torah itself, however, provides no indication that the practice of giving a parting kiss to the dead was censured. Quite the contrary, it was deemed an admirable practice, for Joseph did this when he parted from Jacob: "Joseph flung himself upon his father's face and wept over him and kissed him" (Gen. 50:1). According to the Midrash, Joseph was following the example that had been set by his father Jacob, who had kissed his father Isaac before his death, an act which had been deemed particularly meritorious. A similar conclusion was reached by the homilist in *Genesis Rabbah*[5] from Isaac's words to Jacob: "'Come close and kiss me, my son' (Gen. 27:26) – He said to him: You, and not others, kiss me when I am buried." This Midrash provides incontrovertible evidence that in the time of the homilist the rabbis saw nothing wrong with giving the dead a parting kiss.

Further evidence of this can be found in a famous story found in the Jerusalem Talmud (*Shabbat* 2.7, 5b) that after the death of R. Eliezer, "Rabbi Joshua removed his phylacteries and flung himself on him, kissing him and crying, 'Rabbi, Rabbi, the vow has been absolved, Rabbi, Chariot of Israel and his horsemen.'" Moreover, according to another Midrash, Jeremiah's fondness for the Jews who perished at the hands of the

---

[2] It should be noted that the standard version of *Genesis Rabbah* does not include this Midrash, but rather a different text which does not mention kissing the dead or Joseph's kiss to his father in particular. See *Genesis Rabbah*, ed. Theodor-Albeck, p. 118. Apparently the source for Rabbi Seba's remarks was *Bereshit Rabbati*, ed. H. Albeck (Jerusalem 1940), p. 752: "'And he kissed him' – this teaches us that one must kiss the dead when parting from them."

[3] See R. Abraham Danzig, *Hokhmat Adam, Hilkhot Avelut*, 157.5.

[4] See also *Ba'er Hetev* on *Shulhan Arukh, Yoreh De'ah* 394.1; *Pithei Teshuvah*, ibid.; *Kitzur Shulhan Arukh* 197.7.

[5] Ch. 65 (ed. Theodor-Albeck), p. 740.

Babylonian warriors caused him to kiss the limbs of the dead that he found scattered by the roadside on his return journey, after Nebuzaradan had taken him "chained in fetters" (Jer. 40:1).[6] Similarly, the Midrash describes those who longed to kiss the blood of saints:[7] "What would the blind say? 'Would that we could see the blood of Zechariah!' And what would the lame say? 'Would that we could have the very place where Zechariah was killed; then we would embrace it and kiss it,' as it is written, 'They wandered blindly through the streets' (Lam. 4:14)."

Various twelfth and thirteenth century Ashkenazic sources, however, attest an opposite viewpoint. The first such source is attributed to Rabbi Judah he-Hasid, whose testament (§4) states:[8] "One should not kiss[9] any of one's sons when they have died, for not a single one of them will remain alive." A similar formulation is found in Rabbenu Yeruham, citing Rabbi Judah He-Hasid in *Sefer ha-Kavod*:[10] "Rabbenu Judah He-Hasid wrote in *Sefer ha-Kavod* that if a person kisses any of his dead sons, not one will remain."[11] Likewise, *Sefer Hasidim* (§236)[12] states that this proscription applies to a mother kissing her dead sons, and notes that neither parent should kiss a dead daughter: "A man whose son or daughter has died should not kiss them, nor should he let his wife kiss them, for that shortens the life of their sons and daughters. The mother and father should be prevented [from doing this]."

From these reports of Rabbi Judah He-Hasid's statements, it is clear that the prohibition against kissing the dead was limited to kissing sons or

---

[6] *Pesikta de-Rav Kahana*, ed. D. Mandelbaum, 1.232.

[7] *Lamentations Rabbah*, 4 [14], p. 941. The printed version in *Midrash Eikhah* is somewhat different and cannot provide conclusive evidence.

[8] *Sefer Hasidim*, ed. Margaliyot (Jerusalem 1957), pp. 11–12.

[9] A variant text reads "one should not grasp" (ibid.), but "not kiss" is the reading cited by Rabbenu Yeruham.

[10] On Sefer ha-Kavod see Y. Dan, *Ha-Basis ha-'Iyyuni le-Torat ha-Musar shel Hasidut Ashkenaz*, Ph.D. thesis (Jerusalem 1964), pp. 76–86, 85–95; Y. Dan, *Tarbiz* 30 (1961), p. 372, n. 2; Y. Dan, *Hasidut Ashkenaz be-Toledot ha-Mahashavah ha-Yehudit* (Tel Aviv 1990), pp. 731–831.

[11] Rabbenu Yeruham Meshulam, *Sefer Adam ve-Havvah*, Havvah, §28, Venice 1553, 231d.

[12] Ed. Margaliyot, p. 210.

daughters who had died, and that the dangers associated with doing so extended only to the other sons and daughters of such a parent. In the process of transmission, however, this statement ultimately evolved into a broader prohibition which applied to kissing any dead person. Thus, a medieval Ashkenazic commentary cites a tradition in the name of Rabbi Eliezer of Worms, the author of *Sefer ha-Rokeah*:[13]

> "Joseph flung himself upon his father's face and wept over him and kissed him" – from Rabbi Eliezer ben Yehudah, of blessed memory, we have the tradition that it is dangerous to kiss the dead, since when the deceased is kissed, the deceased, in his fondness for the person who kissed him, will lead him to the grave, except for a father or mother [who may be kissed]. Any person who kisses his son after his death will, it is known, have all his sons die in his lifetime. Hence Joseph was able to kiss his father. Moreover, Jacob never died, as follows from the first chapter of *Ta'anit* (5b).

Analyzing this source, we see that it contains two strata: the initial ruling attributed to R. Judah the Hasid, according to which "any person who kisses his son after his death will, it is known, have all his sons die in his lifetime," and a later extension, which prohibited kissing the dead in general. Taking the evidence at face value, it seems that this extension of the prohibition is attributable to Rabbi Eliezer of Worms, author of *Sefer ha-Rokeah*, who was a close disciple of Rabbi Judah the Hasid. According to the formulation here – "it is dangerous to kiss the dead" – no distinction is made between dead people whom it is permissible to kiss and dead people whom it is forbidden to kiss, except for the special case of kissing a parent after his or her death, which will be discussed below.

The danger resulting from such conduct according to this version of Rabbi Eliezer of Worms' ruling differs from that described in the traditions attributed to Rabbi Judah He-Hasid above. It would seem that the danger

---

[13] *Perush Rabbenu Ephraim b. R. Shimshon u-Gedolei Ashkenaz ha-Kadmonim 'al ha-Torah*, I (Jerusalem 1993), p. 168, s.v. *va-yipol*.

discussed here is a personal one, affecting the person who gives the kiss: "When the deceased is kissed, the deceased, in his fondness of [the person kissing him], will lead him to the grave." However, this source also preserves the original formulation of Rabbi Judah He-Hasid, according to which the prohibition against kissing the dead applied only to kissing one's sons, and the resultant danger extended only to the siblings of the person who had died, as stated further on: "Any person who kisses his son after his death will, it is known, have all his sons die in his lifetime."[14]

Thus it seems that the special dispensation given to kiss one's mother or father was meant to justify the medieval custom which prohibited kissing the deceased, since this custom seems to conflict with the plain sense of the Bible, which ostensibly permits parting from the dead with a kiss, as Joseph did to his father. Therefore, even if it is forbidden to kiss other dead people, as reported in the name of Rabbi Eliezer of Worms, one's parents are an exception.

However, since this text claims that the reason for the danger to the person who gives such a kiss is that the deceased, out of love for the person who kissed him, will draw him to the grave, we are left wondering: don't a person's parents love him? And assuming they do, why wouldn't they draw the person who gave them a kiss to the grave? Here we clearly see the tension between the ancient sources and the new custom that was gradually spreading through the Jewish community, with the seeming conflicts being smoothed out so the new custom would not contradict the earlier sources.

Sometimes, however, a new custom gains so much strength that it can openly contradict earlier ancient sources. In such cases commentators usually reinterpreted the earlier sources, in order to eliminate the tension between current custom and earlier tradition. This stage, as well, is evident in the last source cited above. After it was argued that kissing any dead person except for one's father or mother is forbidden, fear of kissing the dead apparently increased to the point that people eventually refrained

---

[14] See the attempt to harmonize these sources made by Rabbi Joseph Isaac Lerner, *Shemirat ha-Guf ve-ha-Nefesh*, 2 (Jerusalem 1988), p. 579, §197: "It is dangerous to kiss any dead person, but the greatest danger lies in kissing one's son."

from kissing parents who had passed away. At this point commentators could no longer claim that Joseph's kissing his father was permissible on the grounds that there is no danger in kissing one's parents. Therefore a new explanation was suggested, based on the aggadic dictum that "Jacob did not die."[15]

An alternative explanation of Joseph's parting kiss was provided by Rabbi Eliezer of Worms:[16]

> One who sees a likeness of the dead or a spirit should not kiss [the departed], since the spirit is a danger to the person, as it is written, "Joseph flung himself upon his father's face and wept over him and kissed him"...as if he were saying, Why should I continue living? In doing so, Joseph acted measure for measure. For Jacob had said earlier, "Now I can die, having seen for myself that you are still alive" (Gen. 46:30). So when [Jacob] died, [Joseph] kissed him, as if to say, "Let me be like you – would that my soul be with your soul."

According to this explanation, the kiss Joseph gave his father was a "suicide kiss," resulting from weakness of heart that temporarily overcame him. In any event, the conclusion to be drawn from both of the traditions attributed to Rabbi Eliezer of Worms is that one must not give a parting kiss to any dead person, even one's mother or father.

Yet another explanation of Joseph's parting kiss is found in a recently published source, which claims that Jacob was not dead. This work, a Bible commentary found in Oxford MS. 862 and apparently written by an anonymous Ashkenazic *Hasid*, states:[17] "'And he kissed him' – whoever

---

[15] See Chaim Milikowsky, "Midrash ha-Aggadah – Metzi'ut o Metaphora," *Mahanayim* 7 (1994), pp. 43–73.

[16] *Hokhmat ha-Nefesh*, p. 68.

[17] Published in Bnai Brak, 1979 as *Perush ha-Rokeah 'al ha-Torah le-Ehad me-Rabboteinu Ba'alei ha-Tosafot...Rabbenu Eliezer me-Garmeiza ha-Noda' be-Shem Ba'al ha-Rokeah*. It has been demonstrated by Y. Dan, *Kiryat Sefer* 59 (1984), p. 446, that this work is not by Rabbi Eliezer of Worms, but by another anonymous rabbi from the *Hasidei Ashkenaz*.

kisses the dead, his sons die. But Jacob was not dead, for his lips moved."[18] This source is particularly interesting, since it unsmoothly conflates the various views surveyed above. On the one hand, it claims that kissing any dead person is forbidden ("whoever kisses the dead"), yet on the other hand, it claims that only the sons of the person who kisses the dead are endangered, which reflects the custom not to kiss a dead son.

In light of this, it is clear why the author of this commentary had to claim that "Jacob was not dead." At this point it could no longer be claimed that kissing one's dead parents was permissible, since custom had forbidden this. Nor could the author of this commentary maintain, as did Rabbi Eliezer of Worms in *Hokhmat ha-Nefesh*, that Joseph was like a person committing suicide. For this commentary claims that the danger in kissing the dead affected this person's sons, but not himself. Hence Joseph would not have been committing suicide, but threatening the lives of his sons. Thus, one could not present Joseph's action as conduct "measure for measure," corresponding to Jacob's words, "Now I can die, having seen for myself that you are still alive." Nor is it conceivable that Joseph, out of love for his father, would risk the lives of his sons.[19] Thus the only option left was to explain that Jacob had not really died, and hence kissing him was not problematic.[20]

---

[18] Ibid. p. 331, s.v. *va-yishak*.

[19] In contrast, see Reuben's words to his father in Gen. 42:37, and the sharp comment aimed at Reuben in the *aggadah* (*Genesis Rabbah*, ch. 91, ed. Theodor-Albeck, p. 1125, and notes there). Note also the embarrassment that this caused traditional exegetes; see Rabbi M. M. Kasher, *Torah Shelemah*, 6 (New York 1948), p. 1590, n. 103.

[20] Interestingly, no mention is made in any of these sources of the question raised in the Jerusalem Talmud about the parting kiss given by Rabbi Joshua to Rabbi Eliezer, which cannot be satisfactorily resolved according to any of the views cited above. Indeed, later rabbinic authorities had no choice but to suggest that a great Torah scholar may be kissed even if he is not one's father. See, for example, R. Nissim Abraham Ashkenazi, *Nehmad le-Mar'eh* on *Yerushalmi Shabbat* 11.2, s.v. *ve-nistalkah*, from which it is clear that the prohibition applies only to kissing sons. On the other hand, he stresses that kissing and hugging a righteous man who died is certainly permitted, suggesting that he might not have permitted kissing other dead people who were not *tzaddikim*. Cf. also R. Shalom Mordechai Schwadron's glosses on *Sefer Hasidim*, in the edition of *Sefer Hasidim* published by Rabbi H. D. Laufer (Jerusalem 1992), p. 60, and Rabbi J. I. Lerner, *Shemirat ha-Guf ve-ha-Nefesh*, §3.

THE MAGIC OF BLESSINGS

Prof. David Henshke
Department of Talmud

ASIDE FROM THE QUESTIONABLE morality of the way Jacob and his mother obtained Isaac's blessings, serious questions arise concerning the significance of these blessings, as noted by Ibn Ezra in his commentary on this week's reading. If the blessing was a form of prophecy, how could Isaac not have known whom he was blessing? Moreover, what force did Isaac's blessing have for Jacob, if Isaac really had Esau in mind?

Prima facie, it seems that Rebecca and her sons thought that Isaac had the power to convey blessings, in accordance with the rabbinic maxim that "the righteous decree and the Holy One, blessed be He, brings it to pass." All Isaac had to do was to lay his hands upon the recipient of the blessing, and that son would become blessed almost automatically, even if Isaac had meant to bless his other son. This explains Isaac's fearful trembling after discovering that he had been deceived: "'Now he must remain blessed' – for I cannot take back the blessing" (R. Joseph Bekhor Shor). Rabbi Joseph ibn Kaspi made this point even more forcefully (*Tirat Kesef, Sefer ha-Sod*, ch. 28): "Just as Jacob and Esau considered the blessings of their father Isaac effective, so too Balak and his followers treated the blessings and curses delivered by Balaam as effective."

However, the principal question is not what Isaac's sons thought about the force of his blessing, but how the Torah itself treats this blessing. Does the Torah actually adopt this almost magical view about the power of a righteous man's blessing? Is the ritual of conferring a blessing sufficient for the recipient to be automatically blessed, without taking into consideration such factors as the appropriateness of the blessing or the intention of the person who bestows the blessing?

In fact, the significance of the story of Isaac's blessings emerges when we realize that these blessings were not realized at all! As R. Jose b. R. Simeon asked R. Eleazar (*Zohar* I, 143b): "Did you learn from your father why the blessings Isaac conferred on his son Jacob were never fulfilled?" For Jacob was blessed with two principal things – in Isaac's words to Esau: "I have made him master over you: I have given him all his brothers for servants, and sustained him with grain and wine" (Gen. 27:37). In fact, though, Jacob was never a farmer blessed with grain and wine. Rather, he spent all his days as a shepherd. As for being master over his brother, the Torah intimates that the opposite was the case; instead of becoming "master over your brothers and letting your mother's sons bow to you" (Gen. 27:29), "Jacob...bowed low to the ground seven times until he was near his brother" (Gen. 33:3), and seven times Jacob called Esau "my lord." Nevertheless, nothing in the Torah is in vain, and ultimately Isaac's blessings will be realized in their entirety, in messianic times (*Zohar*, ibid.).

Parashat Vayetze

DO THE DEAD TELL NO TALES?

Prof. Daniel Sperber
Department of Talmud

THIS WEEK WE READ that "Rachel stole her father's household idols [Heb. *teraphim*]" (Gen. 31:19). The talmudic rabbis and certain medieval Jewish commentators associate the word *teraphim* with various peculiar traditions. For example, R. Menahem Zioni (14th century, Worms, Franco-Germany, whose commentary was composed in 1386) writes on this verse:

> A firstborn red person would be taken and slaughtered, and his head would be cut off and salted with salts and well-known herbs. Then they would write on a golden frontlet the name of impurity and place it under his tongue, and put [the head] in the wall or in a window in the city wall, and two lamps would be lit in front of it. Then it would speak, as it is said, "For the *teraphim* spoke delusion" (Zech. 10:2).

This tradition is based on *Pirkei de-Rabbi Eliezer* (ch. 36), which is based on *Midrash Tanhuma* (*Parashat Vayetze*, 12):

> Why were they called *teraphim*? Because they were the product of lewdness (*ma'ase toref*), of impurity. How did they make them? They would take a firstborn man, slaughter him and salt him with salts and herbs, and write on a golden frontlet the name of a spirit of impurity, and place the frontlet with spells under his tongue, and place him in the wall and kindle lights before him and bow

down to him, and he would speak to them in a whisper. As the Bible says, "For the *teraphim* spoke delusion." Therefore Rachel stole them.

Here we find all the same elements as in Zioni, except for the claim (found in relatively late sources) that the first-born person (*adam*) was red (*adom*)! In addition, this source tells us why Rachel stole the *teraphim* from her father: they revealed unknown information, and hence Rachel feared that the *teraphim* might reveal the deeds of Jacob and his family to Laban.

As indicated, the later sources, such as Zioni, state that the embalmed person was red, while earlier sources do not include this detail. It would seem that this detail is a later addition and not an essential element of the tradition. However, I would argue precisely the opposite: the ancient source spoke of a red (*adom*) firstborn person, but later sources omitted this word because it appeared strange, or perhaps because it appeared to be an erroneous repetition of the word *adam*, "person."

This text describes how a firstborn is slaughtered in order to make a magical device that can tell the future. Interestingly, other ancient sources recount how the Phoenicians used to slaughter their firstborns in times of trouble. We know that the Phoenicians believed that it was possible to consult with the dead by throwing into a tomb a rolled-up lead plate bearing a magical inscription; then the dead would speak to them from the grave. Furthermore, "Phoenicians" means "red (people)," as this word is derived from the Greek *phoinix*, "red." This name was given to the Phoenicians because they manufactured red (and blue) pigments.

However, the Phoenicians did not generally embalm corpses in the manner described in the texts above. The description of treating the corpse with salt and herbs is reminiscent of the practice of embalming found in Egypt, where salt-water and various herbs were used in preserving a corpse.

After preserving the corpse, a technique had to be found to make the embalmed body speak, in fulfillment of the aforementioned verse cited from Zechariah. Indeed, from rabbinic sources we learn of the practice of inserting a metal plate under the tongue. For example, *Sotah* 47a: "And some say that [Jeroboam] inscribed the Divine Name in the mouth of [the golden calf], and the calf would recite, 'I am the Lord your God, You shall have no other gods beside Me.'" Similarly in *Song of Songs Rabbah* 7.9: "What did that wicked man (Nebuchadnezzar) do? He took the frontlet of the High Priest and placed it in the mouth (of the idol), and (the idol) said, 'I am the Lord your God.'" Thus we have identified all the components of this legend. Although they originate from a variety of places and cultures, they were woven together by the author of the *aggadah* into a single coherent unit.

We still have to determine how the author of the legend arrived at the idea that these *teraphim* were embalmed. The answer is simple. The Hebrew word *teraphim* might appear to come from the Greek verb *therapeuo*. This word commonly means "to serve" or "to heal," although it has another, less well known meaning, which is found in Egyptian papyri: "to embalm." Thus one could claim the *teraphim* were embalmed corpses that spoke (according to Zechariah) by means of a frontlet placed under the tongue (rabbinic sources). These *teraphim* were made of corpses of the firstborns of the red people, who were slaughtered for this purpose. Rachel feared that they might reveal to Laban what Jacob was doing, and therefore she stole them and hid them from her father.

By analyzing all the elements of this strange legend, we can better understand how it came into being. The author of the *aggadah* collected assorted notions from Israel's neighboring cultures (Greece, Egypt, Phoenicia) that echoed the distant past, and applied the generally accepted homiletical technique of associating similar words from distant sources (Genesis and Zechariah), interpreting them by using folk etymology, a technique commonly used in aggadic literature. Thus our author concluded that the *teraphim* were embalmed corpses that foretold the future and were made of the firstborns of the red people. Combining all these elements yielded a new midrashic creation that had cohesiveness and internal logic.

Last, we note that the principal magician here is the author of the legend himself. He took a story that describes the matriarch Rachel, who had little respect for her father and stole from him what he held dearest – his household gods (Gen. 31:30). Afterwards she lied to him and even concealed things from her husband. Are we to emulate such a figure? However, after reading the above legend we arrive at quite a different conclusion. Our matriarch Rachel is portrayed as a brave woman who sought to protect her husband and family from her wicked father, an idolater who consulted the dead in a most cruel way. Rachel, in her great wisdom, foiled his evil plans and protected her family by stealing the abominable *teraphim*. Such a brave woman is indeed worthy of emulation.

Parashat Vayishlah

JACOB AND ESAU: A PARTING OF WAYS

Menahem Ben-Yashar
Department of Bible

THE BEGINNING AND END of *Parashat Toledot* – practically the entire *parashah* – deal with the struggle between Jacob and Esau, the sale of the birthright and Jacob's blessing; in short, who would carry on Abraham's line and destiny. Since *Parashat Toledot* concludes with Jacob's flight from Esau and from the land of Canaan, it seems as if Esau won the struggle, since he remained in Canaan, his ancestral homeland. Indeed, at the beginning of this week's reading, when Jacob returns from his prolonged and difficult exile, he is compelled to acknowledge the victory of his older brother: Jacob sends Esau an offering, a tribute of submission, referred to as a gift sent "to my lord Esau" from "your servant Jacob" (see Gen. 32:18).

Yet in the final analysis, Jacob carries on the heritage of Abraham and builds Abraham's line, for only Jacob and his household remain in the land of Canaan. Now, Jacob's victory might be attributed to divine intervention. Indeed, in addition to the blessings that Isaac bestowed on Jacob as a result of Jacob's deceit, Isaac later added another blessing of his own will, and blessings serve as agents of the Divine. Moreover, God Himself confirms the blessings both when Jacob went into exile (Gen. 28:13–15) and shortly before his return (31:3, 12–13). Also, a miraculous figure contends with Jacob and blesses him (32:24–30), and it is clear from the prophet Hosea that this figure was an angel ("He strove with an angel and prevailed," Hos. 12:5).

In the Bible, Divine destinies and promises come to pass through human endeavor. Direct intervention by God through miracles is relatively rare. Usually things happen naturally, with Divine providence operating behind the scenes. The real story of Esau's retreat in the face of Jacob is told towards the end of this week's reading (36:6–8). It does not attract our attention, since it is secondary to the history of Esau and his clan. To the casual reader, who is not attuned to the finer nuances of the Torah, the passage appears fairly inconsequential. It reads as follows, beginning with the end of verse 5:

> [5] Those were the sons of Esau, who were born to him in the land of Canaan. [6] Esau took his wives, his sons and daughters, and all the members of his household, his cattle and all his livestock, and all the property that they had acquired in the land of Canaan, and went to another land because of his brother Jacob. [7] For their possessions were too many for them to dwell together, and the land where they sojourned could not support them because of their livestock. [8] So Esau settled in the hill country of Seir – Esau being Edom.

To this we must add the contrasting verse which opens chapter 37 and *Parashat Vayeshev*: "Now Jacob settled in the land where his father had sojourned, the land of Canaan."

This passage resembles a parallel passage in Genesis 13, which speaks of Lot leaving Abraham. Even the language used there is similar; note especially the similarity of Genesis 13:6 to verse 7 above: "the land could not support them staying together; for their possessions were so great that they could not remain together." Both subject matter and language are similar, although it is not clear why Esau had to leave. In *Lekh Lekha*, chapters 12–13, the sequence of events is clear: When Abraham and his household were in Egypt because of the famine, Pharaoh treated him well, bestowing economic benefits on him after he took Sarah into his house. Thus both Abraham and Lot, who accompanied him, amassed extensive flocks. While the areas of lush vegetation in Egypt could support all of their livestock, the meager vegetation on the edge of the desert in Canaan could not, so Abraham had to part ways with Lot. Similarly, we read that both Esau and Jacob had much livestock, as with Abraham and Lot.

In any event, the acts of buying the birthright and deceitfully stealing the blessing about which we read in *Parashat Toledot* teach us about the character and aspirations of the two brothers. One brother scorns the birthright, while the other struggles to obtain it, and along with it the blessing – who would continue Isaac's line. But these actions – buying the birthright for a bowl of lentil soup and obtaining the blessing by putting on a strange disguise – do not seem to have the power to determine the brothers' status. So how was Jacob to achieve these things that he desired?

As a result of these unfruitful attempts to achieve his desires, Jacob was forced to flee from his home and his country and become indentured to Laban, serving him industriously. By working hard, day and night (Gen. 31:38–41), Jacob acquires flocks of his own, and from these he sends offerings to his brother Esau. With these he appeases Esau and, thanks to the abundance of flocks and paucity of grazing land, Jacob finally brings about Esau's departure from Canaan (which Esau scorned, just as he had scorned the birthright) and moves to the land of Seir.

From this analysis we see that the important messages of the Torah, the explanations for crucial turning points in history, are not necessarily found in the major biblical events that are carefully read and heavily interpreted (for example, the stories of Jacob's encounter with Esau, his struggle with the angel, or the story of Dinah or the death of Rachel). The great and fateful turning point of our story is concealed, as we have shown, at the end of the weekly portion, in the course of listing the members of the clan of Edom.

Furthermore, we learn about symmetry in the Torah. The first separation between "brothers" in the Torah – Abraham and Lot – takes place in the same manner and is described in similar language as the last separation between brothers, between Jacob and Esau.

Parashat Vayeshev

TAMAR

Yael Tzohar
Department of Bible

THE STORY OF Judah and Tamar (Gen. 38) begins with details about Judah's first marriage to the daughter of Shua the Canaanite and the birth of his three sons, Er, Onan and Shelah. This is followed by the account of the death of his two older sons and his wife. One may accordingly ask whether there is any significance to this exceptionally detailed description of Judah's family, almost all of whom died, or whether this description only provides the functional setting for the appearance of Judah's daughter-in-law Tamar.

According to Avraham Kariv,[1] the Torah seeks to describe the home that Judah established, a home that ended in heartbreak and disappointment because Judah's Canaanite wife was not worthy of establishing his line. His wife, explicitly described as being "the daughter of a certain Canaanite" (v. 2), was wiped off the face of the earth along with her sons, and another woman, who would be worthy of establishing the dynasty descending from Judah, took her place. Kariv's suggestion explains why the Torah goes into such detail regarding Judah's marriage to the daughter of Shua the Canaanite and the birth of their sons (vv. 3–4).

Judah's eldest son, Er, married Tamar and then died, as the Torah states: "But Er, Judah's firstborn, was displeasing to the Lord, and the Lord took his life" (v. 7). Onan ought to have married his deceased brother's widow to provide offspring for his brother, but he shirked his duty, as it is

---

[1] A. Kariv, *Shiv'at 'Amudei ha-Tanakh* (Tel Aviv 1968), p. 43.

written, "What he did was displeasing to the Lord, and He took his life also" (v. 10).

The verbatim repetition of the phrase "displeasing to the Lord," coupled with the penalty of death, foretells the continuation of the story, in which Judah accuses Tamar of the death of his two sons and is unwilling to let her marry his third son. The details that the Torah provides about Tamar's husbands and the circumstances of their deaths indicate that Tamar played no part in their demise, but rather was the innocent victim of a marriage to evil people.

Judah, having incorrectly interpreted the tragedies that befell him, accused Tamar of responsibility for the death of his sons. He saw her as a woman who brings disaster:[2] "Then Judah said to his daughter-in-law Tamar, Stay as a widow in your father's house until my son Shelah grows up" (v. 11). In a parenthetical remark, the Torah reveals that Judah had no intention of ever giving Tamar to Shelah: "For he thought that he too might die like his brothers." Given the painful circumstances of the death of his two sons, Judah was unwilling to put his only surviving son at risk.

So Tamar waited. She candidly accepted what Judah said and expected to be given Shelah in marriage. But as time went by, she observed that Shelah was not being given to her. Tamar wished to bear a son who would continue the line of Judah,[3] and having realized that she had been deceived by Judah, she took the initiative in a daring and dangerous way. Disguising herself as a harlot, she sat on the main road and seduced Judah (who did not recognize her), taking as a pledge his seal, cord, and staff, and then she conceived by him. When Judah found out that his daughter-in-law had seemingly become pregnant by harlotry, he proclaimed without hesitation, "Bring her out and let her be burned" (v. 24).

As the story continues, our sympathy goes increasingly to Tamar, who is portrayed both as the victim of her two husbands and as the victim of

---

[2] According to talmudic law, a woman who lost two husbands endangers other, future husbands: "If a woman married a man, and he died, and she married a second husband and he also died, she must not marry a third husband" (*Yevamot* 64b). "If she was widowed twice, she is not fit for marriage" (*Ketubbot* 43b).

[3] For Tamar's lofty motives, see Benno Jacob, *Das erste Buch der Tora, Genesis* (Berlin 1934), pp. 261–263.

her father-in-law's mistake, as a refined woman who is even willing to be burned, so long as she does not publicize Judah's disgrace: "As she was being brought out, she sent this message to her father-in-law: 'I am with child by the man to whom these belong.' And she added, 'Examine these; whose seal and cord and staff are these?'" (v. 25). She did not make a public proclamation or utter harsh words of anger, but rather presented the pledge in a manner that intimated to Judah what had happened, thereby leaving the matter at his discretion.[4]

At the end of the story, it is Judah, who had initially held Tamar responsible for the death of his sons, who recants and says explicitly, "She is more in the right than I, inasmuch as I did not give her to my son Shelah" (v. 26). Judah, too, is shown to be a great person, capable of admitting error. He admitted to having acted deceitfully by promising Tamar Shelah without truly intending to give him to her, and hence her deeds were justified. Furthermore, Judah expressed his recognition of Tamar's good intentions – her desire to continue the name of her deceased husband and bear a son for the family of Judah.

Chapter 38, which begins with the details of Judah's first family, concludes with the birth of Tamar's twins. One of them reached out and the midwife tied a crimson thread to his wrist, but then the other suddenly burst forth "and she said, 'What a breach (Heb. *peretz*) you have made for yourself!' So he was named Peretz." This was the Peretz who became ancestor of the Davidic line. What does this story teach us?

The conclusion of the story is the inverse of its beginning. The beginning describes Judah's failed attempt to establish a family, while the end indicates that he had established a family.

This story about the struggle over the birthright reminds the reader of many similar struggles over birthrights in the book of Genesis – for example, the conflicts between Cain and Abel, Isaac and Ishmael, Jacob

---

[4] Rashi comments: "'As she was being brought out' – to be burned. 'She sent this message to her father-in-law' – she did not wish to embarrass him and say, 'I am with child by you,' so instead she said, 'I am with child by the man to whom these belong.' She thought, 'If he confesses, he will do so of his own accord, and if not, I shall be burned, but I shall not embarrass him.' Hence it is said (*Sotah* 10b), 'Better for a person to be thrown into a fiery furnace than to publicly embarrass someone else.'"

and Esau, Joseph and his brothers. Moreover, the story of the birth of Tamar's twins serves as a "correction," as it were, of the story of the birth of Jacob and Esau. Peretz succeeded in coming out first, whereas Jacob did not, despite his grasping the heel of Esau. Zerah, Peretz's twin brother, also became one of the forefathers of the tribe of Judah, whereas Esau was excluded from the Israelite dynasty.

Significantly, Judah's first two sons are never again mentioned, whereas Shelah is mentioned among the families belonging to the tribe of Judah (see Num. 26:20, I Chron. 4:21–23). Nevertheless, the family of Shelah was not considered an important part of the tribe of Judah, and in Chronicles it is listed only briefly, after a detailed description of the families descended from Peretz and Zerah. Radak commented on this as follows: "All the genealogies mentioned thus far were descended from Peretz and Zerah. Thus far the sons of Shelah had not been mentioned, so now, when completing the genealogy of Judah, brief mention is made of the sons of Shelah."

In conclusion, Judah's statement indicates that Tamar was in the right, having good intentions and a righteous personality, and that Peretz, Tamar's son, would become one of the ancestors of the House of David. To be sure, this is not explicitly mentioned in the Torah, but it is made fully clear in the Book of Ruth, in the people's blessing to Boaz: "May your house be like the house of Peretz whom Tamar bore to Judah, through the offspring which the Lord will give you by this young woman" (Ruth 4:12). In the Book of Ruth, Tamar is blessed retroactively and given full credit for her deeds.

Parashat Vayeshev

JACOB AND SONS

Prof. Nathan Aviezer
Department of Physics

THE GREATEST DRAMA in this week's reading is undoubtedly the plot by Joseph's brothers to kill him. The theme of murder is found elsewhere in Genesis; Cain killed Abel, and Esau planned to kill Jacob. However, Cain did not belong to the family of patriarchs, and Esau was traditionally considered wicked. By contrast, our reading deals with the sons of the patriarch Jacob, the progenitors of the Jewish people. How could these eminent figures have plotted and almost succeeded in carrying out the murder of their younger brother?

An answer is given in the Torah, but it is utterly incomprehensible: "They said to one another, 'Here comes that dreamer! Come now, let us kill him and throw him into one of the pits...We shall see what comes of his dreams!'" (Gen. 37:19–20). Could the fact that Joseph had a dream or two which the brothers did not like be a sufficient motive for murder? Is that a reason for killing Joseph in cold blood?

The cruelty of Jacob's sons is revealed by a close reading of Scripture. This week's reading describes the attempted murder only from the point of view of the brothers. Now, how did Joseph respond when his brothers fell upon him in order to kill him? The answer is found in *Parashat Miketz*, where Joseph, then vizier of Egypt, meets Jacob's sons, who had come to Egypt to obtain food. Recognizing his brothers, while they did not recognize him, Joseph begins to give them a hard time: "You are spies, you have come to see the land in its nakedness" (Gen. 42:9). Later Joseph even incarcerates his brothers. Joseph's brothers interpret their hardships as divine retribution: "Alas, we are being punished on account of our brother, because we saw his anguish, yet paid no heed as he pleaded with us" (Gen. 42:21). According to this account, Joseph pleaded with his brothers, but their hearts remained hard as stone.

The Torah make it clear just how cruel their conduct was. Immediately after they cast Joseph into the pit to die of hunger, the brothers "sat down to a meal" (Gen. 37:25). In other words, they felt no pangs of conscience, no second thoughts or remorse. The brothers took action which would lead to the death of their younger brother and immediately thereafter sat down to feast. How is this dreadful behavior to be understood?

Family Relationships

Understanding the story of Joseph and his brothers depends upon understanding the relationships in Jacob's family. As we know, Jacob made no secret of his special love for Joseph, and "he made him an ornamented tunic" (Gen. 37:3). The Torah reveals how Jacob's preference for Joseph affected his other sons. After the second trip which Jacob's sons made to Egypt, Joseph had a silver chalice hidden in Benjamin's sack and then sent his servant after the brothers to accuse them of theft. The cup was indeed found in Benjamin's sack, and as punishment he had to remain in Egypt as a slave. In the wake of this catastrophe, all the brothers returned with Benjamin to Egypt, and Judah embarked on a desperate attempt to obtain mercy from the vizier, a cold and cruel man. On the doorstep of the vizier's house, in the most dramatic speech in the entire Torah, Judah entreated Joseph, setting forth the entire history of his family, including the special bond which his father had with Joseph and Benjamin. Judah explained that Joseph had died and that all of Jacob's love was focused on Benjamin – "his life is bound up with his" (Gen. 44:30). If Benjamin would not return, tragedy would surely befall his father: "When he sees that the boy is not with us, he will die...For how can I go back to my father unless the boy is with me? Let me not be witness to the woe that would overtake my father!" (Gen. 44:31–34).

Judah, Son of Leah

This speech is remarkably successful. Joseph could hardly hold back his tears. Having succeeded thus far, the moment finally arrived for Judah to present his request. We might expect Judah to tell Joseph something like the following: "Have mercy on the father, have mercy on the son; let Benjamin return home, even though he was caught with the cup in his sack." However Judah said something altogether different; he asked Joseph to take him as a slave instead of Benjamin. What sort of proposal is this? Is Judah any less Jacob's son than Benjamin? The answer is clear. In Jacob's eyes, Judah is the son of Leah, the "unloved" wife (Gen. 29:31), whereas Benjamin is the son of his beloved Rachel (Gen. 29:20). If Judah would never return, life would go on; but if Benjamin were never to return, Jacob would die of heartbreak, plain and simple. Judah was not exaggerating in the least when he described how tragic it would be for his father if Benjamin would remain in Egypt.

What About Simeon?

Elsewhere we learn of Jacob's favoritism to his children precisely from what the Torah neglects to mention. After the brothers returned home from their first trip to Egypt, having been told not to return unless they brought their brother Benjamin with them, they tried to persuade Jacob to let Benjamin go to Egypt. Among all the arguments which they made, one argument is glaringly absent: Benjamin should be sent to Egypt to help secure Simeon's release. Simeon was imprisoned in Egypt and would not be released until Benjamin was brought there, yet none of the brothers mentioned this to Jacob. The rest of the family knew that it was inconceivable that Jacob would risk his dearly beloved son Benjamin in order to free Simeon, and therefore it was pointless to mention the matter.

These two events underscore the sad reality, known to all, in the house of Jacob. In this family there were two classes, two categories of sons: the sons of the beloved Rachel, and the sons of all the others.

Jacob's sons were well aware of this point, but they were incapable of changing the situation. It never occurred to them to complain to their father, the head of the family, the lofty personage who had a special relationship with God. Jacob's discrimination naturally led to jealousy, hatred, and frustration, but before Joseph's reporting his dreams, these feelings had not been translated into action. After all, was it the fault of Joseph and Benjamin that Jacob favored them over the rest of the brothers? Thus, Joseph's brothers were left to suffer constant frustration.

Joseph's dreams opened the brothers' eyes, revealing to them what he really felt. Now they knew that not only did Jacob consider Joseph his favorite son, but Joseph himself was party to this unhealthy favoritism. Now there was an outlet for their pent-up frustration of many years. In an instant, in the wake of Joseph's dreams, the brothers' frustration turned into unbridled hatred, and the outbreak of this animosity is what led the brothers to plot to murder Joseph, later accepting the idea of selling him as a mere compromise.

Parashat Miketz

REUBEN AND JUDAH: A STUDY IN CONTRASTS

Yonah Bar-Maoz
Department of Bible

THE COMPETITION BETWEEN Reuben and Judah for leadership makes comparison between them natural. Overall, Judah comes out the victor in this competition. However, closer examination reveals that Reuben ultimately played a major role in shaping the course of Jewish history, since Reuben's initiative at the beginning of the Joseph story made it possible for later events to occur.

When Joseph arrived unexpectedly in Dothan, where his brothers were herding the sheep, his appearance evoked great anger. They did not know what we, the readers, know: that Joseph had come at his father's bidding, not to spy on them and report back to their father. They must have ruefully observed that even the great geographic distance between them did not suffice to prevent trouble. While the Midrash blames Simeon and Levi for plotting to kill Joseph, the plain meaning of the biblical verse "they said to one another" (Gen. 37:19) suggests that all of the brothers were equally guilty.

The First Challenge

Only one brother, Reuben, took exception to the brothers' plot, and his role at the time was of crucial importance. In the heat of the moment murder might have been committed, and while it was ultimately Judah who persuaded the brothers not to kill Joseph, had it not been for Reuben's immediate intervention, Judah would not have been able to accomplish what he did.

The Second Challenge

In this week's reading Reuben and Judah again take action in similar fashion: first Reuben responds unsuccessfully to the situation, and then Judah takes action and succeeds. Both brothers try to persuade Jacob to send Benjamin with them. Reuben says, "You may kill my two sons if I do not bring him back to you. Put him in my care, and I will return him to you" (Gen. 42:37). Jacob refuses, and only after Judah's intervention does he agree.

Judah said, "I will be surety for him; you may hold me responsible. If I do not bring him back to you and set him before you, I shall stand guilty before you forever" (Gen. 43:9). In fact, though, Judah gave no tangible surety for Benjamin's well-being. He only states that he will suffer pangs of conscience if something happens. By contrast, Reuben's reference to losing two of his sons arouses the hope that he will try especially hard to save Benjamin. Indeed, a rabbinic midrash offers a different reason for Judah's success where Reuben failed: proper timing. The same holds true for Judah's proposal to sell Joseph, made after the brothers had cooled off somewhat and sat down to eat. Judah's success proves his powers of leadership, but at the same time it reflects a moral failing, on which we read in Bavli *Sanhedrin* 6b:

> Rabbi Eliezer says: What blessing is recited by a person who has stolen a *se'ah* of wheat, ground it into flour, baked it into bread and taken *hallah* from it? Such a person does not say a blessing; rather, he blasphemes, as it is said: "The grasping man (Heb. *botzea'*, which also means "breaking bread") reviles and scorns the Lord" (Ps. 10:3). [The word for "reviles" is *berekh*, "blessed," a euphemism for "reviles" when speaking of God. The Midrash parses the verse differently, reading "If he who broke bread had stolen the wheat" – taking *botzea'* in both its meanings of breaking bread and "grasping" or "stealing" – "then his blessing over the *hallah* which he tithed is blasphemy" – taking *berekh* in both its senses, "bless" and "revile."]
>
> Rabbi Meir says: "The word *botzea'* refers to Judah, as it is written, 'Then Judah said to his brothers: What do we gain (Heb. *mah*

betza') by killing our brother?' (Gen. 37:26). Whoever praises Judah is guilty of blasphemy, as it is written: 'The grasping man reviles and scorns the Lord.'"

The Midrash also finds Judah's treatment of his father objectionable (*Tanhuma Mikketz* 8): "Judah said to them: Let the old man be until his bread runs out. For it is written, 'And when they had eaten up the rations...'" The Midrash considers Judah's treatment of his father disrespectful, for Judah treated his father as weak-minded because of his age.

Judah's Initiative

Initially Jacob did not react at all to Judah's offer, so Judah spoke again, trying to persuade him:

> But Judah said to him, "The man warned us, 'Do not let me see your faces unless your brother is with you.' If you let our brother go with us, we will go down and procure food for you, but if you will not let him go, we will not go down...Then Judah said to his father Israel, "Send the boy in my care, and let us be on our way, that we may live and not die – you and we and our children. I myself will be surety for him; you may hold me responsible. If I do not bring him back to you and set him before you, I shall stand guilty before you forever. For we could have been there and back twice if we had not dawdled" (Gen. 43:3–10).

In the end Jacob accepted the unpleasant reality, but even then he did not respond directly to Judah's remarks or to his offer of surety, just as he did not respond to Reuben's earlier offer. This is evident from the fact that he spoke in the plural, addressing all his sons. After Reuben's proposal, Jacob said, "My son must not go down with you...you will send my white head down to Sheol in grief" (Gen. 42:38). Similarly, after Judah's proposal, Jacob said: "If it must be so, do this...take your brother too, and go back at once to the man" (Gen. 43:11–14).

Reuben's and Judah's Character

Thus we see that on two occasions each of the sons responded in his own characteristic fashion, in a manner which combines favorable and unfavorable elements. In Jacob's blessing on his deathbed, he characterizes Reuben as "unstable as water," responding hastily without waiting for the proper moment, although this haste was invaluable when Reuben was faced with imminent danger. Judah, on the other hand, had the patience of a lion laying in wait for its prey, who only leapt into action when the time was ripe, generally achieving his objective. However, the considerations of profit that underlay Judah's actions were not always commendable.

Reuben's and Judah's subsequent actions are also noteworthy. When the brothers recalled their mercilessness – "They said to one another, Alas, we are being punished on account of our brother, because we looked on at his anguish, yet we paid no heed as he pleaded with us. That is why this distress has come upon us'" (Gen. 42:21) – Reuben immediately reproached his brother: "Didn't I tell you, Do no wrong to the boy? But you paid no heed. Now comes the reckoning for his blood" (Gen. 42:22). This reproach might seem like a petty and foolish provocation, since it was of no avail at the time, although it does reveal Reuben's great pain over what happened to Joseph.

Reuben's emotional outbreak also absolves him of any possible suspicion of secretly rejoicing over Joseph's disappearance. It should be recalled that Reuben, as the firstborn, suffered most from Joseph's haughty behavior, since it was Joseph who would presumably become the leader of the Israelites after Jacob. And while Reuben did save Joseph, he might have been suspected of doing so only out of a desire to keep proper relations with his father. Reuben's distress over Joseph's fate more than twenty years later attests to the purity of his heart, and shows that he was free of jealousy towards his other brothers, whether Joseph or Benjamin, who had taken his place in Jacob's heart. In contrast, Judah's silence at this juncture is noticeable. His voice is swallowed up in that of the group: "They said to one another, 'Alas, we are being punished.'"

Later on, at the end of *Parashat Miketz*, the picture is reversed: Reuben is the one who blends into the background with the other brothers, while Judah is the one whose voice stands out, as he speaks on his own behalf and on behalf of his brothers: "When Judah and his brothers reentered the house of Joseph, who was still there, they threw themselves on the ground before him...Judah replied, 'What can we say to my lord? How can we plead, how can we prove our innocence? God has uncovered the crime of your servants. Here we are, then, slaves of my lord, the rest of us as much as he in whose possession the goblet was found'" (Gen. 44:14–16).

Judah immediately rose like a lion. He found the inner strength to stand up to the tyrannical despot on his own, evincing moral conduct, responsibility for his brother and empathy for his plight. Significantly, Judah was always able to find the perfect timing to ensure that his action would bear fruit. He could change plans on the spur of the moment, and he offered himself as a slave to prevent all the other brothers from becoming slaves in exchange for Benjamin's release.

How could Judah have hoped to convince the ruler to accept such a minimalist offer after Joseph had already turned down a more generous offer? The answer is that Judah saw a soft spot in Joseph's conduct. Despite Joseph's seeming cruelty, he said: "The rest of you go back in peace to your father" (Gen. 44:17), so Judah seized the opportunity. Fourteen times in his speech Judah mentioned the word "father," playing on Joseph's feelings of pity for the elderly, suffering father. Judah's remarks could be construed as calculated emotional manipulation, if not for the utter devotion and self-effacement which he showed in accepting the assumption that in his father's eyes, his life was not as important as Benjamin's.

Through this conduct Judah finally atoned for suggesting that Joseph be sold into slavery without any feelings of brotherly love or sensitivity to his father's feelings. If we also consider Judah's exemplary behavior regarding his daughter-in-law Tamar, as he publicly admitted his responsibility and absolved her of guilt, we can well understand why "the scepter shall not depart from Judah, nor the ruler's staff from between his feet" (Gen. 49:10), for "Judah became more powerful than his brothers and a leader came from him" (I Chr. 5:2).

Reuben lacked the ability to lead his brothers in difficult times. However, his warmth and sensitivity to the suffering of his brother and father earned him a place of honor among his brothers, assuring him that despite his sin in defiling his father's bed, he would be blessed: "May Reuben live and not die" (Deut. 33:6); "May Reuben live in this world, and not die in the world to come" (*San.* 92a); "May Reuben live on the merit of what he did for Joseph, and not die for his act with Bilhah" (*Avot de-Rabbi Nathan*, version B, 45).

Parashat Vayigash

"YOUR ANCESTORS WENT DOWN TO EGYPT SEVENTY PEOPLE IN ALL"

Dr. Rivka Raviv
Department of Talmud

IN THIS WEEK'S TORAH READING we read about the beginning of the Israelite exile in Egypt, about which Abraham had been foretold years ago: "Know well that your offspring shall be strangers in a land not theirs, and they shall be enslaved and oppressed" (Gen. 15:13). This sad moment in history is aptly described by the verse "These are the names of the Israelites, Jacob and his descendants, who came to Egypt...The total of Jacob's household who came to Egypt was seventy people" (Gen. 46:8–27). Justifiably, the book of Exodus begins by repeating this information: "These are the names of the sons of Israel who came to Egypt with Jacob...The total number of people from Jacob's offspring came to seventy" (Ex. 1:1–5).

Why did the Torah count the number of people who came to Egypt? An answer can be found in Moses' speech in Deuteronomy: "Your ancestors went down to Egypt seventy people in all, and now the Lord our God has made you as numerous as the stars of heaven" (Deut. 10:22). Thus, we see that God's promise to Abraham, "I will make of you a great nation" (Gen. 12:2), was fulfilled, for from the seventy people who went to Egypt the Jews increased to a nation of six hundred thousand.

The list of Jacob's family members who came to Egypt is organized according to the names of the mothers: the sons of Leah, the sons of Zilpah, the sons of Rachel, and the sons of Bilhah. After each mother, the sum total of children is given (Gen. 46:8–27):

These are the names of the Israelites, Jacob and his descendants, who came to Egypt. Jacob's firstborn, Reuben; Reuben's sons...Simeon's sons...Levi's sons: Gershon, Kehath, and Merari. Judah's sons: Er, Onan, Shelah, Peretz, and Zerah – but Er and Onan had died in the land of Canaan...Issachar's sons...Zebulun's sons...Those were the sons whom Leah bore to Jacob in Paddan-Aram, in addition to his daughter Dinah. All the people, male and female, were thirty-three. Gad's sons...Asher's sons...These were the descendants of Zilpah, whom Laban had given to his daughter Leah...sixteen people. The sons of Jacob's wife Rachel were Joseph and Benjamin. To Joseph were born...Benjamin's sons...These were the descendants of Rachel who were born to Jacob – fourteen people in all. Dan's son [Heb. "sons"]: Hushim. Naphtali's sons...These were the descendants of Bilhah, whom Laban had given to his daughter Rachel. These she bore to Jacob – seven people in all. All the people belonging to Jacob who came to Egypt – his own issue, aside from the wives of Jacob's sons – all these people numbered sixty-six. And Joseph's sons who were born to him in Egypt were two in number. Thus the total of Jacob's household who came to Egypt was seventy people.

This list raises a most perplexing question: thirty-four names are listed as the sons of Leah. Excluding Er and Onan, who died in the land of Canaan, we are left with only thirty-two names. Why is the total of Leah's children in 46:15 given as thirty-three? Some commentators explained this by claiming that the thirty-three people mentioned in this verse include Jacob himself.[1] As proof, they cite the concluding verses of the list: "All the

---

[1] So e.g. Ibn Ezra on Gen. 46:23, Rashbam ad loc., and R. Joseph Bekhor Shor ad loc. Ibn Ezra mentions another way of resolving the question, according to which seventy is a round number. However, he rejects this interpretation because the difficulty with the verses ultimately stems from the number 33 mentioned in Gen. 46:15, and this is obviously not a round number. Rabbi Mordechai Breuer made an interesting attempt to resolve this difficulty by arguing that the thirty-three sons of Leah refer to her offspring in the land of Canaan; hence this number includes Er and Onan but not Dinah. Later, when the Israelites came to Egypt, the count of thirty-three was

persons belonging to Jacob who came to Egypt – his own issue, aside from the wives of Jacob's sons – all these persons numbered sixty-six. And Joseph's sons who were born to him in Egypt were two in number. Thus the total of Jacob's household who came to Egypt was seventy persons." According to these verses, "Jacob's issue" who came to Egypt included only sixty-six people, to which Joseph and his two sons born in Egypt should be added, and Jacob, bringing the total to seventy. Evidence for this interpretation goes back to the Book of Jubilees (44:11–34). There, too, the overall figure is seventy, although there are differences between the subdivisions of the two lists. Particularly relevant to our discussion is the fact that in Jubilees, the verse listing the total number of Leah's sons explicitly mentions Jacob as one of the people counted:

> These are the names of the sons of Jacob who came to Egypt with their father Jacob: Reuben, Israel's firstborn; and these are the names of his sons...Simeon and his sons...Levi and his sons...Judah and his sons...Issachar and his sons...Zebulun and his sons...these are the sons of Jacob and their sons who came to Egypt with Jacob their father – twenty-nine, and Jacob their father along with them comes to thirty.

The same solution can be found in rabbinic teaching. Thus, *Genesis Rabbah* ch. 94 (ed. Albeck, p. 1181) states: "Some say that Jacob completed the count." The same source, however, suggests other ways of solving the problem (pp. 1180–1182):[2]

> "All the persons belonging to Jacob who came to Egypt...And Joseph's sons who were born to him" (vv. 26–27). R. Levi said in the name of Samuel bar Nahman: Did you ever see a person give his friend sixty-six cups, then give him another three, and count

completed by Dinah and Jacob. See M. Breuer, *Pirkei Bereshit* (Alon Shevut 1999), 2.697–704.

[2] See also *Pesikta de-Rav Kahana*, ed. Mandelbaum, pp. 188–189; Bavli *Sotah* 12a; *Bava Batra* 120a, 123b; *Tanhuma Buber, Bemidbar*, 19; *Tanhuma, Bemidbar*, 16; *Midrash Shmuel*, 32.5 [3]; *Aggadat Bereshit*, 22.5 [1]; *Pirkei de-Rabbi Eliezer*, ch. 38; *Exodus Rabbah*, ch. 1.

them as seventy? Rather, it was Jochebed who completed the count of the Israelites in Egypt. R. Levi said in the name of R. Samuel bar Nahman: Jochebed was conceived in the land of Canaan and born in Egypt, as it is written, "The name of Amram's wife was Jochebed [daughter of Levi, who was born to Levi in Egypt]" (Num. 26:59)...R. Levi said in the name of R. Samuel bar Nahman: The Holy One, blessed be He, instructed us to count this tribe even while it was in its mother's womb, as it is written: "Jeduthun – the sons of Jeduthun: Gedaliah, Zeri, Jeshaiah, Hashabiah, Mattithiah – [six]" (I Chron. 25:3). Five are listed, yet there are six in all, for the Holy One, blessed be He, also counted Shimei while in his mother's womb...Some say that the Holy One, blessed be He, Himself completed the count...and some say that Dan's son Hushim completed the count...and some say Serah daughter of Asher completed the count.

The last three solutions – that God completed the count, that Dan's son Hushim completed the count, and that Serah daughter of Asher completed the count – are patently homiletic. The first solution is apparently related to the idea that God is with the Jews in times of trouble, a notion that developed from God's promise to Jacob before he went down to Egypt: "I Myself will go down with you to Egypt" (Gen. 46:4). Dan's son Hushim can complete the count only if Hushim is counted twice and thus considered as two sons, a possibility alluded to by the Torah's use of the plural form *benei Dan* ("Dan's sons") in connection with Hushim.[3] Serah daughter of Asher is to be counted twice because of her unusually long life.[4]

---

[3] See Albeck's note in his edition of *Genesis Rabbah*, p. 1181, on line 7. Interestingly, the Book of Jubilees mentions other sons of Dan aside from Hushim. Cf. A. Kahana, *Ha-Sefarim ha-Hitzoniyim*, 1 (Jerusalem 1970), p. 305.

[4] See Albeck's note in his edition of *Genesis Rabbah*, p. 1182, on line 4. Heinemann suggests that the expression "completed the count" [Heb. *hishlim 'imahem et ha-minyan*], which occurs throughout this Midrash, emerged in the context of midrashic interpretation of the verse "I am one of those who seek the welfare of the faithful in Israel" (II Sam. 20:19; Heb. *anokhi shlomei emunei Yisrael*), as "I am he who completed (Heb. *shalamti*) the count of all Israel" (*Yalkut Shim'oni* 2.152). However, that passage

The suggestion that Jochebed the daughter of Levi completed the count is the best solution to the difficulty raised by the Torah's list. Jochebed was a descendant of Leah, and including her in the total would complete the count of Leah's children, bringing it to thirty-three. All the other solutions bring the total to seventy, but do not solve the problem of the thirty-three descendants of Leah. Indeed, *Seder 'Olam* (ch. 9) states: "Jochebed was among those who came to Egypt and who came to the Land of Israel and was the name of Amram's wife [who was born to Levi in Egypt]" (Num. 26:59).

The biblical prooftext from Num. 26:59 includes the incomplete sentence, "who was born to Levi in Egypt" (literally, "who bore her (Jochebed) to Levi in Egypt"), whose implied subject, the wife of Levi, differs from the subject of the preceding clause ("the name of Amram's wife was Jochebed daughter of Levi") and of the following clause ("she [Jochebed] bore to Amram Aaron and Moses and their sister Miriam"). Thus, this obscure bit of information about Jochebed being born in Egypt, which draws attention both on substantive and syntactic grounds, can be readily understood if we fill in the details of the story and assume that Jochebed was conceived before the descent to Egypt.

Combining the assumption that Jochebed daughter of Levi was born just as the children of Israel came to Egypt with the assumption generally accepted in rabbinic literature[5] that the Jews spent 210 years of exile in Egypt, we may conclude that Jochebed must have been 130 years old when Moses was born. Ibn Ezra accordingly inquires, "Why didn't the Torah mention the miracle that happened to her?" Nahmanides answers this question in the context of a general discussion about the treatment of miracles in the Torah (in his commentary on Gen. 46:15):

Let me point out something that is obviously true in the Torah, namely, that miracles wrought by a prophet who prophesied

---

deals with completing the count of those who came to Egypt, and not with completing the count of seventy people. Heinemann claims that later midrashists transferred this interpretation about "completing" to the count of seventy people. See Joseph Heinemann, *Aggadot ve-Toldoteihen* (Jerusalem 1974), pp. 57–59.

[5] See Heinemann, *Aggadot ve-Toldoteihen*, pp. 65–73.

beforehand or by an angel...are mentioned in the Bible, and those that occur of themselves to aid the righteous or to fell the wicked are not mentioned in the Torah or the Prophets...Here is reliable proof of what I have said. We know that from the time the Israelites came to the land of Israel until the birth of King David was some 370 years. This period may be divided into four generations – those of Salmon, Boaz, Obed, and Jesse, each of whom lived about 93 years – so that all of them were close to the age of Abraham, and each begot a son the year he died, contrary to the natural way of the world, for the life span in their day was not one hundred years.

Perhaps this observation about Jochebed's conception teaches us something else as well. The birth of Jochebed on the Egyptian border served, as it were, as an antidote to exile. For Jochebed gave birth to Moses, who led the Israelites out of Egypt. In other words, as the Israelites went into exile the instrument of their deliverance was born.

The notion that even at the most difficult of times, the tool for deliverance from hardship is created, is found repeatedly in the Bible. Two examples will suffice here:

1. In *Parashat Vayeshev*, between the story of the sale of Joseph (Gen. 37) and the story of Joseph in Egypt (ch. 39 ff.) the Torah includes the story of Judah and Tamar. Although this story can be related to the stories about the sale of Joseph and later stories, it really seems to be an interruption in the narrative rather than a continuation. This interruption was made in order to allude to tidings of better days, for the story of Judah and Tamar leads to the birth of Peretz, the son of Judah and Tamar, one of whose descendents was King David (cf. Ruth 4:18–21 and *Genesis Rabbah*, ch. 85, ed. Albeck, p. 1030).

2. A similar thing happened regarding Absalom's rebellion. Absalom's entry into Jerusalem is mentioned twice in the Bible, once at the end of the story of how Hushai the Archite was sent by David to foil Ahithophel's counsel – "And so Hushai, the friend of David, reached the city as Absalom was entering Jerusalem" (II Sam. 15:37) – and a second time in the ugly scene where Absalom has intercourse with his father's concubines:

"Meanwhile Absalom and all the people, the men of Israel, arrived in Jerusalem, together with Ahitophel. When Hushai the Archite, David's friend, came before Absalom..." (16:15–16). Both passages mention Hushai the Archite in connection with Absalom arriving in Jerusalem. As we know, Hushai the Archite is a key figure in the story, for it was his intervention that foiled Ahitophel's second piece of advice, turning the battle in David's favor. Here, too, we see that the remedy was provided before the ailment, for as Absalom was entering Jerusalem to celebrate his victory over David, Hushai the Archite had already been brought into the picture, prompting the course of events which led to Absalom's fall.

From these and other passages we may infer that the same applies to this week's Torah reading: as the children of Israel were on their way to Egypt, the ground was being laid for their exodus through the birth of Jochebed, Moses' mother. There is indeed good reason for selecting Ezekiel 37:15–28 as the *haftarah* of *Parashat Vayyigash*, since this selection includes the encouraging words: "You shall declare unto them, Thus said the Lord God: I am going to take the Israelite people from among the nations where they have gone, and I will gather them from every quarter and bring them to their own land" (v. 21).

Parashat Vayehi

"HIS EYES ARE DARKER THAN WINE"

Prof. Aaron Demsky
Department of Jewish History

JACOB'S BLESSING TO JUDAH (Gen. 49:8–12) can be divided into two parts. The first part (vv. 8–10) promises Judah dominion over his brothers and the crown in years to come. Here Judah is compared to a lion's whelp (Heb. *gur aryeh*), words which have been preserved in traditional Jewish names such as Gur Aryeh and Aryeh (Leib) Judah. In the second part of the blessing, Jacob blesses Judah with excellent vineyards in the Judean hills (vv. 11–12):

> He tethers his donkey to a vine,
> His donkey's foal to a choice vine;
> He washes his garment in wine,
> His robe in blood of grapes.
> His eyes are darker than wine;
> His teeth are whiter than milk.

The first distich praises the strength of his vines, which can be used to tether a young donkey, which is quite an unruly beast. The second distich explains that the land of Judah will flow with great quantities of wine, so plentiful that one could wash one's garments in it.

The last distich, *hakhlili einayim mi-yayin, u-leven shinayim me-halav*, and especially the rare word *hakhlili*, which occurs only twice in the entire Bible (here and in Prov. 23:29–30), has been interpreted in a variety of ways. R. Saadiah Gaon interpreted it as "eyes redder than wine and teeth whiter than milk." He took the preposition *mi* (*min*) as a comparative, meaning "more than," and not as a causative, viz., "from," "as a result of," "because of" (cf. Rashi, Ibn Ezra, Rashbam), or "from large quantities of" (cf. Targum Onkelos).

As for the word *hakhlili*, it is generally agreed to refer to the deep red of wine, and indeed this is the meaning of this word in modern Hebrew. This interpretation is supported by the two previous distichs that mention the "blood of grapes" and *sorekah*, one of the choicest varieties of grape vines, whose fruit is deep red.

Opposing these exegetes is Nahmanides, who derives *hakhlili* from the root *k-h-l* (= blue) with a transposition of the letters *het, kaf, lamed*. Support for his view may be adduced from the biblical expression *kahalt 'einayikh*, "you painted your eyes" (Ezek. 23:40); from mishnaic Hebrew, "not until he write and tattoo with ink or with blue [Heb. *kahol*] or with anything that leaves a mark" (Mishnah *Makkot* 3.6); and from Arabic, *el-kahul*, "substance for darkening the eyes." Having *hakhlili* eyes means that they are *kahlili*, "eyes blue [e.g., black, dark] from wine; he cannot disguise his drunkenness, so his eyes must be painted constantly." Nahmanides concludes, surprisingly, that no blessing was meant here: "The Bible speaks disparagingly of wine and of its bad outward effects, causing discoloring and sores." According to this interpretation, our distich not only yields the word pair "tooth and eye," but it also draws a contrast between black and white.

In 1972 an ancient wine jar finely engraved with a Hebrew inscription was discovered. The jar had apparently been found in illegal excavations in one of the villages in the Judean Hills. Its inscription was deciphered by Prof. Nahman Avigad as follows: "For Yehezyahu. Wine. *Kahol*," along with a sign giving its measure (perhaps an *'issaron*). The jar is dated to the seventh–eighth century B.C.E. and is now on display at the Israel Museum in Jerusalem. Avigad interpreted the new term, "wine *kahol*" as designating the vineyard from which it came, that is, "wine from the village Beit-Kahil," which is approximately four kilometers northwest of Hebron.[1]

In light of Nahmanides' interpretation of *hakhlili 'einayim*, we could also interpret this inscription as referring to a type of wine classified by its dark color, for the talmudic rabbis stated that "Black is similar to *kahol*" (*Kiddushin* 12a). Thus, the wine mentioned here would have a dark, almost black color. Compare Mishnah *Niddah* 9.11: "There are grapes that produce red wine, and there are grapes whose wine is black." In Akkadian as well, the word *ekelu*, equivalent to the Hebrew root *h-kh-l*, refers to the dark color of eyes (the modern sense of *kahol* as blue is a later development, possibly dating to the Middle Ages).

I believe this to be a highly instructive example of the Bible shedding light on our understanding of an archaeological finding, and of the archaeological finding casting new light on an ancient exegetical problem. By combining the interpretations of R. Saadiah Gaon, Nahmanides, and *Genesis Rabbah* 98.10 – "*Hakhlili 'einayim mi-yayin* – these are the people from the south, whose eyes are dark (*kehulot*) and whose talent lends itself to Torah study" – our distich could be interpreted as a blessing and not as expressing disapproval of wine. The blessing would be that the eyes of the descendants of Judah should be darker and more beautiful than the deep color of the excellent wine derived from the grapes that grow in the Judean Hills.

---

[1] N. Avigad, "Two Hebrew Inscriptions on Wine Jars," *Israel Exploration Journal* 22 (1972), pp. 1–5; A. Demsky, "Dark Wine from Judah," *Israel Exploration Journal* 22 (1972), pp. 233–234.

Sefer Shemot – The Book of Exodus

Parashat Shemot

AN HOUR OF FAVOR

Devorah Ganz
Department of Bible

THE TEACHINGS OF THE TORAH and the Prophets repeatedly stress the importance of divine providence – there is no reward without good deeds, and repentance precedes deliverance. Given these beliefs, earlier and later rabbinic authorities have asked on what merit the Israelites were delivered from Egypt.

Our Parashah, *Shemot*, which from the very beginning presents the dual themes of slavery and redemption, provides no evidence of change, either moral or religious, in the behavior of the Israelites that might warrant their deliverance as its reward. Quite the contrary, until 2:23 the name of God is strikingly absent from the text. Nechama Leibowitz suggested that this reflected the low level of religiosity in that generation: the oppressed and downtrodden masses did not feel the presence of God in their midst at all. "Suddenly the darkness was pierced by a powerful beam of light. The impenetrable barrier that had separated the upper and lower worlds fell down. The heavens opened."[1] The heavens opened despite no real change in the behavior of those who were enslaved and were now about to be redeemed.

The Sages were aware of the sharp transition from bondage to redemption, as we read in *Exodus Rabbah* (1.42):

---

[1] Nechama Leibowitz, *Studies in Shemot*, 1 (Jerusalem 1976), p. 18.

"God looked upon the Israelites": they had no good deeds to present as reason for being delivered, as is written in Ezekiel (16:7): "I let you grow like the plants of the field...and your hair grew," and when the time came for redemption, "you were still naked and bare," without good deeds. Therefore the Torah says, "God looked," for they had no good deeds by which to merit redemption.

If the Israelites lacked good deeds, by what merit were they redeemed? The talmudic rabbis, and subsequently the medieval commentators, answered this question in various ways.

One approach was indeed to seek some merit in the Israelites, as we find in *Exodus Rabbah* (1.16): "According to Rabbi Akiva, by virtue of the righteous women of that generation the Israelites were delivered from Egypt." The righteousness of these women manifested itself in the measures they took to bear sons in spite of the harsh conditions and decrees of Pharaoh.

Another example of this approach is found in *Leviticus Rabbah* 32:

> They were redeemed on four merits: for not changing their names, their language, for not speaking gossip, and for not having a single woman among them who was improper in her sexual behavior.

Some commentators attribute the Exodus to the patriarchs' merits.[2] Even Sarah the Matriarch is credited in the Midrash[3] for the Exodus from Egypt. Similarly, but in more general terms, the Sages and later Ibn Ezra claimed that the redemption stemmed from the Israelites's repentance. One example is found in the *Mekhilta*: "'And God took notice of them [lit. "and

---

[2] *Exodus Rabbah*, 8: "Go tell them in My name, which is the quality of mercy with which I treat them because of the merits of their ancestors."

[3] *Leviticus Rabbah*, 32.

God knew"]' – He knew that they had repented, but they themselves did not know it."[4]

Ibn Ezra's commentary on Ex. 2:23 offers a similar line of reasoning: "The Israelites had repented." Ibn Ezra's remark is based on a verse in Ezekiel, which states that the Israelites worshipped abominations in Egypt and that God therefore oppressed them. They repented for committing this sin before being redeemed.

The explanations that claim that the Israelites had some sort of merit, such as that of the Patriarchs, do not explain why that particular generation was rewarded with deliverance rather than an earlier generation. As for repentance before the Exodus, the Torah provides no evidence of this, at least not in the conventional sense.[5]

Rashi takes a totally different approach. He suggests seeking the answer to our question not in the Jews' past but in the future. Rashi understands Moses' question, "Who am I...that I should...free the Israelites from Egypt?" (Ex. 3:11) as meaning "By virtue of what do they merit being redeemed?" This is followed by God's response: "And when you have freed the people from Egypt, you shall worship God at this mountain" (Ex. 3:12), which means:

> I have a great purpose in this – My bringing them forth. For they are destined to receive the Torah on this mountain three months after they leave Egypt (Rashi ad loc.).

In other words, God delivered the Israelites from Egypt on the merit of their future behavior, not because the generation of the Exodus was any better than its predecessors. The justification for redemption lay not in their past actions, but in their future destiny. The shortcoming of this interpretation lies in the fact that while God knew beforehand that the Jews would accept His Law at Sinai, He also knew of all the negative things they would do along the way, for which they surely did not deserve to be given such credit. Indeed, the Sages commented about this (*Exodus Rabbah*, 3.3):

---

[4] *Mekhilta Ba-Hodesh*, s.v. *Rabbi*.

[5] As set forth by Maimonides in *Hilkhot Teshuvah*.

Ra'oh ra'iti ("I have surely seen") – God said to Moses: You see only one thing, but I see two. You see them coming to Sinai and accepting My Torah...*ra'oh ra'iti* – this refers to seeing the incident of the golden calf.

In short, we see that none of the commentaries provides a conclusive solution, and each proposed explanation raises additional questions. We therefore suggest looking elsewhere in the Torah to find an answer to this question.

In fact, at least twice in the course of Jewish history we find redemption that was contingent neither on repentance nor on the outcome of repentance. These redemptions did not fit into the pattern of "return to Me and I shall return to you," but were rather encapsulated in the words, "Come back to Me, for I redeem you" (Isa. 44:22). Both in the Exodus from Egypt and in the return to Zion from Babylon, redemption preceded repentance.

Isaiah, in his tidings of redemption to the exiles, did not stipulate repentance as a condition for redemption. His emphatic call, "Comfort, oh comfort My people," was not preceded by a demand to return to God. The prophet was well aware that it is problematic to bring tidings of redemption to a people who lived in exile as punishment for their misdeeds. He therefore did not speak of reward and punishment, notions so familiar to the people from the words of the other prophets. Isaiah told the people in exile of a new concept, a "time of grace." God, who had turned away from the Jews in other eras, now wished to redeem His people. This was a "window of opportunity" between God and the Jewish people. This was God's decree, which was to be accepted without questioning.

In answer to our initial question, we can explain that in fact the Jews did not merit redemption. However, a new age had arrived – a time of grace in the eyes of God. He rules history, and we must submit to and accept His decrees. We are not able to grasp His will, just as a son cannot grasp the will of the father who sired him, nor can matter grasp its creator. The ways of God, in punishment as in mercy, are beyond our human comprehension. We must therefore accept the answer of the prophet (Isa.

45:11): "Thus said the Lord, Israel's Holy One and Maker: Will you question Me on the destiny of My children, will you instruct Me about the work of My hands?"

This is how we are to understand the Exodus from Egypt, and likewise the exodus from Babylon. In both instances, the period of punishment had come to an end and the age of redemption had arrived: "Thus said the Lord: In an hour of favor I answer you, and on a day of salvation I help you" (Isa. 49:8).

Parashat Va'era

SIGNS AND WONDERS

Menahem Ben-Yashar
Department of Bible

THE PASSAGE IN THE Passover Haggadah, "these are the ten plagues," has accustomed us to thinking of ten plagues that were inflicted upon the Egyptians. However, the word *makkot*, which refers to these "plagues" in the Haggadah and in rabbinic writings, appears only once in all of the Bible, where it is used by the Philistines: "He is the same God who struck the Egyptians with every kind of plague [*makkah*]" (I Sam. 4:8).[1] This expression occurs in the Bible only when spoken by non-Jews; the Torah itself always refers to these events as wonders (*mofetim*) or as signs and wonders (*otot u-mofetim*). This is the case in the account of the Exodus from Egypt (Ex. 7:3–11:10), and throughout the remaining books of the Torah (Deut. 6:22; 26:8), as well as the Prophets (Jer. 32:21), Psalms (Ps. 78:43; 105:27; 135:9), and elsewhere in the Writings (Neh. 15:10).

The last plague is an exception: this is the only one referred to as a *nega'* (Ex. 11:1), and in Psalms it is described by the root *m-k-h* (to strike): "He struck Egypt through their firstborn" (Ps. 136:10). This usage is justified, for this action ultimately caused Pharaoh to let the Israelites go.

---

[1] I did not cite the concluding words of this verse, "in the wilderness," which are problematic. Rashi's interpretation seems plausible, namely, that the reference is to the blow struck against the Egyptians at the Red Sea, which is located in the wilderness. Of all the miracles that happened in Egypt, the only one mentioned by Rahab, the harlot who had sheltered Joshua's spies, was the splitting of the Red Sea, an event that was well known to all the peoples of the region, as noted in the Song on the Sea: "The peoples hear; they tremble..." (Ex. 15:14).

The plague of the firstborn was destined from the outset to punish the Egyptians, as Moses was told when he set out on his mission: "Thus says the Lord: Israel is My first-born son. I have said to you, 'Let My son go, that he may worship Me,' yet you refuse to let him go. Now I will slay your first-born son" (Ex. 4:22-23).[2]

However, the plague of the firstborn remains one of the "signs and wonders," and serves a double purpose. All the plagues function as signs attesting God's dominion over the world. This was clear to both the Egyptians, who represent the pagan world: "And the Egyptians shall know that I am the Lord, when I stretch out My hand over Egypt" (Ex. 7:5), and to the Israelites: "that you may recount to your sons and to your sons' sons how I made a mockery of the Egyptians and how I displayed My signs among them, that you may know that I am the Lord" (Ex. 10:2). By singling out the Hebrews and protecting them against the swarms of insects, pestilence, hail, darkness, and finally from slaying the firstborn, God proved that He had chosen Israel.

For the Israelites themselves, the plague of the firstborn was an additional sign, since God only saved from death those firstborn Israelites whose households offered the Passover sacrifice and indicated this publicly by daubing their doorposts and lintels with blood. In other words, only those who attested by their own actions that they would henceforth be servants of God were delivered from the last plague. The Passover sacrifice demonstrated the Jews' covenant with God to the Egyptians, since the Israelites had asked earlier, "If we sacrifice that which is untouchable to the Egyptians before their very eyes, will they not stone us?" (Ex. 8:22). Presumably only these families would leave Egypt, as we read in the Passover Haggadah regarding the wicked son, who held the Passover sacrifice in disdain: "Had he been there (in Egypt), he would not have been delivered."

Moses was instructed about the first plague – blood – at the burning bush (Ex. 4:9), to give him credibility in the eyes of the Israelites as God's messenger. Turning water to blood at this time served only as a sign, not a plague. At the burning bush Moses was given an additional sign to show

---

[2] See the commentary of R. Obadiah Sforno on Ex. 4:23.

the Israelites, namely, turning his rod into a snake (Ex. 4:2–4). Later, when he returned from Midian to Egypt, Moses was commanded to perform these signs before Pharaoh as well (Ex. 4:21). Indeed, Moses performed them before Pharaoh and his servants,[3] but instead of turning into a snake, his rod turned into a crocodile (*tannin*), the serpent-like creature characteristic of the Nile. One other difference: whereas Moses' rod's turning into a frightening creature was only a sign for Pharaoh, blood, the last of the signs God instructed Moses to perform before the Israelites, later became the first plague to strike Egypt.

Thus, counting the sign of the serpent at the beginning and the death of the firstborn at the end, we actually have eleven signs and wonders. If we include the final and most severe blow of all, which was also the greatest wonder of all – drowning Pharaoh and his army in the Red Sea after the sea had parted to let the Israelites pass through – there were a total of twelve signs and wonders. Twelve is a symbolic number; there are twelve months and zodiac signs, and twelve tribes. Similarly, ten is not an incidental number: it is the base for our mathematical computations, human beings having ten fingers.

How is it, then, that the number ten became associated with the plagues, requiring us to count only the signs that were blows against Egypt, and only those blows that were performed in Egypt itself? In rabbinic literature, the notion of "ten plagues" first appears in two Tannaitic sources: Mishnah *Avot* and *Sifre* on Deuteronomy, as well as in a parallel text in *Midrash Tannaim*. In *Sifre* the reference appears as part of an interpretation of the passage concerning first fruits (Deut. 26:5–9). This interpretation is recited as part of the Haggadah, in fulfillment of the commandment to relate the Exodus from Egypt while eating the Passover sacrifice, as stipulated in Mishnah *Pesahim* 10.4: "One is to recite the text from 'My father was a wandering Aramean' until the end of the passage." Deut. 26:8 states: "The Lord freed us from Egypt with a mighty hand, with an outstretched arm and awesome power, and by signs and wonders." The verse discusses those signs and wonders that manifest both "a mighty hand

---

[3] The sign of the leprous hand was not performed before Pharaoh, perhaps because it did not reflect honorably on Moses and Aaron.

and an outstretched arm," that is, those which brought destruction and were effective in getting the Israelites out of Egypt. These were the ten plagues. By applying literary and numerical *derashot* to this verse, the homilist shows an allusion to the number ten.

In order to include the last blow, namely, the splitting of the Red Sea, the Haggadah adds a series of Tannaitic homilies (see *Mekhilta Beshallah*, 6, ed. Horovitz-Rabin, p. 113, and the parallel in *Mekhilta de-Rashbi*) that multiply the plagues to fifty, two hundred, and even two hundred and fifty. It seems reasonable that these homilies, as well as many others in *Midrash Tannaim* about the splitting of the Red Sea and the Song on the Sea, were proposed by the rabbis as they sat at the Seder table on Passover eve. Presumably the Tannaim who used to sit and tell stories about the Exodus all through the night, as described in the Haggadah, developed such homilies.

The other Tannaitic source for the idea of ten plagues is Mishnah *Avot* 5.4. This chapter of the Mishnah lists eleven items, each of which had ten elements, including ten plagues in Egypt and ten miracles that happened to the Israelites, who were saved from the plagues.[4] A closer look at this list shows that only three of the sets of ten are truly accurate: ten generations from Adam to Noah, and ten from Noah to Abraham, and ten times that our ancestors tried God's patience in the wilderness, as related in Num. 14:22.[5]

All the other sets of ten mentioned in the Mishnah are problematic. One, for example, is, "The world was created with ten sayings," but in Genesis the phrase "God said" appears only nine times, leaving the commentators with the task of trying to find a tenth "saying." Neither the ten plagues on Egypt nor the ten miracles by which the Israelites were

---

[4] This is assuming that the Israelites were delivered from all the plagues in Egypt, not only from the five that the Bible mentions explicitly.

[5] Nevertheless, according to the plain meaning of the text, ten is not an exact number, but a formulaic one. See Rashbam and Ibn Ezra on this verse. According to Rashi, who treats the number as exact (see *Arakhin* 15a–b), the reckoning here is not complete because it does not include the sins after the sin of the spies.

delivered at the Red Sea are listed in detail in the Bible or in the Mishnah.[6] They were apparently mentioned in the Mishnah only in order to contrast them to the miracles in Egypt. Thus the entire series in Mishnah *Avot* is more schematic than realistic. The same applies to the ten plagues in Egypt in that list. Had the Mishnah listed a series of elevens or twelves, the plagues in Egypt could equally well have been included there, as explained above.

The idea that there were ten plagues in Egypt is ancient, dating to the Book of Jubilees (40.7). It also appears in the writings of Philo of Alexandria (*Life of Moses*, 1.94–139). According to Jubilees (40.5–6), however, boils and pestilence were apparently counted as a single plague, and the alternate tenth plague was "He meted out punishments to all their gods and burned them in fire."[7]

Perhaps the Sages' insistence on ten plagues, with Rabbi Judah even developing a mnemonic device, *detzakh, adash, be-ahab*, to remember them, was intended to contrast them with the mention of the plagues in Psalms, where the number and order of the plagues differ from those found in the Torah. Ps. 78:43–51 lists seven plagues, and Ps. 105:27–36 refers to eight. The Mishnah's emphasis on the number ten and Rabbi Judah's mnemonic device were apparently intended to indicate that the correct number and order are those written in the Torah, not in Psalms. In other words, the rabbis meant that the psalmists were using poetic license. They were not historians and were under no obligation to list all the facts in their precise order.

As for the internal arrangement of the ten plagues, the first nine (which did not result in the Israelites' release) are divided by Rashbam into three groups of three (Ex. 7:26). Abarbanel follows this approach of three groupings, basing his interpretation on the mnemonic signs of R. Judah. As for the nature of the plagues, they can be arranged in pairs: blood and frogs

---

[6] *Avot de-Rabbi Nathan* (version A, 33) states explicitly that the ten plagues and miracles on the Red Sea corresponded to those in Egypt. However, the text only lists six plagues on the Egyptians at the Red Sea, and then the miracles that happened to the Israelites.

[7] In his edition, A. Kahana renders this as "the Lord meted out revenge," but the Hebrew source of Jubilees, following Ex. 12:12, reads "punishments."

came from the Nile, vermin and beasts are troublesome creatures of dry land, pestilence and boils are diseases, hail and locusts are a blow to agriculture, and darkness and the death of the firstborn go together since darkness signifies death (one example is Job 18:18). The Sages (*Mekhilta Beshallah*, introduction) also associated death with the plague of darkness, telling us that it was during this plague that the wicked Israelites died.

In the final analysis, the plague of the firstborn and the miracle of the Red Sea were the two decisive plagues and wondrous signs that delivered the Israelites. The Israelites took an active part only in these two events, and were passive observers during all the other plagues.

The plague of the firstborn saved the Israelites from bondage in Egypt, but the people could not free themselves from bondage to Pharaoh without becoming servants of their new master, God. Therefore the Passover sacrifice, through which the entire community of Israel worshipped God while still on Egyptian soil, took place before the plague of the firstborn and the Exodus from Egypt. As the rabbis noted, spiritual deliverance preceded physical deliverance. However, only after the crossing of the Red Sea and the drowning of the Egyptian army were the Israelites outside of Egyptian territory and the strong arm of Pharaoh. Only then were they truly free to sing the praise of God, the Song at the Sea, which Moses and the children of Israel sang together.

Parashat Bo

THE JEWISH CALENDAR

Prof. Aaron Demsky
Department of Jewish History

"THIS MONTH SHALL MARK for you the beginning of the months; it shall be the first of the months of the year for you" (Ex. 12:2). This commandment, the first given to the Israelites as a nation, conveys the essence of the Jewish calendar. Here we shall attempt to investigate the inner significance of this calendar. We have often heard the expression "new year," but this is a relative concept: the first of January marks the beginning of the year in the Gregorian calendar, and it is the beginning of the fiscal year in many countries. In China the new year is celebrated on the first new moon that generally occurs in the month of February, and in ancient Babylonia the new year was celebrated during the first ten days of the month of Nissan, which falls at the spring equinox.

The description of the Hebrew calendar in Mishnah *Rosh ha-Shanah* 1.1 is surprising. Not one, but four different days are given as the beginning of the new year:

> The first of Nissan is the new year for kings and festivals. The first of Elul is the new year for the tithe of cattle. R. Eleazar and R. Simeon say: the first of Tishrei. The first of Tishrei is the new year for years, for sabbatical and jubilee years, for planting and for [tithing] vegetables. The first of Shevat is the new year for trees according to the House of Shammai. The House of Hillel say: the fifteenth of Shevat.

The first of Nissan is the new year for kings, i.e., the beginning of the civil year. In biblical times the kings of Israel counted the years of their reign from this date. For example, if a king died in the month of Sivan, two months after the beginning of Nissan, the son who succeeded him would rule for the next ten months of that year, but would start counting his first year of rule only from the beginning of the next Nissan. The Mishnah adds that this date is also the beginning of the year for the religious calendar described in the Mishnah with regard to pilgrimage festivals, since the year's cycle of festivals begins with the pilgrimage to Jerusalem for Passover.

Unlike most ancient calendars, which were based on natural phenomena, the Hebrew calendar chose a historical event – the exodus from Egypt – to mark the beginning of the year. (This innovation was adopted by the other monotheistic religions, which also incorporated a historical element in their calendars, as is evidenced by the celebration of Christmas, by observance of the millennium in the Christian world, and by the Moslems reckoning their years from the *hegira*.) The Exodus from Egypt is the beginning of the year for the people of Israel: "This month shall mark for you the beginning of the months." The first commandment of the people as a whole charts a new and original understanding of time, measured from a point that characterizes and emphasizes the identity of the people of Israel as a free nation. A slave does not control his time, and therefore the commandment to establish a calendar constituted a kind of declaration of independence for the people who had just won their freedom.

The second new year mentioned in the Mishnah is the first of Elul, the sixth month (counting from Nissan); this month marks the time for tithing flocks and herds. According to the talmudic rabbis, when a person brings tithes and gifts to the Temple and the priests, the animals born before this date belong to the previous tax year, whereas all animals born after the first of Elul must be tithed in the current year. It should be noted, however, that this date was disputed; Rabbi Eleazar and Rabbi Simeon believed that the new year for such tithes should begin on the first of Tishrei, after the last birthings of the summer.

The first of Tishrei, the seventh month, is yet another new year listed in the Mishnah. This date marks the day from which the years are reckoned, and it is the "official" beginning of the year (e.g., the transition from the year 5760 to 5761). According to one opinion, this date was chosen because it was the beginning of the year for other ancient peoples. For example, in ancient Canaan the year began in the autumn, when the rainy season started. During the Hellenistic period, even the Seleucid kingdom began its calendar year from Tishrei. According to another view, central in Jewish tradition, this date was chosen because it marks the creation of the universe. The Mishnah notes that the sabbatical year, when tilling the soil is forbidden, also begins on this date, and so does the jubilee year. The age of a tree is counted from this date, which is important for determining the three years during which the fruit of a young tree may not be eaten. If a tree is planted even one month before the first of Tishrei, the tree is considered to be one year old, and it accordingly begins its second year, halakhically speaking. All of these matters are important to agriculture, and hence the new year for them is at the beginning of the year in nature, namely, autumn, when the rainy season begins.

The fourth and final new year mentioned in the Mishnah is the first of Shevat, the eleventh month. This is the new year for trees, since the winter is drawing to a close, the sap is beginning to flow again, and the trees are awakening from their winter slumber to begin a new season in their life cycle. The House of Shammai holds that this date determines the beginning of the new year for trees. The House of Hillel, however, maintains that the date is the fifteenth of Shevat, when the winter rainy season is more than half over. The *halakhah* follows the House of Hillel, and indeed the State of Israel celebrates the fifteenth of Shevat, *Tu bi-Shvat*, as a festival for planting trees.

The Mishnah clearly does not speak of four "new years" which divide the year into equal parts, nor does it maintain that the various "new years" have equal weight in Jewish life. The "new years" fall into two categories. The first of Elul and the fifteenth of Shevat pertain to tithes of animals and plants, and the fact that these dates are disputed suggests that they are dates of lesser significance. The other two dates are central in Jewish life, and have not diminished in significance even after the destruction of the Second Temple. They both emphasize fundamental values and themes of the Jewish people. These dates, close to the spring and fall equinox, are undisputed, and divide the year into two equal, six-month segments.

What lies behind these dates? Calendars in the ancient world often reflected the world of nature. In the pagan world nature and religion were always intertwined. The sun and moon, the fields, forests, rivers, storms and fertility – all were viewed as manifestations of the gods and were reflected in the calendar. The ancient world, in which the Israelite people lived, had two major centers of civilization, Mesopotamia and Egypt. Both of these, like such other great civilizations as India and China, began their history as river civilizations. They harnessed the might of the river to their needs, using it to establish political power and developing religious observances around it. Mesopotamia's economy and culture were based on irrigation from the Tigris and Euphrates, just as Egypt's was based on the Nile. These societies set their time cycles accordingly: the year began in the spring, after the snow had begun melting in the mountains and flowing into the rivers. Using this date, they established their relationship with nature, religion, and civil government.

The ancient Israelites lived in Canaan, a region with no central river; hence their agricultural life was dependent on the rain: "But the land you are about to cross into and possess, a land of hills and valleys, soaks up its water from the rains of heaven" (Deut. 11:11). Canaan, which later became the land of Israel, begins its natural year with the onset of the rainy season. The Hebrew name for this season, *setav*, is borrowed from an Aramaic word meaning winter (a similar word in Arabic, *sita*, means rain). This season follows summer, *kayitz*, whose name might allude to the end, *ketz*, of the cycle of the year (cf. Amos 8:1–2). Ancient Canaanite religion mythically expressed the transition from season to season in terms of their primary deity, Baal or Hadad, the storm god who brings the rain and causes the soil to be fertile. This connection finds expression in the term *sedeh ba'al* [lit. "field of Baal"], which denotes a field watered by the rain. Even though this phrase is used in rabbinic Hebrew as a technical, secular term, its pagan religious origins are obvious.

In the land of Israel, the natural year begins on the first of Tishrei. But for the Jews this date has both natural and supernatural significance. The Jewish new year and the Day of Atonement are sacred days on a cosmic level, when all mankind is judged and the world of nature is created anew. In the Rosh ha-Shanah liturgy we stress the universality of the day in our repetition of the words *ha-yom harat 'olam*, "this is the day the world was conceived," meaning that this is the day of Creation. Likewise, we proclaim the Day of Atonement as "judgment day for all living things." These points attest to the first of Tishrei as the beginning of the natural year in Judaism. On this date the lives and physical needs of Israel and of the entire world face judgment, with special emphasis on the central role played by the Jewish people in determining the fate of mankind.

In contrast to this universalistic perspective, Nissan was chosen as the beginning of the Jewish year to reflect a particularistic perspective. As noted above, this was the first time in history that a calendar was based not on nature but on a historic event. Beginning the year in the spring was exceptional in a society where most beginnings were connected with the fall. The implicit message is that Judaism is not based on nature. Jews live in another dimension. We celebrate and sanctify historic events, and do not necessarily celebrate the transitions between the seasons that were sanctified in the pagan world around us. We do not deny nature, but neither do we champion a god of nature. The agricultural significance of the land of Israel finds expression in the three festivals, all of whose names reflect events associated with the Exodus and the Jews' wanderings in the wilderness: Passover takes place at the time of the barley harvest, Shavuot marks the wheat harvest and the offering of first fruits, and Sukkot celebrates the gathering of the fruits of the trees.

The Hebrew calendar balances the paradoxical complexity of life's events. It lends expression to our desire for a unique and special identity on the one hand, while strengthening our bonds with all of mankind on the other. The particularistic aspect (e.g. kingship and faith) finds expression in the new year beginning in Nissan, while the universalistic (i.e. natural) aspect is manifest in the new year beginning in Tishrei. The Mishnah confirms this duality and the harmony of the two new years that divide the year into equal halves.

Parashat Beshallah

"AND MIRIAM CHANTED FOR THEM" – KOL ISHAH?

Dr. Admiel Kosman
Department of Talmud

From the plain sense of the biblical text we may infer that women used to sing in the presence of men and occasionally even together with them, as is evident from the Torah's account of the Song of Miriam in this week's reading: "Then Miriam the prophetess, Aaron's sister, took a timbrel in her hand, and all the women went out after her in dance with timbrels. And Miriam chanted for them [using the masculine suffix]: Sing to the Lord, for He has triumphed gloriously; horse and driver He has hurled into the sea" (Ex. 15:20–21).

Likewise, Deborah sang a victory song with Barak for vanquishing Sisera and his army: "On that day Deborah and Barak son of Abinoam sang" (Judg. 5:1).[1] Similarly, women sang and danced before King Saul after David slew Goliath: "The women of all the towns of Israel came out singing and dancing to greet King Saul with timbrels, shouting and sistrums" (I Sam. 18:6). Ecclesiastes describes choral groups of "male and

---

[1] Ralbag wrote on Judges 4:25: "She sang over the miracle that God wrought for Israel through the hand of Deborah, and the mention of Barak does not mean that he assisted her in making the song, for she herself composed it. Rather, Barak is mentioned along with her, like 'Then Moses sang.'" In other words, according to Ralbag the prophetess Deborah composed the song herself, and she was assisted by Barak only in singing the song. Similarly, the verse in our Torah reading, "Then Moses and the Israelites sang this song," should be understood as meaning that Moses composed this song; the Israelites only assisting him in singing it. See Yehezkel Kaufmann, *Sefer Shofetim* (Jerusalem 1962), p. 133, on v. 1.

female singers" (Eccl. 2:6),[2] and the song of men and women is also mentioned in the farewell words of Barzillai the Gileadite to David (II Sam. 19:36). In the Book of Ezra, the people who returned to the land of Israel after permission was first granted by Cyrus included "200 male and female singers" (Ezra 4:65).

The picture presented by the Talmud is quite different. There we find the statement, attributed to Samuel, that "a woman's voice is indecent" (*Berakhot* 24a). Indeed, this has not always been interpreted as an absolute prohibition against listening to female singing, but in actual practice, following various developments which we cannot discuss here at length,[3] later rabbinic rulings viewed this as a comprehensive proscription against listening to a woman's singing voice.[4] Nor was joint singing of men and women viewed favorably, as reflected in the remarks of R. Joseph bar Hiyya in *Sotah* 48a:

> If men sing and women respond [in song to the singing of the men], this is licentiousness; and if women sing and men respond [in song to the singing of the women], this is like setting fire to chaff, for it kindles desire like a flame set to linen.

Clearly the discrepancy between the implication of the biblical sources and the view cited above requires explanation. An attempt to resolve this discrepancy can be found in *Mekhilta of Rabbi Ishmael, Beshallah* (ed. Horowitz-Rabin, p. 152):

---

[2] The *Zohar* compares this chorus with Miriam's chorus of women at the Red Sea: "Rabbi Jose said: For it is written, 'singing [fem.],' as it is said, 'And Miriam chanted for them.'" (Ex. 15:20; *Zohar*, Exodus, 19a).

[3] Saul J. Berman, "Kol Isha," in Leo Landman, ed. *Rabbi Joseph H. Lookstein Memorial Volume* (New York 1980), pp. 45–66.

[4] See the various opinions cited in Rabbi Yehiel Michael Epstein, *'Arokh ha-Shulhan, Even ha-'Ezer* 21.3. It should be noted that several later *posekim* took a more lenient stand, with some permitting mixed singing of sacred songs by men and women in certain circumstances. See, for example, R. Yehiel Jacob Weinberg, *Seridei Esh*, 2.8. Cf. also Joel B. Wolowelsky, "Modern Orthodoxy and Women's Self-Perception," *Tradition* 22 (1986), pp. 65–81.

And Miriam chanted for them: "Sing to the Lord, for He has triumphed gloriously; horse and driver He has hurled into the sea." The Torah relates that just as Moses recited the song for the men, so Miriam recited the song for the women, as it is written, "Sing to the Lord."

This homily apparently assumes that Miriam sang only for the women; she did not sing for the men either in solo or as part of a choir of women singing with Moses' choir.[5]

Among traditional commentaries we find other opinions, according to which listening to a woman's voice may, under certain circumstances, have spiritual dimensions, and these circumstances applied to Miriam's song. For example, the *Zohar* says (*Shelah* 167b):

"Then Miriam the prophetess...took a timbrel in her hand." All the righteous in the Garden of Eden listen to her[6] sweet voice, and several holy angels give thanks and praise along with her to the Holy Name.

These commentaries, according to the thesis I shall present below, share what might be called a spiritual-utopian bent. Halakhically these commentators had to view the spiritual potential of the female voice in utopian terms. In other words, those commentators who sensed great spiritual potential in the female voice assumed that it could only be present

---

[5] Cf. Philo's interpretation in *Life of Moses*, 2.256, ed. Susan Daniel-Nataf (Jerusalem 1991), p. 321. Interestingly, *Zayit Ra'anan* on the *Mekhilta* suggests that the correct reading here is Miriam sang the "song for two [*li-shenayim*]" instead of "song for women [*le-nashim*]." In other words, Miriam sang with two women who responded in chorus after her. Other commentators attempted to solve this problem by claiming that Miriam took the timbrel in hand not to improve the music she made, but to spoil it, as the sound of the timbrel would interfere with men listening to the women's voices. Cf. R. Issachar Eilenburg, *Tzedah La-Derekh* (Jerusalem 1998), p. 82, on Ex. 15:20, and R. Jacob Kuli, *Yalkut Me-'Am Lo'ez, Shemot, Beshallah* (Jerusalem 1967), p. 360. Rabbi Joseph Rosen suggested that Miriam and the women who accompanied her only played instruments, but did not sing. See *Tzafenat Pa'neah 'al ha-Torah*, ed. Menahem M. Kasher (Jerusalem 1961), p. 10.

[6] Apparently Jochebed's; see ibid.

under special future conditions, when there would no longer be any evil inclination. At present, though, the *yetzer ha-ra* "throws up a smokescreen" of physical attraction that makes it impossible to sense the powerful spiritual vitality of the female voice.

For example, Rabbi Menahem Azariah of Fano[7] (1548–1620), who assumed that Miriam and the women who sang in chorus did indeed sing before men,[8] claimed: "Song was her intention, and one should not be strict [=forbidding listening to female singing] under all circumstances, since the evil inclination does not exist in that world."[9]

In other words, Rabbi Menahem Azariah assumed that the moment of spiritual elation in which Miriam and the women sang before the men on the shore of the Red Sea was an exceptional moment in which the quality of the World to Come penetrated this world, making it possible to deviate from the general prohibition against women singing before men. Hence the female voice at that special moment was both prophetic and divine, enabling the men to attain special spiritual elation.[10] This is apparently what R. Menahem meant when he wrote that "Song was her intention," namely, song in the sense of the spiritual revelation that prompted this singing. Moreover, it should be stressed that Rabbi Menahem Azariah was not referring here to a quality of song that was specific to women, but rather to the general prophetic quality of song, which could be male or female. In

---

[7] R. Menahem Azariah of Fano, *Kanfei Yonah* (Lemberg 1884), 4.36, 99b. R. Menahem Azariah's remarks are more familiar from a secondary source which cites them, *Yalkut Ha-Reuveni* on Exodus (Warsaw 1884), *Parashat Beshallah*, p. 78, although the citation of R. Menahem Azariah's remarks there is not fully accurate. This anthology was edited by Rabbi Abraham Reuben Hakohen Sofer, who lived in Poland in the seventeenth century.

[8] This is actually the second possibility suggested by R. Menahem Azariah; the first possibility is that the women who joined Miriam did so only to provide a sort of accompaniment to the main melody sung by Moses and the men. According to R. Joseph b. Hiyya in *Sotah* 48a, this is not strictly forbidden, but is deemed licentious behavior, which people did not always avoid.

[9] I.e., the spiritual world. Compare this with the statement attributed to Abraham's servant Eliezer in *Bava Batra* 58a: "It is well-known that desire does not exist in that world [the World to Come]."

[10] A similar interpretation was suggested by Rabbi Issachar Eilenburg in *Tzedah la-Derekh* (above, n. 5).

fact, in such song the distinction between male and female disappears completely, since it is altogether divine.

Another possibility suggested by Rabbi Menahem Azariah is that only Miriam sang before the men; the rest of the women only joined her with musical accompaniment, but not with song. Why was Miriam's singing considered permissible? R. Menahem explains that the other women were ordinary people, incapable of "directing their minds to the *'Attika* ["Old One],"[11] whereas Miriam was a prophetess, and as such she knew that at this precise moment it was the will of God that a woman – namely, herself – should sing before the men, even though the *halakhah* generally forbade this.

The last possibility, the most remarkable of those offered by Rabbi Menahem Azariah, is that behind every woman stood an angel to whom Miriam turned when she requested to be joined in song; it was these angels who sang along with Miriam, not the rest of the women. Perhaps this interpretation should be viewed as a reflection of the idea that when an angel stands behind a woman her song becomes inspired, so that even men can become spiritually elated by her singing.

A different approach to this problem was taken by R. Ephraim of Luntshitz (d. 1619), author of *Keli Yakar* on the Torah. He maintained that the status of women's singing changed in this week's Torah reading because the women themselves changed momentarily, climbing to the spiritual level of men in their "receptiveness of prophecy." Furthermore, at this particular time the men were presumably in no danger of becoming aroused by the women's voices. R. Ephraim's interpretation is based on a seeming grammatical error which he found in the biblical text. Miriam turned to the women, asking them to join her in song, in the following words, "And Miriam chanted for them (Heb. *lahem*, masculine): Sing to the Lord" (Ex. 15:21). Seemingly, the text should have read "Miriam chanted for them" (Heb. *lahen*), using the feminine form, since she was addressing

---

[11] *'Attika Kadisha* is the term used in mystical literature for the One God Himself. See Judah Liebes, *Torat ha-Yetzirah shel Sefer Yetzirah* (Jerusalem 2001), p. 51.

the women. Hence R. Ephraim concluded:[12] "At the Red Sea the women attained the level of men in their receptiveness of prophecy. Therefore Scripture says *lahem*, as if talking to men, and indeed of the End of Days it is written, 'A woman shall court a man'" (Jer. 31:22).[13]

The principal difference between the approaches of these two rabbis regarding a woman's voice can be summarized as follows: R. Menahem Azariah emphasized the change that occurred at this specific, miraculous moment in the inner world of the men, as they rose to a level of spirituality where they could sense the spirituality of the female voice, whereas R. Ephraim of Luntshitz viewed the change as having occurred within the women themselves, as they rose to greater spiritual heights, identical to the level of the men. Thus their voices would no longer entice men into sinful thoughts.[14]

---

[12] R. Luntshitz assumes that according to our verse, women will rise in the future to the level of men. This position is expressed by R. Chaim Joseph David Azulai in various places in his works; see e.g. *Nahal Kedumim le-Parashat Beshallah* (Jerusalem 1976), §21.

[13] In this connection it is worth noting Rabbenu Bahya's comment on our verse: "One ought not to wonder that prophecy should come to a woman, for she is of human kind, and is called man, as it is written: 'He...called them Man'" (Gen. 5:2). Rabbenu Bahya proceeds to list numerous women who, according to tradition, received prophecy, as well as several tenets of the faith that were revealed by women according to the Midrash. He concludes, "All this indicates that womankind is not totally vapid, but has substance" (Rabbenu Bahya, *Be'ur 'al ha-Torah*, ed. C. B. Chavel, 2 [Jerusalem 1994], p. 135).

[14] Cf. also Tovah Cohen, "Yihudah shel Miriam ke-Manhigah," *Bar-Ilan Daf Shevu'i*, Beshallah 5760.

Parashat Yitro

"YOU SHALL NOT MURDER" – YOU SHALL NOT COMMIT SUICIDE

Dr. Israel Zvi Gilat
School of Education

THE TALMUDIC RABBIS interpreted the biblical verse "you shall not kill" not just as a prohibition against killing others, but also against killing oneself. Thus, a *baraita* in the Talmud (*Bava Kamma* 90b) states: "But for your own lifeblood I will require a reckoning" (Gen. 9:5) – R. Eleazar said: For your life [=soul] I shall require [a reckoning of] your blood." This prohibition is inferred by other sources from the verse "You shall not kill" (see *Pesikta Rabbati* on Exodus, ch. 24), viz.: "You shall not kill – you shall not cause yourself to be killed."[1] Thus, the verse "you shall not kill" applies not just to taking another person's life, but even to taking one's own life, whether directly, by committing suicide, or indirectly, by taking undue risk.

The idea that a person is not entitled to cause his own end provides an answer to a question that has perplexed experts in criminal law: Does the prohibition against murder have any intrinsic significance, aside from fear of punishment? What if, heaven forbid, a person wished to risk dying by committing a crime that is subject to the death penalty? Is he allowed to do so? An answer to this question is given in the Midrash:[2]

---

[1] Meir Ish-Shalom, *Perush Meir 'Ayin*, ad loc.

[2] *Mekhilta de-Rashbi* on Ex. 20.13 (ed. Epstein-Melamed, p. 152).

> How do we know that if one commits murder with the intention of being executed, he is considered forewarned [and hence punishable]? As it is written: "You shall not murder." How do we know that if one is about to be executed and he says: I will commit murder, that he is considered forewarned? As it is written: "You shall not murder."

This interpretation clearly reflects the view that a person's life does not belong to him, and therefore one is not allowed to decide what to do with one's body[3] – a view patently contradictory to all notions of civil liberty in which the freedom of the individual and his supreme rights over his own body are sacrosanct.[4]

Nevertheless, these rulings forbidding self-harm are not undisputed. The Bible, the Apocrypha, and even history books written after the destruction of the Second Temple and the subsequent revolts provide numerous examples of important figures who willingly put an end to their own lives, whether by suicide or by dying in optional battles – for example, Samson, King Saul, Hannah and her seven sons, the "four hundred children who were taken captive to be disgraced" (*Gittin* 57a), the zealots in Jerusalem, the fighters at Masada, the victims of Beitar, and others.[5] Moreover, some rabbis even praised these people.

Indeed, the sweeping proscription against self-harm has evoked serious disputes among halakhic authorities, beginning with the *Rishonim*. Is killing oneself forbidden even if one is forced to commit a sin that falls into the category of "be killed, rather than transgress"? Is such a person forbidden to avert the calamity that lies in store and to kill himself "if he

---

[3] See Radbaz's commentary on Maimonides, *Hilkhot Sanhedrin* 18.6.

[4] For such views, see Leon Shelef, "Bein Kedushat ha-Hayyim li-Kevod ha-Adam – 'Al Yissurei Guf, ha-Kidmah ha-Refu'it, Regishut Enoshit ve-ha-Mishpat ha-Pelili," *Mishpatim* 24 (1994), pp. 207–240.

[5] These include such rabbinic stories as the story of Beruriah, the wife of R. Meir, who strangled herself (*Avodah Zarah* 18b; see also Rashi ad loc., s.v. *ve-ikka de-amrei*), and Yakum of Tzerorot, the nephew of R. Jose ben Joezer of Tzeredah, who "went and carried out [on himself] the four methods of execution available to the court" (*Genesis Rabbah*, 65.22). His uncle remarked (ibid.), "In but a fleeting moment he reached Heaven before me."

sees that he will not be able to withstand the test," as the Tosafists phrased it? Or is he then "commanded to inflict injury upon himself," as maintained by Rabbenu Tam? Or is neither the case, with the decision left to the person himself?[6]

It should be noted that the Torah itself is not fully clear on this issue, and indeed different interpretations of the examples cited above have been offered by commentators.[7] King Saul, for example, asked a necromancer to summon the ghost of the prophet Samuel. According to the Bible, Samuel reproved Saul, concluding with the words, "Further, the Lord will deliver the Israelites who are with you into the hands of the Philistines. Tomorrow your sons and you will be with me" (I Sam. 28:19). Later we read about the battle that was waged the following day: "The battle raged around Saul, and some of the archers hit him, and he was severely wounded by the archers. Saul said to his arms-bearer, 'Draw your sword and run me through, so that the uncircumcised may not run me through and make sport of me.' But his arms-bearer...refused, whereupon Saul grasped the sword and fell upon it" (I Sam. 31:3–4). How could Saul have taken his own life?

A prevalent view among Jewish scholars is that Saul did not sin "because he knew he was destined to die in battle, for Samuel had told him."[8] In other words, Saul acted as he did because he knew with certainty that he would die in that battle. Hence, any other person whose death is uncertain has no right to take his own life. This view is based on *Yalkut Shim'oni* (ibid. 141):

---

[6] Tosafot *Avodah Zarah* 18a, s.v. *ve-al yehabbel*; Tosafot *Bava Kamma* 91b, s.v. *ha-hovel be-'atzmo*.

[7] For further discussion, see Yehezkel Lichtenstein, *Issur ha-Hit'abdut be-Mahalakh ha-Dorot*, M.A. thesis (Ramat Gan 1991). For suicide in connection with martyrdom in medieval Franco-Germany, see the important study of Haym Soloveitchik, "Religious Law and Change – The Medieval Ashkenazic Example," *AJS Review* 12 (1987), pp. 205–221; Avraham Grossman, "Shorashav shel Kiddush ha-Shem be-Ashkenaz ha-Kedumah," *Kedushat ha-Hayyim ve-Heruf ha-Nefesh* (Jerusalem 1993), p. 99; idem, "Bein 1012 le-1096: Ha-Reka' ha-Tarbuti ve-ha-Hevrati le-Kiddush ha-Shem be-1096," *Yehudim Mul ha-Tzelav: Gezerot 1096 be-Historiah u-ve-Historiografiah* (Jerusalem 2000), p. 55. See also Yisrael Yuval, "Ha-Nakam ve-ha-Kelalah, ha-Dam ve-ha-'Alilah: Me-'Alilot Kedoshim la-'Alilot Dam," *Zion* 58 (1993), p. 33, and the responses to this article by other scholars which appeared in *Zion* 59 (1994).

[8] As formulated by R. David Kimhi in his commentary on I Sam. 34:4.

Samuel prophesied during his lifetime and after his death. He said to Saul: If you take my advice and die by the sword, then your death will atone for you and you will share the same place as I do. So Saul took his advice and was killed along with his sons.

Thus Saul's act should not be treated as a binding precedent for later generations, but as a momentary dictate to atone for his sins, based on the prophecy he had received.

Another explanation is that Saul's act was not considered suicide "because the archers had found him and he had no escape. Better for him to have killed himself than for the Gentiles to have made sport of him."[9] This explanation, too, rests on the uniqueness of Saul as King of Israel. Alternatively, he might have reasoned that if he fell into their hands alive, they would make sport of him and torture him. Obviously the Israelites would not have been able to tolerate seeing and hearing their king in trouble without rising to save him, thereby causing tens of thousands of Israelites to fall. Alternatively, Saul's suicide might have been justified because it was not befitting for him to die at the hands of the uncircumcised, who would contemptuously torture him to death, thereby desecrating God's name.

Still other authorities maintained that King Saul was not exempt from the strict regulations of the *halakhah*, and that his status as king did not exempt him from the usual prohibition against suicide. Nahmanides, and subsequently R. Asher, held that Saul's action was permitted because he was pursued, so he was not guilty of committing suicide.[10] R. Joseph Karo, in his *Beit Yosef*,[11] also discussed Saul's act in the context of a debate among

---

[9] R. Shlomo Luria in *Yam Shel Shelomo, Bava Kamma* 8.59.

[10] Nahmanides, *Torat ha-Adam, Sha'ar ha-Hesped* (ed. Chavel, 2.84); R. Asher (Rosh), *Mo'ed Katan*, 3.94. Both comment on *Genesis Rabbah*, ch. 34: "'But for your own life-blood I will require a reckoning – from your life [=soul] I shall require [a reckoning of] your blood.' Does this apply even to someone pursued, like Saul? That is what we are taught by the word 'but.'" Note that the word "pursued" is a later addition to the text, which does not appear in our editions of the Midrash.

[11] *Yoreh De'ah* 157, s.v. *ve-ha-Rambam*.

the *Rishonim*. Some of these scholars, such as Rabbenu Tam,[12] held that "when there is concern that pagans will cause one to commit a transgression – for example, by torture that one cannot withstand – one is obligated to harm himself," but others disagreed.

> We maintain that in times of persecution a person may deliver himself to death and take his own life if he knows that he will not be able to withstand [torture]...Evidence for this is provided by those who killed babies in times of persecution. Some authorities forbid this, maintaining...that a person may not kill himself. Hananiah, Mishael and Azariah delivered themselves to others but did not harm themselves. Saul son of Kish acted contrary to what the rabbis ordained.[13]

Later generations of scholars also analyzed this issue. In *Teshuvot Hayyim Sha'al* by R. Chaim Yosef David Azulai, the following question was discussed:

> A Jew was captured, brought to trial, and incarcerated in the same place as the king's prisoners, but was kept in a room by himself. After several days the prison guards said that they found him strangled, a scarf around his neck. The question is whether this should be considered suicide, and hence the deceased should not be mourned, or whether one should mourn for him.
>
> Here is my answer: One could argue that since it had been publicized that [the man on trial] was the murderer, this poor

---

[12] Cited in Tosafot on '*Avodah Zarah* 18a.

[13] *Beit Yosef*, ibid. The text there continues, "Once there was a rabbi who slaughtered many babies during a time of persecution, for he was afraid lest they be forced to betray their religion. There was another rabbi with him who was angry at him and called him a murderer, but the former did not listen to him. The latter rabbi, who wished to restrain him, said: If I am right, may that rabbi die a strange death. And so it was that he was captured by the gentiles, who tore off his skin and stuffed sand between his skin and his flesh. Later the evil decree was annulled, and had [the rabbi] not slaughtered [his children], they might have been saved and not killed." See the discussion of R. Shlomo Luria, *Yam Shel Shelomo, Bava Kamma* 8.59.

person feared he would be abused and sentenced to death by torture, and therefore he chose to die on his own, without torture. In *Beit Lehem Yehudah*, R. Zvi b. R. Azriel wrote:

If a person puts himself to death for fear of having to face great torture, as is the practice with pagans...then surely this is not considered suicide[14]... Regarding what is said in *Genesis Rabbah* on the verse, "But for your own life-blood" etc., one may ask whether this also applies to people in circumstances like King Saul's...Regarding Saul, the Bible states that he was afraid that the Amalekites would make sport of him. From this we learn that a person who takes his own life for fear of being tortured is not considered a suicide.

Hence we see that fear of torment warrants special leniency, even in cases where suicide was not committed to avoid violating a prohibition where one is ordinarily obligated to "be killed rather than transgress."[15]

Rav Kook (*Mishpat Kohen*, §144) sought to infer from Saul's act, as from the other cases of illustrious people who endangered themselves or committed suicide, that Saul was not simply afraid of torture, but "he was afraid that the uncircumcised Philistines would abuse him sexually...if one fears being defiled sexually, he may take preemptive action and take his own life." This seems to imply that one may not take his own life merely

---

[14] *Yoreh De'ah* 345.3. Various related laws are cited there: "If someone committed robbery and is subject to the death penalty according to the law of the kingdom, he is mourned...and is not considered a suicide...If one accepts [upon himself any of] the four death sentences meted out by a rabbinical court in penitence for his sins, and consequently he drowns himself in the river, he is not considered a suicide. It also seems to me that one who commits suicide because he is afraid of great torture of the sort imposed by pagan law is not considered a suicide. This follows from what is written in Tosafot [=Tosafot *Gittin* 57b, s.v. *kafetzu*]: "They jumped into the sea because they were afraid of being tortured."

[15] It might be argued that this is merely a *de facto* justification of suicide, but even Saul's conduct was analyzed by halakhic authorities from a *de facto* perspective: should he have been eulogized after what he did? (Some authorities maintained that the fact that Saul fell on his sword should not have prevented people from eulogizing him.)

out of fear of bodily suffering, unless the fear is accompanied by an element of coercion to commit a transgression.[16]

Saul's act evoked considerable interest in the framework of a famous rabbinic debate some forty years ago. The question was whether the suicide at Masada was permitted according to the *halakhah*. Rabbi Shlomo Goren, then Chief Rabbi of the Israel Defence Forces, ruled that "the heroism of the fighters on Masada was in accordance with *halakhah* as we understand it today."[17] He offered the following arguments in support of his opinion:

1. When a person falls into the hands of a cruel enemy who is about to kill him in battle, and he fears that he will be tortured into transgressing a commandment regarding which it is obligatory "to be killed rather than to violate the law" (e.g., idolatry, incest, or bloodshed), one is obligated to die at his own hands and not fall into the hands of the enemy.

2. When falling into the hands of the enemy would lead to desecration of God's name, e.g., because it would give the enemy something to boast of, and when the potential victim would be killed anyway, he is obligated to die at his own hands rather than falling into the hands of the enemy, as was the case with King Saul – and the zealots at Masada.

To substantiate his claim that the mass suicide on Massada was halakhically acceptable, R. Goren cited the example of Saul's suicide:

> Saul did not act entirely on his own initiative. As as we read in
> *Yalkut Shim'oni,* "Samuel said to Saul: If you take my advice to fall
> by the sword, then your death shall be your atonement." This

---

[16] Ibid. §144 (p. 326). Rav Kook relied on R. Asher, but if one carefully examines Rav Kook's remarks, one sees that his ruling does not reflect the plain sense of R. Asher. For R. Asher wrote *me-hamat she-mafkirin oto,* "since he is abandoned," whereas Rav Kook interpreted this as *minhag hefker nahagu ba,* i.e., "one was treated as something *hefker,*" i.e., he was abused. Likewise, Rav Kook explains his claim that Saul was afraid that he would be sexually abused as follows: "Like the concubine in Gibeah...where there was also an issue of illicit sexual behavior." Rav Kook thereby sought to bring Maimonides' ruling (*Hilkhot Yesodei ha-Torah* 5.4) that "anyone who is required to transgress rather than be killed and allows himself to be killed is guilty of giving up his life" into conformance with Saul's conduct in committing suicide. Later, however, Rav Kook alludes to another possible explanation of Saul's conduct – "it is permitted to endanger oneself in danger in wartime, although in my opinion this is a special law pertaining uniquely to kings."

[17] *Or ha-Mizrah* 7 (July–Aug. 1960), pp. 22–27.

makes it clear that the advice to fall on the sword came from Samuel, who gave this advice as a prophecy from the Almighty.

It follows that under such circumstances, taking one's own life is not only permissible *de facto*, but obligatory *de jure*.[18] Note too that according to Rabbi Goren, King Saul's suicide was carried out in response to a prophetic command.

R. Moshe Tzvi Neriah sharply opposed this ruling in a pamphlet entitled "The Suicide on Massada in the Halakhah":[19]

> This interpretation is most peculiar. Where did Samuel tell Saul to fall *on* his sword? The verse says to fall *by* the sword, meaning to go to war and die in battle.

R. Neriah raised a second objection: If Samuel commanded Saul to "fall on his sword," why did Saul order his arms-bearer, "Draw your sword and run me through"? Third, if Saul fell on his sword in response to a prophetic command, this would contradict the assumption that the Masada suicide was normative, since prophets are not allowed to introduce halakhic innovations. Thus Samuel's instructions could not serve as a basis for rendering halakhic decisions for later generations.

R. Neriah took the argument further, maintaining that Rabbi Goren's verdict about the fighters on Massada was not accepted by most *Rishonim*

---

[18] Note, however, that when there is fear of "terrible torture if one falls into enemy hands" which is not accompanied by coercion to betray the faith or to desecrate God's name, "and the enemy is cruel and will surely kill the victim in the end with unbearable torture," Rabbi Goren rules as follows: "Some permit dying at one's own hands even in these circumstances." Thus, while Rabbi Goren permits suicide under such circumstances, he does not claim that it is obligatory. Rabbi Goren also ruled that "when there is reason to fear that prior to death the enemy will attempt to extract through torture important classified information which one must safeguard with his life – for a person who divulges such information is considered a *rodef* (=one who threatens the life of another Jew)...then we are obligated to avoid this. Hence a person in such a position must choose death rather than violate this law."

[19] *Hit'abdut Anshei Metzadah ba-Halakhah = Tznif Melukhah* (Kefar Ha-Ro'eh 1992), pp. 196–198.

and some *Aharonim*. Even Rabbenu Tam was cited in other sources as permitting suicide, though not viewing it as imperative.

R. Neriah's reservations accordingly indicate his hesitancy to draw halakhic conclusions from the historical sources without relying on reliable interpretation by authoritative scholars. As he put it:

> What happened in ancient times on top of Masada requires further investigation, in light of the conditions of Roman captivity and knowing what lay in store for these fighters if they surrendered...Even if we assume that the circumstances justified their conduct, we must take explicit issue with the arguments given by their commander, Eleazar ben Yair, in whose opinion suicide was the only path not only for the heroes of Masada, but for the entire people, for "long ago God issued this judgment to the entire Jewish people, and there is no escaping it," "God has sent this decree upon us," and "this is what the Torah ordains."
> Needless to say, these words have no basis, for the laws of our Torah command us to safeguard our existence and our life, even in times of captivity. For God has planted everlasting life within us...Had our brethren who were in distress and captivity, in ghettos and death camps where they were likely to be tortured, abused, and made to betray their faith, followed this ruling, not one of them would have survived.

Parashat Mishpatim

Cruelty to Animals in Jewish Tradition

Dr. Yael Shemesh

Department of Bible

IN THEIR DISCUSSIONS of whether cruelty to animals is prohibited by the Torah or only by rabbinic injunction, most *Rishonim* ruled that this prohibition applies according to Torah law.[1] Support for this viewpoint is frequently adduced from the commandment that appears in this week's reading: "When you see the donkey of your enemy lying under its burden and you want to refrain from raising it, you must nevertheless raise it with him" (Ex. 23:5, and similarly Deut. 22:4).

This article does not purport to be a comprehensive halakhic discussion of animal rights, but rather attempts to present a few of the many classical Jewish sources that reveal a compassionate attitude towards animals, viewing them as creatures to be treated with consideration.[2] Following this investigation of the sources we shall also consider some practical applications in our own daily lives.

---

[1] Cf. Yehudah Altschuler, *Ha-Yahas le-Ba'alei Hayyim ve-ha-Tipul Bahem le-Or ha-Halakhah*, M.A. thesis (Ramat Gan 1996), pp. 153–156; Avraham Steinberg, "Tza'ar Ba'alei Hayyim le-Or ha-Halakhah," *Sefer Assia*, 1 (Jerusalem 1989), pp. 263–269.

[2] For further information and additional sources, see Richard H. Schwartz, *Judaism and Vegetarianism* (Marblehead, Mass. 1988), pp. 13–30; *Judaism and Animal Rights – Classical and Contemporary Responses*, ed. Roberta Kalechofsky (Marblehead, Mass. 1992); Masha Matias Sarid, "Mivhano shel Moshe – ha-Yahas le-Ba'alei Hayyim be-Moreshet Yisrael," *Teva, On u-Beriut* 102 (2000), pp. 29–30; ibid. 103 (2000), pp. 30–31.

Compassion and Decency Towards Animals

The reason given in this week's *Parashah* for observing the Sabbath is "that your ox and your donkey may rest, and that your bondman and the stranger may be refreshed" (Ex. 23:12). The Torah acknowledges that animals have needs that must be considered and respected, and protects their right to a day of rest just as it protects the rights of the bondman and the stranger – the weak and exploited in human society. Sensitivity to the needs of animals can be seen in other biblical passages as well. For example, "You shall not muzzle an ox while it is threshing" (Deut. 25:4); "You shall not plow with an ox and an donkey together" (Deut. 22:10), because "the Lord had compassion on all His creatures, insofar as a donkey does not have the strength of an ox" (Ibn Ezra ad loc.).

Similarly, limitations were placed on the use of animals, the aim of these precepts being to instruct men to shun the cruelty that finds expression in the cynical exploitation of animals:[3] "You shall not boil a kid in its mother's milk" (Ex. 23:19; 34:26; Deut. 14:21); "No animal from the herd or from the flock shall be slaughtered on the same day with its young" (Lev. 22:28); "If, along the road, you chance upon a bird's nest...do not take the mother together with her young. Let the mother go, and take only the young" (Deut. 22:6–7).

Various sources indicate that animals are to be treated as individuals, whose needs should be considered. This is implied by the verse "A righteous man knows the needs of his beast" (Prov. 12:10), as well as by the homily describing Moses and David as devoted shepherds who gave their flocks personal attention. It was this character trait that made them worthy in God's eyes of leading the Jewish people.[4]

The following astonishing story, with its revolutionary message, is told of Rabbi Judah ha-Nasi (here known by his common appellation, "Rabbi"). A calf that was led to slaughter pushed its head under the corner of Rabbi's garment and began bleating woefully. Rabbi, however, pushed it away, saying, "For this you were created." For this act he was punished measure for measure: since he did not have mercy on the calf, it was decreed that he

---

[3] Cf. S. D. Luzzatto's commentary on Ex. 23:19 and Lev. 22:28.

[4] Cf. *Exodus Rabbah* 2.2.

should suffer many years of terrible pain. His healing was also measure for measure. Many years later, when he had mercy on a litter of mice and did not allow his maidservant to sweep them out of the house, God had mercy on him, and his pain disappeared.[5]

The approach revealed by these sources is diametrically opposed to that of the modern food industry,[6] which frequently exploits animals, with no concern for their welfare. The result is that animals are overcrowded in order to economize on expenses, and hens' biological clocks are fooled by artificial lighting to make them lay more eggs. Clearly, one cannot expect individual care of animals in such settings.

Vegetarianism in Judaism

It is generally accepted that the first ten generations of mankind were vegetarian and that only after the generation of the flood did God allow human beings to eat meat.[7] The Talmud states (*Sanhedrin* 59b): "Rabbi Judah quoted Rav: Eating meat was not permitted to Adam, as it is written, '[All the green grasses]...shall be yours for food, and for all the animals on land' (Gen. 1:29–30); He did not permit you the living creatures. But when the sons of Noah came, He permitted them to eat animals, as it is written, 'As with the green grasses, I give you all these'" (Gen. 9:3).

R. Joseph Albo (ca. 1380–1444) explains the retroactive permission to eat meat as "an attempt of the Torah to combat the evil inclination, just as beautiful women were permitted to them" (*Sefer ha-Ikkarim*, 3.15). Albo's view about eating meat is expressed in strong language: "Aside from the cruelty, rage and fury in killing animals, and the fact that it teaches human

---

[5] *Bava Metzia* 85a; Yerushalmi *Kilayim* 9.3; *Genesis Rabbah* 33.3; *Yalkut Shim'oni* on Psalms, §888, s.v. *tehilah le-David*. For a more detailed discussion, see my "Min ha-Mekorot – R. Yehudah ha-Nasi Lomed le-Rahem 'al Ba'alei Hayyim," *Teva, On u-Beriut* 102 (2000), pp. 27–28.

[6] For the intolerable conditions suffered by animals in the modern food industry cf. Peter Singer, *Animal Liberation* (New York 1990), ch. 3. Several of his points are presented below.

[7] For more on the connection between Judaism and vegetarianism, see Richard Schwartz (above n. 2), which is entirely devoted to this subject. See also *Rabbis and Vegetarianism: An Evolving Tradition*, ed. Roberta Kalechofsky (Marblehead, Mass. 1995); a bibliography is found in Rinah Lee, *Agnon ve-ha-Tzimhonut – Iyyunim bi-Yetzirotav shel S. Y. Agnon min ha-Hebet ha-Tzimhoni* (Tel Aviv 1994), pp. 20–22.

beings the bad trait of shedding blood for naught, eating the flesh even of select animals will give rise to a mean and insensitive soul" (ibid.).

Similarly, Don Isaac Abarbanel (1437–1508) explained in his commentary on Ex. 16:4 why God provided the Israelites in the wilderness "bread from heaven" (i.e., manna) and not meat:

> God said to Moses: Eating meat is not essential for one's nutrition. Rather, it is a form of gluttony, of filling one's belly and increasing one's lust. Meat also gives rise to a cruel and evil temperament in men. Therefore you will find that the animals and birds of prey that eat meat are cruel and evil. But sheep and cattle, hens, turtledoves and doves that sustain themselves on the grass of the field have neither cruelty nor wickedness in them. Therefore the prophet declared that in the future era of redemption "the lion, like the ox, shall eat straw" (Is. 11:7; 65:25)...Therefore God did not tell Moses that He would give the Israelites meat, but bread, which is a fitting food and is essential for the human temperament. Hence [it is written], "I will rain down bread for you from the sky."

Vegetarianism and Peace in Rav Kook's Vision of the Future

R. Abraham Isaac Hakohen Kook (1865–1935), himself a vegetarian, wrote in various places about the proper attitude to take towards animals. These passages, which appear in his *Afikim ba-Negev* and *Talelei Orot*, were compiled by Rabbi David Cohen (also known as the Nazir) into a work entitled *Hazon ha-Tzimhonut ve-ha-Shalom me-Behinah Toranit*, from which the citations discussed below are taken.

Rav Kook accepted the rabbinic view (*Sanhedrin* 59b) that eating meat was forbidden to Adam, and that men were only allowed to kill animals and eat their flesh because of the subsequent decline in human caliber over the generations (p. 49). His views about the reprehensibility of eating meat are expressed in no uncertain terms: "It is an overall moral shortcoming of mankind. For it does not promote good and lofty sentiments to take the life of any living creature for one's own needs and pleasures" (p. 7). Likewise, "It is impossible to imagine that the Lord of all, blessed be He, who takes pity on His creatures, would make such an everlasting law in his very good work of creation, that mankind could not survive except by violating its sense of morality in shedding blood, even if it be the blood of animals" (p. 8).

Rav Kook finds "implied rebuke" in the wording of Deut. 12:20, "when...you have the urge to eat meat." This verse allows eating meat "if your inner sense of morality is not revolted at eating the flesh of animals in the same way you are already revolted by the thought of eating the flesh of human beings" (p. 11). This state of human moral degeneracy is a temporary condition. "For when the time comes when our sense of morality will make eating the flesh of animals repulsive, because of the moral disgust in doing so, you will no longer have the urge to eat meat, and you will not eat it" (ibid.).

Why, then, did the Torah not forbid us to eat meat? Rav Kook explains that the moral development of humanity must take place gradually. First men must eliminate hatred and war among themselves, and only afterwards can they reach the high level of morality of treating animals morally and justly: "At the present time, when morality is greatly lacking and the spirit of impurity has not yet passed from the earth, there can be no doubt that such a thing [a blanket prohibition against eating meat] would cause many a mishap. When the animalistic urge to eat meat increases, it does not distinguish between human flesh and animal flesh" (p. 14).

Allowing people to eat meat is therefore a "moral concession" destined to be eliminated in the future (p. 18).[8] In the current system of commandments, however, higher moral values trickle down gradually, providing the basis for future change in human behavior towards animals (p. 23). For example, we are commanded to cover animal blood after slaughtering in order to remind us that taking the life of an animal is a morally reprehensible act, of which we ought to be ashamed (pp. 23–24).

Rav Kook stresses that in the future, human morality concerning animals will not stem from a sense of mercy or "righteous concession," but will be part of "absolute justice and firmly established law" (p. 22).

---

[8] He also says that these are "concessions made under pressure," and that "the Torah included them only as [countermeasures] against the evil inclination" (p. 20).

Moreover, he maintains that in the future there will be no more animal sacrifices, but only offerings from the vegetable kingdom.[9]

Practical Suggestions to Reduce Cruelty to Animals

Even people who do not want to become vegetarians can, with minimal effort, reduce the suffering they cause animals. For example, one can refrain from eating *paté de fois gras* or veal, whose preparation entails especial cruelty to animals, and one can eat organic eggs or eggs from free-range chickens instead of eggs from industrial egg farms. Below I shall explain why one ought to refrain from eating the foods mentioned above.

Eggs from Hens in Industrial Chicken Coops[10]

Hens naturally live in small groups, with social stratification whereby each hen knows its place and identifies the others in its group. The hens enjoy taking sand baths, running about the yard and flying around. They lay their eggs in privacy, in nests that they build. None of this, of course, is true of commercial chicken coops, where hens are packed, row upon row, into overcrowded coops. The area allotted to each hen is no larger than the hen herself. The hens cannot move around, let alone spread their wings. The wire netting on which they stand often wounds their feet. Laying eggs in industrial chicken coops without an ounce of privacy has been described by the zoologist Conrad Lorenz as the cruelest form of torture for a hen. Overcrowding and tension cause hens to pick at their own feathers as well as those of other hens with them in the coop. To prevent this, their beaks are often snipped while they are still chicks. This procedure is done with a guillotine-like instrument with blades heated red hot. Since chicks have nerve endings in the tissue of their beaks, this procedure causes the chicks prolonged and intense pain.

What can we do? Even those of us who have no intention of refraining from eating eggs can buy eggs produced by hens grown in

---

[9] Cf. David Sperber, "Korbanot le-'Atid la-Vo be-Mishnat ha-Re'ayah," in *Re'ayot ha-Re'ayah – Massot u-Mehkarim be-Torato shel ha-Rav Kook* (Jerusalem 1992), pp. 97–112.

[10] Cf. Singer, ibid.; Russanah Berghoff, "Ma Ba Kodem, ha-Betzah o ha-Tarnegolet?" *Anonymous (li-Zekhuyot Ba'alei Hayyim)* (Fall 1999), pp. 8–10.

relative freedom. Such eggs are often labeled "free-range" or "organic." Free-range eggs are preferable because the Society for Farm Animals supervises the conditions under which the hens are raised. It is important to keep in mind that eggs labeled "fresh farm eggs" are not organic eggs, but eggs from commercial chicken coops. Likewise, one should not be misled by the deceptive pictures of happy, free-roaming hens printed on certain egg cartons, when the eggs they contain were actually laid by battery hens. Eating eggs laid by free-range hens is not only morally preferable but also better for one's health.

Paté de Fois Gras [11]

The process for making *paté de fois gras* is particularly cruel. Geese are held in tight cages where they cannot move around, so that all the food forced into their bodies goes to fattening them. The geese are force-fed through a tube used to insert vast quantities of food. Geese that are fattened for the express purpose of enlarging their livers (up to ten times the normal weight) suffer severe health problems, including tears in the esophagus from insertion and removal of the tube, severe breathing difficulties, swelling of the liver, and internal bleeding. The enlarged, diseased liver presses on other internal organs. A handbook published by Israel's Ministry of Agriculture says such that geese "breathe heavily, have pale beaks, have difficulty even walking to the drinking trough, and are no longer able to digest food" (*Pitum Avazim*, Rishon Le-Ziyyon 1970). Approximately 12% of these geese die while being force-fed. The product obtained at the end of this cruel process of force-feeding is a diseased liver, rich in poisons and cholesterol, derived from a tortured, dying goose. The cruelty of the process it has led to its being banned in the United States, England, Sweden and other countries.

What can we do? Very simply, avoid this product, which causes geese so much suffering.

---

[11] From *Pitum Avazim* ("Force-feeding Geese"), published by the *'Amutah le-Ma'an Hayot Meshek* (Rishon le-Ziyyon 1997).

Veal[12]

Veal comes from calves that have been torn away from their mothers shortly after birth and intentionally raised in a way that makes them ill. In order to make their flesh tender and pale, they are fed a liquid diet of milk substitute, without any iron or fiber, causing them to contract anemia. The calves are kept in dark, tight wooden stalls, with insufficient room to move around. All they can do is stand or lie down. The purpose of these minimally sized stalls is to prevent the calves from using their muscles, thereby yielding more tender meat and preventing what the calves' owners would consider an unnecessary waste of calories. No straw lines the floors of these stalls. This is to prevent the calves from eating straw and thereby obtaining iron, a nutrient essential to their health but detrimental to the flavor of the meat they produce. The calves' stalls are so narrow that in their last days they can hardly stand comfortably. The calves' life of misery comes to an end at the age of about four months, when they are slaughtered.

What can we do? Simply refrain from consuming unhealthy meat, which can be produced only at the cost of causing severe suffering to young calves.

Conclusion

The most appropriate conclusion to this article is the verse from Ps. 145:9, "The Lord is good to all, and His mercy is upon all His works," as well as the famous midrashic dictum, "The Omnipresent is merciful, so you too should be merciful; God shows kindness, so you too should be kind" (*Sifre Devarim*, 45, s.v. *la-lekhet be-khol derakhav*).

---

[12] Cf. Singer, ibid., pp. 166–173.

Parashat Mishpatim

"WHEN MEN QUARREL, WHEN MEN FIGHT"

Yossi Peretz
Mikra'ot Gedolot Ha-Keter Project

THE TALMUD YERUSHALMI (Nazir 9, 58a) inquires about the relationship between the verses "when men quarrel [Heb. *yerivun*]" (Ex. 21:18) and "when men fight [Heb. *yinnatzu*]" (Ex. 21:22) in this week's reading:

> Is a fight a quarrel and a quarrel a fight? What does the Torah wish to teach by saying "when men fight" and "when men quarrel," if not to contrast the case of one who acted with intention and one who acted without intention?

In other words, the two verbs, "quarrel" and "fight," are not synonyms, but rather refer to distinct actions. Each pertains to a different situation and entails different legal consequences.

Below we briefly review the attitudes of the Talmudic rabbis and the medieval commentators to synonyms in the Bible, to determine whether seemingly synonymous biblical expressions have different meanings.[1]

Synonyms in Rabbinic Literature
Some of the talmudic rabbis held that similar biblical expressions are not truly synonymous, while others disagreed. In *Rosh Hashanah* 6a, the Talmud asks what difference there is between a votive offering (*neder*) and a freewill

---

[1] For further discussion, see my "'Al ha-Milim ha-Nirdafot ba-Mikra," *Talelei Orot* 10 (1992), pp. 11–26.

offering (*nedavah*), concepts mentioned in Lev. 7:16: "If the sacrifice one offers is a votive or a freewill offering." The Talmud answers: "One is responsible for a votive offering if it dies or is stolen, but one is not responsible for a freewill offering if it dies or is stolen." This example, like the one cited above from the Yerushalmi ("quarreling" vs. "fighting"), show that similar words are not true synonyms; each term means something different, halakhically speaking.

The rabbis also found interpretative distinctions between similar terms found in the Bible's prose and poetry. For example, *Mekhilta de-Rabbi Ishmael, Shirata* 2:

> One passage reads: "Horse and driver He has hurled [Heb. *ramah*] into the sea" (Ex. 15:1), and another passage reads: "Pharaoh's chariots and his army He has cast [Heb. *yarah*] into the sea." How can these two passages coexist? *Ramah* means that they were tossed upward, and *yarah* means that they sank down to the deep.

Similarly, regarding the verse "the Lord your God will put the dread and the fear of you over the whole land" (Deut. 11:25), *Sifre* Deut. 52 asks: "If they are in dread, then do they not fear? Rather, those near you will be in dread of you, and those who are farther away will fear." A similar interpretation was suggested for Ex. 15:16, "Terror and dread [*emata va-fahad*] descend upon them" – "Terror on those who are far, and dread on those who are near" (*Mekhilta de-Rabbi Ishmael, Shirata* 9).

Other rabbis, however, did not attribute different meanings to such word pairs. Regarding the words "wine" and "intoxicant" in the laws of the nazirite (Num. 6:3), the Midrash asks, "Is not wine an intoxicant and an intoxicant [the same as] wine?" The answer given there is that the Torah used two ways of describing the same thing (*Sifre* Num., 23). The Midrash proceeds to cite other examples:

> Likewise, one says that "slaughtering" is "sacrificing" and "sacrificing" is "slaughtering"; *kemizah* is the same as *haramah* and *haramah* the same as *kemizah*; "deep" (*amukah*) is the same as "shallow" (*shefelah*) and "shallow" the same as "deep"; a "sign" (*ot*)

is a "wonder" (*mofet*) and a "wonder" a "sign"; the Torah simply used two ways of speaking. Here, too, the Torah states that [the nazirite] should abstain from wine and intoxicants, but wine is an intoxicant and an intoxicant means wine; the Torah simply used two different expressions.

Additional examples can be found in many Midrashim which list synonymous terms for a particular notion. For example: "There are eight nouns that denote a poor person: *'ani, evyon, misken, rash, dal, dakh, makh, helekh*" (*Lev. Rabbah* 34.6); "Many terms have been used to refer to prayer: *tefillah* (prayer), *tehinah* (beseeching), *tze'akah* (shouting), *ze'akah* (crying), *shav'ah* (wailing), *renanah* (singing), *pegi'ah* (touching), *ne'akah* (moaning), *keri'ah* (calling), *'atirah* (petitioning), *'amidah* (standing), *hilui* (appealing)" (*Tanhuma Vaethanan*, 3). Similarly, "There are seven words for lion: *aryeh, ari, kefir, lavi, layish, shahal, shahatz*" (*Avot de-R. Nathan*, Version B, ch. 43), and "Four names were given to the snake: *nahash* (the generic term for snake), *peten* (adder), *ef'eh* (viper) *seraf, tzif'oni, tannin* (crocodile), *shefifon* (viper, horned snake)" (ibid.); "There are ten terms for a prophet"; "Idolatry has ten pejorative names," etc.

Medieval Exegetes on Biblical Synonyms

Almost all the medieval biblical exegetes realized that the Bible uses synonyms. They frequently use expressions such as "there is a duplication of the subject using different words," or "the same idea is repeated in different words," etc. Rashbam comments on the verse, "My might and the first fruit of my vigor" (Gen. 49:3), that "There is one statement here; it is the Bible's manner to double expressions." On the word pair "my person" and "my being" [literally "my honor"] in the verse "Let not my person (*nafshi*) be included in their council, let not my being (*kevodi*) be counted in their assembly" (Gen. 49:6), Ibn Ezra wrote: "R. Moses ha-Kohen the Sephardi says that *kevodi* is the same as *nafshi*, and there are many similar instances in Psalms. His interpretation is reasonable, for the meaning is duplicated, as is customary in prophetic writing." Similarly Ibn Ezra commented on the verse, "Come, curse me Jacob; come, tell Israel's doom" (Num. 23:7): "'Tell Israel's doom' – this is a repetition of the same idea, for it is a manner of speaking to express one idea in different formulations, and the repetition is for emphasis." In contrast to the talmudic rabbis, who interpreted the words *yarah* and *ramah* as denoting different things, Ibn Ezra interpreted them as synonyms, writing in his short commentary on Exodus (15:4): "*Yarah* means the same as *ramah*."

Radak, too, recognized the use of synonyms and employed this exegetical tool in many of his commentaries. On the second half of the verse from Jeremiah, "Erect markers, set up signposts" (Jer. 31:21), Radak wrote: "It is a repetition of the idea in different words, for signposts are the same as markers." Likewise, Ralbag commented on the verse, "His bones are like tubes of bronze, his limbs like iron rods" (Job 40:18): "The idea is repeated in different words."

Just how often synonyms are used in the Bible can be ascertained through examination of the commentaries of two noted commentators:

1. Ibn Ezra, in his commentary on the Bible, notes several hundred places where synonyms occur; in most of them he uses the phrase "the meaning is repeated," and in some cases "a repetition of the idea."

2. Radak notes the use of synonyms in about two hundred places in his commentary, generally using the phrase "a repetition of the idea" and sometimes "the idea (verse) is repeated."[2]

In contrast to these exegetes, a small group of commentators ascribed different nuances of meaning to word pairs. The earliest of these is R. Joseph Ibn Caspi (1279–1340) from Provence. In his interpretation of synonyms he followed the approach of Maimonides, who maintained that no two words are absolutely synonymous.[3] One of the examples discussed

---

[2] It is interesting to note that Metzudat David, which appears in the standard editions of *Mikra'ot Gedolot*, remarks on "repetition of the subject" more than 600 times.

[3] The presence of synonyms intrigued Maimonides (1135–1204), as is evident from his introduction to *Guide of the Perplexed* (ed. M. Schwartz [Tel Aviv 1969], p. 4). He does not treat this as a question of style and esthetics, but as an issue of theological significance: "The primary objective of this book is to explain the meaning of nouns appearing in the prophets." On the pair of words *temunah* and *tavnit* he writes: "*Temunah* and *tavnit* are thought to be one and the same in the Hebrew language, but this is not so" (p. 23). He also distinguishes between the verbs *ra'ah* ("saw"), *hibit* ("looked"), and *hazah* ("beheld in a vision"; see ch. 4, p. 24). In another of his works, *Millot ha-Higayon* (ed. M. Ventura, Jerusalem 1969, p. 67), he writes: "*Adam – ish – enosh*

by Ibn Caspi pertains to three words used to denote an implement with a blade made of metal: *herev* (sword), *sakkin* (knife) and *ma'akhelet* (knife):

> Even though the one implement is called *herev*, *sakkin*, or *ma'akhelet*, one might think that all three refer to the same thing. Nevertheless, one noun is not like the other. This implement is called *herev* when it is used to destroy (*yeherav*) the one struck with it. It is called *sakkin* when the one struck by it is endangered (*mesukan*), and it is called *ma'akhelet* when the one struck by it is consumed (*ne'ekhal*) and slaughtered. The three different roots are evidence of these subtle differences.[4]

Thus, even though all three words refer to the same object, Caspi suggests they are not absolutely synonymous, since each one emphasizes a different nuance.

Two more recent commentators who suggested that biblical terms with similar meanings refer to different concepts are the Vilna Gaon (1720–1797) and Malbim (1809–1879). Thus, the Vilna Gaon distinguished between the words *tikvah* ("hope") and *tohelet* ("ambition") in Prov. 11:7: "At death the hopes of a wicked man are doomed, and the ambition of evil men comes to nothing," and between *simhah* ("rejoicing"), *gil* ("exultation") and *sason* ("gladness") in Job 3:22.[5] Malbim, who discussed this subject extensively, also maintained that there are no true synonyms in the Bible. In the introduction to his commentary on Isaiah (*Mevo Ha-Mahberet*), he presented the basics of his approach and the "three pillars on which his commentary rests":

(all meaning "man") – these are indeed basically synonymous, but not identical in all their shades of meaning."

[4] I would like to thank Prof. Hannah Kasher for calling my attention to Ibn Caspi's exegetical approach to synonyms. See her doctoral thesis, *Joseph Ibn Caspi ke-Parshan Philosof* (Ramat Gan 1983), p. 132.

[5] Pinchas Hakohen Peli collected a list of more than one hundred groups of synonyms from the Vilna Gaon's works, including groups of three, four, and even more synonymous words. See *Sefer ha-Gra*, 1 (Jerusalem 1954), pp. 333–342.

In the language of the prophets there is no duplication of the same subject matter in different words – neither duplication of the subject, nor duplication of the utterance, nor duplication of the expression, nor two sentences whose subject is one and the same, nor two parables proving the same point, nor two words that duplicate each other.

In his study of words with similar meaning, Malbim established the following principle: "Similar words always intensify from light to harsh, from small to large, from few to many, and never the reverse." He applied this rule to Is. 1:4, in which seven expressions describe the people abandoning God: "Ah, sinful nation! People laden with iniquity! Brood of evildoers! Depraved children!," etc. In his opinion there is no duplication here. Rather, the prophet describes a series of acts with different degrees of severity, each expression adding to the gravity of the previous one. In Malbim's words, "the prophet ascends a scale, increasing the extent of the people's sins step by step."[6]

We conclude with a brief look at the fate of synonyms since the renewal of the Hebrew language. One of the greatest challenges encountered by those who revived the Hebrew language was a serious lack of terms for expressing concepts found in daily life. One way of solving this problem was to use semantic differentiation, giving different meaning to groups of words that were originally equivalent or close in meaning. The importance of this use of the available sources to enlarge the Hebrew lexicon is evident in the proposal made by Klausner, a contemporary of Ben-Yehuda:

In the Bible there are some twenty words, all of which denote "thorn": *na'atzutz, nahlol, shamir, shayit, 'akrav, kotz, serev, silon, barkan, hedek, sirpad*, and others. What would our language lose if we were to reserve one or two words for the meaning of "thorn,"

---

[6] See Eleazar Touitou, "Bein Peshat le-Derash – 'Iyyun be-Mishnato ha-Parshanit shel ha-Malbim," *De'ot* 48 (1970), pp. 193–198, n. 10.

and use the other nouns to denote various plants that resemble thorns in appearance or nature?[7]

Indeed, this process accelerated in modern Hebrew. Many synonyms, primarily biblical Hebrew words which have parallels in Mishnaic Hebrew,[8] underwent a process of semantic differentiation in modern Hebrew. Some examples are *yeled* (which has come to denote child) vs. *tinok* (now denoting an infant); *kalkalah* (economy) vs. *parnasah* (livelihood) and *shofet* (judge) vs. *dayyan* (judge in a rabbinic court).

---

[7] Joseph Klausner, *Ha-Lashon ha-'Ivrit – Lashon Hayah* (Jerusalem 1949), ch. 2: "Mekorot le-Harhavat ha-Lashon," p. 32.

[8] See the detailed discussion of Abba Ben-David, *Leshon Mikra u-Leshon Hakhamim*, 1–2 (Tel Aviv 1967).

Parashat Terumah

AN ALTAR OF EARTH OR GOLDEN CHERUBS?

Dr. Hayyim Borgansky
Department of Talmud

THE COMMANDMENT TO BUILD the Tabernacle and its implements,[1] which appears in *Parashat Terumah* and *Parashat Tetzaveh*, is not the first commandment in the Torah that deals with worship. At the end of *Parashat Yitro*, immediately after the revelation at Mount Sinai, the Torah commands us to build an altar on which to offer sacrifices:

> Thus shall you say to the Israelites: You yourselves saw that I spoke to you from the very heavens: With Me, therefore, you shall not make any gods of silver, nor shall you make for yourselves any gods of gold. Make for Me an altar of earth and sacrifice on it your burnt offerings and your sacrifices of well-being, your sheep and your oxen. In every place where I cause My name to be mentioned I will come to you and bless you. And if you make for Me an altar of stones, do not build it of hewn stones, for by wielding your tool upon them you have profaned them. Do not ascend My altar by steps, that your nakedness may not be exposed upon it (Ex. 20:19–23).

---

[1] Some of the ideas here stem from a conversation I had with R. Mordechai Breuer. I do not follow the Talmud's approach to the interpretation of the biblical passages discussed here (see below). This article is part of a broader investigation of Leviticus' attitude toward sacrifice compared with the treatment of the Tabernacle in Exodus, as well as the significance of the revelation at Mount Sinai.

Now, there are numerous differences between this passage and the commandments concerning the Tabernacle in *Parashat Terumah*:

1. *Parashat Terumah* speaks of an altar that is part of an organized and established Tabernacle, whereas *Parashat Yitro* speaks of an altar that is not part of a complete ritual complex at a designated site, and which may be erected anywhere.[2]

2. According to *Parashat Yitro*, the altar should be made of earth or unhewn stones, whereas *Parashat Terumah* states that the altar should be made of wood and brass.[3]

3. In *Parashat Yitro* there are no restrictions regarding who may serve at the altar, whereas in *Parashat Terumah* only the priests [*kohanim*] may serve in the Tabernacle.

4. *Parashat Yitro* forbids ascending the steps of the altar "lest your nakedness be exposed upon it," whereas *Parashat Terumah* states that the priests wear linen breeches "to cover their nakedness."

5. *Parashat Yitro* implies that silver and gold should not be used in worshipping God,[4] whereas *Parashat Terumah* states that these materials should be used for building certain parts of the Tabernacle and its implements.

6. *Parashat Yitro* commands us to erect an altar (without specifying when and where), whereas in *Parashat Terumah* the Torah commands us to build the Tabernacle.[5]

These differences can be understood by examining the essential distinctions between two types of worship. The first type is an expression of a spontaneous urge to worship God, which stems from a strong desire

---

[2] See Nahmanides on v. 21, s.v. *ve-ta'am ve-im*. Compare Rashi's commentary on v. 20, s.v. *be-khol makom asher azkir et shemi*.

[3] The Sages already noted this contradiction. See, for example, *Mekhilta de-R. Yishmael*, *Ba-Hodesh*, 11 (ed. Horowitz, p. 242), and see Rashi on Ex. 20:21, s.v. *mizbah adamah*.

[4] Halakhic midrashim associate the injunction "You shall not make any gods of silver, nor shall you make for yourselves any gods of gold" with the restrictions placed on using these materials in worshipping God. Cf. *Mekhilta de-R. Yishmael*, ch. 10 (ed. Horowitz, p. 241). Cf. also Rashi on v. 19, s.v. *elohei kesef* and *velohei zahav*.

[5] See Ibn Ezra's commentary on Ex. 20:21, s.v. *mizbah avanim*, which associates the passage about the earthen altar with the altar that Moses built at the foot of Mount Sinai in *Parashat Mishpatim*.

to commune with God, to thank Him for His daily kindness, or to request an answer to personal needs. Such worship is described in the story of Cain and Abel, when Noah leaves the Ark, when the Patriarchs thank God for His promises and publicly call on His name. This sort of worship stems from an inner need that is unrestricted in time and place. It involves the feelings of a specific individual and is not bound to the service of priests and Levites. Such worship is of great value precisely because of its authenticity: it expresses a person's deepest feelings for his Creator, and is not the compulsory performance of a duty, executed without any true emotion or desire for closeness to God.

The danger inherent in this type of worship is that it can become remarkably similar to pagan worship, as the worshipper might view the sacrifices offered on the altar as a present to God from which He derives pleasure. Someone who thinks that he is pleasing God by giving Him presents might build a magnificent altar adorned with silver and gold and offer on it the finest sacrifices. Ultimately, though, such a person would be worshipping his personal pride rather than God, and this would lead to the moral degeneracy that accompanies paganism. Inebriation would replace spiritual elation, and celebration of the flesh would replace the spiritual rejoicing in the Living God.

The passage in *Parashat Yitro* about the earthen altar refers to this individual form of spontaneous worship, which is free of priests and priestly vestments, of obligatory measurements and procedures, and is not restricted in time or place. Due to this danger, the passage in *Parashat Yitro* commanding us to build an altar is introduced by the words, "You yourselves saw that I spoke to you from the very heavens." These words serve as a guide for the ensuing commandments.

God is not a god of silver or gold, for He has no representation at all. An altar of the most primal materials, unaltered by the pride of human hands, properly expresses the position of man vis-à-vis God: "God is in heaven and you are on earth." This is why the altar should be built of earth and unhewn stones. Later we are commanded to season every offering with salt rather than with honey,[6] for making offerings of a natural substance will prevent us from priding ourselves on the gifts we make to Heaven.

The prohibition against offering leaven on the altar has a similar aim.[7] The commandment not to ascend the altar's steps, "lest your nakedness be exposed upon it," reflects the fact that this text deals with a private altar, where a person might worship without wearing special garb. Moreover, the phrase "that your nakedness not be exposed" warns against the sensuous ways of pagan worship that were so common in the ancient world.

Parashat Terumah, in contrast, does not deal with private worship of God. The purpose of the Tabernacle is stated at the beginning of the passage: "Let them make Me a sanctuary that I may dwell among them" (Ex. 25:8). This elaborate structure, with its wide variety of implements and materials, is a dwelling place for God; when made according to all the divinely ordained fine details, with its precious materials and specific dimensions, the Glory of God will dwell in it. Furthermore, God will speak to the Israelites from between two golden cherubs.

The Tabernacle is the site of divine revelation in the world, where the revelation at Mount Sinai continues.[8] We can infer this from the similarity between the verse "Now the Presence of the Lord appeared in the sight of the Israelites as a consuming fire on top of the mountain" (Ex. 24:17), and the verse "For over the Tabernacle a cloud of the Lord rested by day, and fire appeared in it by night, in the view of all the House of Israel" (Ex. 40:38). The fire and cloud that appeared to the Israelites in the revelation at

---

[6] Lev. 2:13. Even though this passage refers to the altar in the Tabernacle, the Book of Leviticus includes references to both types of worship, as manifest by the two types of altars. The obligatory personal sacrifices in Leviticus apparently entailed a combination of private sacrifice on the earthen altar and obligatory public sacrifice on the altar in the Tabernacle. Apparently, a distinction must be drawn between the obligatory burnt offerings that were offered before the theophany at Mount Sinai, which were handled by the priests, and the burnt offerings and sacrifices of well-being (*shelamim*) that were offered after the theophany, when the covenant in *Parashat Mishpatim* was sealed, with the assistance of "young men among the Israelites." Cf. Ibn Ezra's commentary mentioned in n. 5 above.

[7] See ibid., and cf. *Sefat Emet*, Pesah, #631, s.v. *matzah zo*. See also see R. Yoel bin Nun's comprehensive article, "Hametz u-Matzah be-Fesah, be-Shavu'ot, u-ve-Korbanot ha-Lehem," *Megadim* 13 (1991), pp. 25–45.

[8] See Nahmanides' commentary on Ex. 40:34, s.v. *va-yekhas he-'anan et ohel mo'ed*.

Mount Sinai would move from the top of the mountain to the Tabernacle, where God is to be worshipped. Men must bring offerings not because of the feelings in their heart, but because of their obligation to worship God. Just as there was a "the regular burnt offering instituted at Mount Sinai"[9] (Num. 28:6), so too in the Tabernacle: "Now this is what you shall offer upon the altar: two yearling lambs each day, regularly...a regular burnt offering throughout the generations" (Ex. 29:38–42). The fact that the offering mentioned in Exodus is a regular burnt offering and not a private offering confirms our previous suggestion: the altar in the Tabernacle was the place for fulfilling the constant duty to worship God, rather than a place for expressing spontaneous feelings towards Him.

God's abode should be magnificent – "in His temple all say, 'Glory!'" (Ps. 29:9), or, as the rabbis put it, "there is no poverty in a place of riches." Only God's chosen priests could approach it after they had sanctified themselves in preparation for their service, as they were commanded at Mount Sinai (Ex. 19:22): "The priests, too, who come near the Lord, must stay pure, lest the Lord break out against them." Even they may not approach the place of revelation in the Tabernacle, the Holy of Holies, just as they were commanded at Mount Sinai: "But let not the priests or the people break through to come up to the Lord" (Ex. 19:24).

Thus, the two passages in *Yitro* and *Terumah* deal with completely different types of divine worship. *Parashat Yitro* deals with spontaneous, voluntary worship of God, Who is concealed in heaven, whereas *Terumah* treats the obligatory worship of God, which was mandated because His glory was revealed to men and His word came forth from between the two cherubs in the Tabernacle, or from within the fire at Mount Sinai. These two types of worship have different characteristics, and hence the differences in wording between the two passages.

Both approaches to worship should be practiced, with obligatory sacrifices being offered on the copper altar in the Tabernacle, and burnt offerings and sacrifices of well-being (*shelamim*) offered voluntarily upon the

---

[9] For the assumption that the words "instituted at Mount Sinai" refer to the burnt offering offered on the mountain itself, cf. *Hagigah* 6b and Tosafot ad loc., s.v. *R. Akiva*. See also Rashi on Num. 28:6, s.v. *ha-'asuyah*. In contrast, note Nahmanides' interpretation of Lev. 7:38 in his commentary ad loc., s.v. *ve-yitakhen ki*.

earthen altar in one's yard. For even though the Glory of God dwells in His Tabernacle and worshipping Him there is obligatory, His Presence fills the entire world, so that worshipping Him anywhere is appropriate. Hence we are commanded concerning the earthen altar in *Parashat Yitro*. However, the inadequacy of human intellect might lead people to think that since God dwells in the Tabernacle, someone who sacrifices in his own yard might be worshipping another god who dwells in the field and not in the Tabernacle. Therefore, both ways of worshipping God are combined in Leviticus, and we are commanded to realize the spontaneous desire to serve Him only where His Glory is revealed (Lev. 17:3–7):

> If anyone of the House of Israel slaughters an ox or sheep or goat in the camp or outside the camp, and does not bring it to the entrance of the Tent of Meeting to present it as an offering to God, before God's Tabernacle, bloodguilt shall be imputed to that man. For he has shed blood; that man shall be cut off from among his people. This is so the Israelites may bring the sacrifices which they have been offering in the open before God, to the priest, at the entrance of the Tent of Meeting, and offer them as sacrifices of well-being to God...so they will no longer offer their sacrifices to the goat-demons after whom they stray. This shall be a law for them for all time, throughout the ages.

Later the Israelites would return to sacrificing on high places (Heb. *bamot*), sometimes with permission but usually without. The altar mentioned in *Parashat Yitro*[10] is a sort of high place, a site for spontaneous worship of God. Such altars were permitted when the Tabernacle did not exist.[11] When God established His holy dwelling in Jerusalem, the prohibition against sacrificing outside His dwelling place was reinstated with redoubled force, as is stated in Deuteronomy (12:13–14):

---

[10] Cf. Mishnah *Zevahim* 14.

[11] See e.g. ibid., Mishnah 10: "Public sacrifices are offered in the Tabernacle, and private sacrifices on a high place."

Take care not to sacrifice your burnt offerings in any place you like, but only in the place that the Lord will choose in one of your tribal territories. There you shall sacrifice your burnt offerings and there you shall observe all that I enjoin upon you.

Today we have neither altar nor sacrificial worship, but the tension between obligatory worship, which often does not lend full expression to the individual's feelings, and alternative expressions of serving God, continues to reverberate in our world.

Parashat Tetzaveh

HYOSCYAMUS AUREUS AND ITS RELATIONSHIP TO THE HEADDRESS OF THE HIGH PRIEST

Prof. Yehuda Feliks

Department of Land of Israel Studies

THE MOST DETAILED DESCRIPTION of a plant in ancient Jewish literature is found in Josephus' *Antiquities of the Jews*. Just as Josephus described the architecture of places such as Masada with great precision, so too he was precise in his botanical description of *Hyoscyamus aureus* (Heb. *shikhron zahuv*) when attempting to describe the headdress worn by the High Priest.

The headdress (Heb. *mitznefet*) is listed among the eight vestments of the High Priest: "These are the vestments they shall make: a breastpiece, an ephod, a robe, a fringed tunic, a headdress, and a sash" (Ex. 28:4). However, very little detail is provided about how the headdress was to be fashioned. The headdress is mentioned again in connection with the description of the frontlet (Heb. *tzitz*): "You shall make a frontlet of pure gold...Suspend it on a cord of blue, so that it may remain on the headdress; it shall remain on the front of the headdress" (Ex. 28:36–37).

What sort of headdress is a *mitznefet*? The word is generally thought to be derived from the root *tz-n-f*, referring to a piece of fabric that is wrapped around the head, like a turban or tarboosh. This hypothesis raises several difficulties, which commentators have attempted to resolve.

Josephus described the head covering of the High Priest in *The Jewish War* and *Antiquities of the Jews*. His description in *The Jewish War* is brief:[1] "On his head the high priest wore a linen mitre wreathed with blue and

---

[1] Book 5, 5.7.

encircled by a crown of gold, which bore in relief the sacred letters – four vowels." In his *Antiquities* he described the headdress in far greater detail, adding that the headdress had a gold finial resembling the petals of *Hyoscyamus aureus*, aside from the gold frontlet mentioned in the Torah. He describes this garment as follows:[2]

> For head-dress the high-priest had first a cap made in the same fashion as that of all the priests; but over this was stitched a second, of blue embroidery, which was encircled by a crown of gold wrought in three tiers, and sprouting above this was a golden calyx recalling the plant which with us is called *saccharon* [=Hebrew *shikhron*], but which Greek experts in the cutting of simples term henbane.[3] In case there are any who, having seen the plant, never learnt its name and are ignorant of its nature, or, though knowing the name, would not recognize it if they saw it; for the benefit of such I proceed to describe it.
>
> It is a plant which often grows to a height of above three spans, with a root resembling a turnip...and leaves like those of the rocket. Now out of its branches it puts forth a calyx closely adhering to the twig...this calyx is as big as a joint of the little finger and resembles a bowl in contour...gradually converging with a graceful re-entrant curve, it broadens out again gently near the rim, where it is indented like the navel of a pomegranate...while the flower which it produces may be thought to be comparable to the broad petals of a poppy. It was, then, on the model of this plant that was wrought the crown extending from the nape of the neck to the two temples; the forehead, however, was not covered by the *ephielis* (for so we may call the

---

[2] Book 3, 4.172–179. The translation here is taken from that of H. St. J. Thackeray, ed., Josephus, *Jewish Antiquities*, The Loeb Classical Library, 4 (London 1930), pp. 399–403. On the flower itself, see my *'Olam ha-Zomeah ha-Mikra'i* (Tel Aviv 1957), p. 198.

[3] A plant (*Hyoscyamus aureus*). The Loeb edition identifies this plant as *H. Nigrum*, henbane. Several varieties of *Hyoscyamus* grow in Israel, but *Hyoscyamus niger* grows only in Europe.

calyx), but had a plate of gold, bearing graven in sacred characters the name of God. Such is the apparel of the high-priest.

The main difficulty with Josephus' description is that he includes a gold finial (*nezer*) that is not mentioned at all in the Torah, but is mentioned in Ben Sira (45:12): "A finial of gold, a headdress, and a frontlet." Josephus may have based his claim on Ben Sira, but in view of his detailed description of the flower that the finial resembled, Josephus, who was a priest himself and had been in the Temple, had apparently seen the headdress and finial at close hand. If so, then the finial on the headdress must have been fashioned like an inverted *Hyoscyamus* flower (pointed end up). Two of its petals must have rested on the High Priest's forehead, with the frontlet tied between them.

Parashat Ki Tissa

"FACE TO FACE, HEART TO HEART"

Dr. Yair Barkai
Jerusalem

IN *PARASHAT KI TISSA*, various forms of the word *panim*, "face," occur about 22 times in the course of 47 verses. Thus, as a key word in this section, "face" should be analyzed in any attempt to reveal the deeper meanings of the Torah here.

Let us begin with a few observations about divine revelation to men. From v. 11 in our reading, "The Lord spoke to Moses face to face, as one man speaks to another, and he would then return to the camp," we learn that the intimacy of the encounter between God and Moses was unique. This is clear, too, from what God said to Aaron and Miriam: "Hear these My words: When a prophet of the Lord arises among you, I make Myself known to him in a vision; I speak with him in a dream. Not so with My servant Moses; he is trusted throughout My household. With him I speak mouth to mouth, plainly and not in riddles, and he beholds the likeness of the Lord'" (Num. 12:6–8); cf. the description of Moses as the man "whom the Lord singled out, face to face" (Deut. 34:10).

God reveals Himself differently to Moses than to others, even the greatest prophets: God is available for Moses whenever Moses asks, and He communicates with Moses without intermediaries. It is therefore surprising to read in this week's Torah reading:

> He answered: "I will make all My goodness pass before you [lit. "before your face"]...But," He said, *"you cannot see My face*, for man may not see Me and live"..."As My Presence passes by, I will put

you in a cleft of the rock and shield you with My hand until I have passed by. Then I will take My hand away and *you will see My back; but My face must not be seen*" (Ex. 33:19–23).

This passage indicates that God did not reveal Himself to Moses "face to face," in apparent contradiction to the previous verses. This seeming contradiction has been explained in many ways, and we present some of the approaches here.

One way of reconciling the difficulty is to note different aspects of the word "face." For example, the rabbis in the Midrash understood *panim* as referring to God's revelation of how He directs the universe:

> He answered: "I will make all My goodness pass" (Ex. 33:19); "But," He said, "you cannot see My face" (Ex. 33:20). Moses sought to understand how good deeds are rewarded and how it is that the wicked go untroubled. God answered him, ["You cannot see My face"] (*Tanhuma Buber, Ki-Tissa*, 16).

Moses sought to learn the secrets of how God manages the world, the solution to the question that has troubled men since time immemorial – the problem of theodicy, of Divine reward, retribution and justice. *Panim* is understood by this Midrash as the "face" worn by Divine Justice, which a human being cannot fathom. We are fated to test our faith on the basis of our acknowledged lack of understanding of how God controls the universe and treats His creatures.

Nahmanides maintained that our passage can only be understood according to its hidden, mystical sense. In his commentary on Ex. 33:14 he writes: "This passage cannot be properly appreciated by those who don't know the hidden meaning *(sod)* of the Torah." According to this interpretation, *panim* represents the inner Torah, its secrets and mysteries. Accordingly, God's "back" *(ahorai)*, which the Torah says was shown to Moses, refers to an understanding of God's ways in the past or the ability to contemplate His providence, as *Or Ha-Hayyim* comments:

Concerning God Almighty, one cannot speak of His having a face and a back. Rather, [this verse] means that all living things in the world wish to behold His light and His being, as God of all living things. However, this is impossible, for no creature can look at the radiance of the Almighty. Hence God prepared a veil through which one could look, and this is called *ahorayim*, "back side," just as in His wisdom He made man a back side, with the *nefesh* as his "face" or front, the spirit as the "face" of the *nefesh*, and the *neshamah* (soul) as the "face" of the spirit. Likewise He created radiance from Himself through which one could look and see God, which was called His back side, and a supreme light, which is beyond the comprehension of any living being, which He called *panim* (face).

Another attempt to reconcile the contradictory verses can be found in *Devarim Rabbah* (ed. Lieberman, *Parashat Ha'azinu*, s.v. *ha-tzur tamim po'olo*):

"The Rock whose deeds are perfect" (Deut. 32:4); "Seek the Lord while He can be found" (Is. 55:6). Isaiah said, "Seek the Lord, and David said, "Turn to the Lord, to His might" (Ps. 105:4). Why should one "seek His presence (*panav*) constantly" (ibid.)? To teach you that God sometimes appears and sometimes does not; sometimes He listens and sometimes not, sometimes He lets Himself be sought and sometimes not, sometimes He is accessible and sometimes not, sometimes He is near and sometimes not. How so? He appeared to Moses, as it is written, "The Lord spoke to Moses face to face; then He became invisible to him again when he asked Him, 'Oh, let me behold Your Presence.'"

Thus, this Midrash interprets *panim* as Divine revelation to man, as the opposite of *hester panim*, i.e., God's "hiding His face" by not answering our prayers or revealing Himself to us.

Sometimes God concealed His face from Moses, as the Torah states: "I will...shield you with My hand" (Ex. 33:22), and sometimes Moses hid his face so as not see God: "And Moses hid his face, for he was afraid to look at God" (Ex. 4:6). This was noted by the Midrash (*Exodus Rabbah*, 3.1):

> "And Moses hid his face." [Moses] said, With the God of my father standing here, how can I not hide my face? R. Joshua ben Korhah and R. Hoshaiah [were conversing] and one of them said: It was not good of Moses to hide his face, for had he not hidden his face, God would have shown him what is above and what is below, the past and the future. In the end [Moses] asked to see this, as it is written: "Oh, let me behold Your Presence" (Ex. 33:18). But then God answered Moses: I came to show [Myself to] you and you hid your face. Now I must say to you that "man may not see Me and live," for when I sought to [show Myself], you did not desire this. R. Joshua of Sakhnin said in the name of R. Levi: Nevertheless, He showed him [Himself] as a reward, since Moses hid his face (Ex. 3:6).
>
> "God would speak to Moses face to face"...R. Hoshaiah Rabbah said: It was good that [Moses] hid his face. God said to him: I came to show you My face, and you paid me respect by hiding your face. By My word, you will be with Me on the mountain for forty days and forty nights, neither eating nor drinking, and you will enjoy the radiance of the Divine Presence, as it is written, "Moses was not aware that the skin of his face was radiant" (Ex. 34:29).

Here God hides His face from Moses, just as Moses had hidden his face from God.

Yet another meaning for the word *panim* is suggested in *Exodus Rabbah* 45.2:

> God, said to [Moses]: That is not what I stipulated with you. When you are angry, My face will assuage yours, and when I am angry, your face will assuage mine. Go back and return to the camp, as it is written: "The Lord spoke with Moses face to face."

Here the word *panim* is understood as denoting a "face" of anger as opposed to a "face" showing grace, once again reflecting the reciprocal relationship between the revelation of the Divine Presence and Moses.

We conclude with Or Ha-Hayyim's explanation of the phrase "face to face":

> Moses' apprehension of God corresponded to how much he had prepared to greet Him, for to the degree that a person prepares himself for sacred influence, so he attains. The saying "as one man speaks to another" may be explained according to our approach in light of the verse, "As a face is reflected in water, so with one man's heart to another" (Prov. 27:19). For hearts secretly know whether to love or hate: just as a person prepares his heart to love his fellow, so too his fellow perceives whether to love him. Thus it is written, "As one man speaks to another," meaning that one will not love another if the latter does not prepare his heart to reciprocate friendship. Likewise, God spoke "face to face." Hence a man can discern his standing with God: if his heart yearns for God and longs to worship Him, this is a sign that God loves him.

From this we see that the extent to which a person reveals his inner self to God is reflected in how God reveals Himself to that person.

Parashat Vayakhel

THE GLORY OF GOD

Prof. Avigdor Hurovitz

Department of Bible and the Ancient Near East
Ben Gurion University of the Negev, Beer Sheba

PARASHOT VAYAKHEL AND *PEKUDEI* conclude the lengthy and detailed description of the construction and erection of the Tabernacle. The function of the Tabernacle was described in the beginning of *Parashat Terumah*: "Let them make Me a sanctuary that I may dwell among them" (Ex. 25:8).

Different interpretations of this verse have been offered by commentators. Onkelos, for example, rendered: "Let them make a sanctuary before Me, and I shall cause my Presence to dwell among them." R. Saadiah Gaon understood the verse similarly: "Let them make Me...a sanctuary; I shall cause my Glory to be among them." A similar interpretation is suggested by Abarbanel, who explains at greater length: "Let them make Me a sanctuary, a holy place, that my Presence be felt among them as it appeared before them at Mount Sinai – the Glory of God, as consuming fire with a cloud surrounding it." However, Rashi explains, "Let them make a place of holiness for My Name." Ibn Ezra was even more explicit: "It was called a Sanctuary because it was the dwelling place of the Holy Name."

The origins of these varying interpretations go back to the biblical books themselves. Various attempts to reconcile the conflicting approaches have influenced our understanding of the character of the synagogue to this day.

The Torah describes how God will dwell among the Israelites: "The cloud covered the Tent of Meeting, and the Presence (*kevod*) of the Lord filled the Tabernacle. Moses could not enter the Tent of Meeting because the cloud had settled upon it, and the Presence of the Lord filled the Tabernacle" (Ex. 40:34–35). The Temple which King Solomon built in Jerusalem is described similarly, as we read in the *haftarah* (according to Ashkenazi custom): "The priests came out of the sanctuary, for the cloud had filled the House of the Lord, and the priests were not able to remain to perform the service because of the cloud, for the Presence of the Lord filled the House of the Lord" (I Kings 8:10–11).

God's removing His Presence from the Temple before its destruction is described in chapter 11 of the book of Ezekiel, and God's return to the future Temple is described in the great prophetic vision at the end of the book (Ezek. 43:2, 9). There, as in this week's reading, God promises: "I will dwell among them forever" (Ezek. 43:9). Zechariah shares Ezekiel's opinion and declares that God will be "a wall of fire" around the rebuilt city of Jerusalem, which "will have...Glory (*kavod*) inside it" (Zech. 2:9).

Until God's Presence entered the Tabernacle in the desert, it dwelled on Mount Sinai (Ex. 24:16). Before the Israelites arrived at Mount Sinai, God sometimes appeared to them in the wilderness in a cloud (Ex. 15:10). When the Tabernacle was at Shiloh God's Glory was present there, and when the Ark was taken away the Glory departed with it, as the wife of Phinehas, daughter-in-law of Eli, said: "The Glory has departed from Israel, for the Ark was captured" (I Sam. 4:22, as correctly interpreted by Yehudah Kiel in *Da'at Mikra*, ad loc.).

Thus we see that God's Glory was present in every sanctuary, and its presence was an indication of God's presence. But what is this "Glory"? All the biblical verses cited above suggest that this Glory is something visible and indeed so bright that one cannot look directly at it; hence it is enveloped in a cloud. Thus, it is written in connection with the theophany at Mount Sinai: "Now the Presence of the Lord appeared in the sight of the Israelites as a consuming fire on the top of the mountain" (Ex. 24:17). Elsewhere Moses seeks to behold the Glory of God, but God cautions him that "man may not see Me and live." When Moses is in a cleft of the rock, shielded by God's Hand, God shows Moses His back, as it were, but not

His face (Ex. 33:18–23). What God would not let Moses see, Ezekiel boldly described, and it was the image of a human form seated on a throne, enveloped in gleaming light, at whose sight Ezekiel flung himself down on his face (Ezek. 1:26–28).

From these passages we may infer that "Glory" is not an abstract notion, as in modern usage, but rather denotes something quite tangible. The "Glory" is the gleaming halo that envelops God, as it were, and emanates from Him. This divine halo, which astounded everyone who saw it and caused them to prostrate themselves, was sometimes called *hod*, *hadar* (magnificence), *ge'ut* (grandeur), or *'oz* (might), and was itself enveloped in a cloud.

In striking contrast to all these texts, in Deuteronomy, when Moses describes the theophany at Mount Sinai, he only mentions the Glory of God once, in passing, as he recounts the people's response: "You...said, 'The Lord our God has just shown us His majestic Presence (*et kevodo ve-et godlo*), and we have heard His voice out of the fire'" (Deut. 5:21). Elsewhere Moses speaks of God's abode as being in heaven (Deut. 26:15), while His presence in the sanctuary is limited to His name dwelling in the place He will choose after the Israelites have become established in the Promised Land (Deut. 12:5, 11; 14:23; 16:2).

Similarly, Solomon said, "I have now built for You a stately House, a place where You may dwell forever" (I Kings 8:13), which implies that God dwells in the Temple. Yet after the Ark of God was brought to the Temple and the Glory of God entered it, King Solomon said: "But will God really dwell on earth? Even the heavens to their uttermost reaches cannot contain You, how much less this House that I have built!" (I Kings 8:27). After this Solomon prayed that God would open His eyes from His abode in Heaven toward the Temple, implying that God does not dwell in the Temple.

When Moses, in Deuteronomy, and Solomon, at his inauguration of the Temple in Jerusalem, exalt God, they describe the earthly sanctuary as a sort of great switchboard, as it were, that relays all prayers directed to the Temple toward heaven. God sees those who pray at the Temple and hears their prayers, but does not dwell there. God Himself confirms this role, saying, "I consecrate this House which you have built and I set My name there forever. My eyes and My heart shall ever be there" (I Kings 9:3).

These two notions – the concrete presence of the Glory of God, on the one hand, and His Name as an abstract entity, on the other hand, or the immanent Glory vs. the transcendental Name – seem, prima facie, to be mutually exclusive. Yet in fact we find various intermediate positions. Thus, the prophet Isaiah saw God sitting on an elevated throne in the Temple, but according to the *serafim*, God's Glory fills the entire earth.

Haggai, too, takes a middle-of-the-road approach. Encouraging the people to go to the hills and bring timber to build a House for God, God says: "I will look on it with favor and I will be glorified" (Hag. 1:8), meaning that the magnificent House will glorify God. Although Targum Jonathan understood the verse as meaning that God will consent to have His Presence dwell there in glory, R. Samuel bar Inni (*Yoma* 21b) emphasized that the glory mentioned here is not the Divine Presence. He midrashically inferred from the deficient orthography of this verse (the word *ikkaveda* lacks the final *heh*) that five things (Heb. letter *heh* = five) that were present in the First Temple were lacking in the Second: the Ark, *kapporet* and cherubs, the fire and Divine Presence, the Holy Spirit, and the *urim* and *tummim*.

Haggai subsequently prophesied that God would "fill this House with glory," reminding us that God would "shake the heavens and the earth, the sea and the dry land" (Hag. 2:6–7). This passage is reminiscent of the descriptions of God's appearing at Mount Sinai and elsewhere. However, Haggai divests "glory" of its theological content, for the glory that will fill the Temple will not be the visible Glory of God that dumbfounds whoever sees it, but rather the great opulence of the Temple (cf. Gen. 31:1; I Kings 3:13; Eccl. 6:2; II Chron. 1:12). Thus, the prophecies of consolation and restoration in the Book of Haggai use the broad semantic range of the word "glory" in order to span the theological abyss separating the two approaches about the Temple: the Temple was magnificent and glorious, although it was not filled with the Glory that was in the Tabernacle.

These two approaches are attested later as well. In the biblical description of the building of the Second Temple after the return from the Babylonian Exile, no indication is given that the Glory of God entered the Temple; the inaugural ceremony was limited solely to offering sacrifices (Ezra 6:16–18). Thus, this Temple was devoid of the Glory of God, as the

Sages noted, and served solely as a place of sacrifice. The idea that God does not dwell in the Temple goes hand in hand with the view that God is omnipresent, and that He can be found and worshipped anywhere. Hence the existence of the synagogue is possible, and this institution took the place of the Temple.

Likewise, the original notion of "glory" changed and developed, becoming part of the rabbinic notion of *Shekhinah* (Divine Presence). According to the Sages, the westernmost light in the Temple candelabrum showed that during the forty years of wandering in the wilderness, the Divine Presence accompanied Israel (*Menahot* 86b; cf. *Megillah* 21b, and see Zech. 4:2, 10). In the Second Temple, if this western light went out, it was relit only with fire taken from the altar, which had originally been lit by God Himself when He revealed His Presence (Lev. 9:24). Thus a memory of the gleaming Glory, God's tangible manifestation, is preserved, if only on a "low flame." The *Shiviti* plaques found in some prayer books and in Sephardic synagogues to this day might reflect this notion. Psalms 67 is written on these plaques in the form of a seven-branched candelabrum, with the Tetragrammaton (four-letter name) appearing above it. By having proper intention during prayer and always being mindful of God's presence, one brings the Glory of God that filled the Tabernacle into the synagogue or wherever one prays.

Parashat Pekudei

FROM MOUNTAIN TO TABERNACLE

Menahem Ben-Yashar
Department of Bible

THE BOOK OF EXODUS can be divided into three parts. The first (chapters 1–16) deals with the Jews' bondage in Egypt and the Exodus. The second (from chapter 17, where Moses ascends to the "rock at Horeb" [17:6] to the end of chapter 24, when the covenant at Sinai is sealed), deals with the Revelation at Mount Sinai. The third part (from chapter 25 to 40) deals with building the Tabernacle. The fundamental importance of this final part, which comprises almost half of Exodus, will be discussed below. Between the commandment to build the Tabernacle and its actual construction there is a discussion of the sin of the golden calf and atonement for that grave sin (Ex. 32–34). The inclusion of this narrative in the middle of instructions on the proper way to worship God in the Tabernacle is significant: the Torah is illustrating the wrong way to worship, namely, through a molten image. In other words, we must worship God the way He commands us, and not as we see fit based on contemporary fashions.

The essence of the Revelation at Mount Sinai, according to the plain sense of the Torah, is not necessarily the giving of the Torah and the commandments. Rather, its significance lies in God's making a covenant with the Jews. The ten commandments, which were given at Mount Sinai, were written on the Tablets of the Covenant, and *Parashat Mishpatim*, also given at Sinai, was recorded in the Book of the Covenant (Ex. 24:4–6).

The Torah's description of the giving of the Torah and the commandments begins with the verse "This month shall mark for you the beginning of the months" (Ex. 12:2), which Rashi, following the talmudic rabbis, identifies as the first commandment given to the Israelites. Rashi comments that the entire Torah ought to have begun with this passage, which commanded the Jews not just to celebrate the Passover in Egypt, but to celebrate Passover in the future as well. The Israelites were also commanded to redeem the firstborn. In addition, the Israelites were commanded concerning the Sabbath before the Revelation at Mount Sinai; otherwise it would not have been possible to command them at Mount Sinai, "Remember *the* Sabbath," with the definite article. After the Israelites journeyed on from Sinai, additional commandments were given to them in the Tent of Meeting.

The principal significance of the revelation at Mount Sinai lies in God's revealing Himself to all Israel, thereby granting the entire people a degree of prophecy. Most of the commandments were given then, in order to show the people that the commandments are from God and to teach them that the commandments previously transmitted by Moses, as well as the commandments which Moses would give them later, were also from God, though transmitted through Moses. Indeed, God said to Moses at Mount Sinai: "I will come to you in a thick cloud, that the people may hear when I speak with you and trust you ever after" (Ex. 19:9).

Thus, the revelation of the commandments at Mount Sinai was continued in the Tent of Meeting, which was so called because it is there that God met with Moses to instruct him about the commandments (see Ex. 29:42). The same tent, however, is also called the *mishkan*, because the *Shekhinah* (Divine Presence) dwells there. Thus, the relevation at the Tent of Meeting continued the unique, one-time revelation at Mount Sinai.

There is another connection between Moses' conversation with God on Mount Sinai and the Tabernacle. Moses ascended to the cloud on top of the mountain (Ex. 24:18), and God said to him, "Tell the Israelite people to bring Me gifts [Heb. *terumah*]" (Ex. 25:2). In other words, to honor God they would have to elevate (*yarimu*) material things, making them sacred: "Let them make Me a sanctuary that I may dwell among them," in the middle of the Israelite camp.

Why did Moses have to receive this command from the cloud of God's Glory on the mountain (Ex. 25:8–30 and 25:40)? Apparently, this was intended to show that the Tabernacle was designed like the heavenly sanctuary, and that it facilitated the continued revelation of God's presence from Mount Sinai. The Israelites, after all, would have to journey on from Mount Sinai to the land of Canaan, so what would happen to the Divine Presence that was revealed to them at Mount Sinai? The answer, of course, is that the Divine Presence would be with them in the man-made Tabernacle; in effect, the Tabernacle served as a sort of portable Mount Sinai. In other words, the revelation at Sinai was intended to prepare the Israelites for the Divine Presence to dwell in their midst, in the center of their camp. The Tent of Meeting was a traveling Mount Sinai, because the central and most sacred objects within the Tabernacle were the two hewn Tablets of the Covenant, from Mount Sinai, on which the details of the covenant were recorded.

The parallel between the heavenly summit of Mount Sinai and the earthly Tent of Meeting is evident from the similarity between the language and content of two brief passages in the Torah, the passage describing Moses entering the cloud on top of Mount Sinai, which extends from the end of *Parashat Mishpatim* to the beginning of *Parashat Terumah* (Ex. 24:12–25:9), and the passage describing Moses entering the cloud of Glory that covered the Tent of Meeting, from the end of the Book of Exodus to the beginning of Leviticus (Ex. 40:34; Lev. 1:1–2).

Moses Ascending Mount Sinai	Moses Entering the Tent of Meeting
"When Moses had ascended the mountain, the cloud covered the mountain" (Ex. 24:15)	"The cloud covered the Tent of Meeting, and the Presence of the Lord filled the Tabernacle" (Ex. 40:34)
"The Presence of the Lord abode on Mount Sinai, and the cloud hid it for six days" (Ex. 25:16)	"Moses could not enter the Tent of Meeting because the cloud had settled upon it, and the Presence of the Lord filled the Tabernacle" (Ex. 40:35)
"On the seventh day He called to Moses from the midst of the cloud" (Ex. 24:16)	"The Lord called to Moses" (Lev. 1:1)

"Now the Presence of the Lord appeared in the sight of the Israelites as a consuming fire on the top of the mountain" (Ex. 24:17).	"When the cloud rose from the Tabernacle the Israelites set out on their various journeys" (Ex. 40:36); "but if the cloud did not lift, they would not set out until it did lift" (Ex. 40:37). "For over the Tabernacle the cloud of the Lord rested by day, and fire appeared in it by night, in the view of all the House of Israel throughout their journeys" (Ex. 40:38)
"The Lord spoke to Moses, saying" (Ex. 25:1)	"The Lord called to Moses and spoke to him from the Tent of Meeting, saying" (Lev. 1:1)
"Tell the Israelite people to bring Me gifts" (Ex. 25:2). "Let them make Me a sanctuary that I may dwell among them" (Ex. 25:8).	"Speak to the Israelite people and say to them: When any of you presents an offering of cattle to the Lord" (Lev. 1:2)

The parallels between these two passages were noted long ago by Nahmanides, and in our time by the commentators Benno Jacob (Germany) and Umberto Cassuto (Italy). Both passages recount how the cloud initially covered the mountain/Tabernacle and the Presence of God abode on the mountain/ffilled the Tabernacle. Then we are told that Moses could not enter the Tent of Meeting because of the cloud of the Presence of God. The parallel passage says that Moses ascended Mount Sinai, but not to its summit, which was filled with God's Presence. On the seventh day God called to Moses from the cloud. It was then that Moses ascended to the summit where, in the midst of the cloud, God revealed His plan for the Tabernacle and its implements. In the corresponding passage God called out to Moses from the Tent of Meeting. Both times, this summons was accompanied by a command to speak to the Israelites. On Mount Sinai the Israelites received the commandment to build the Tabernacle, where God's Presence would continue to abide. And from the Tent of Meeting came the commandments regarding sacrificial worship, the operative content of the Tabernacle.

Moses apparently did not enter the Tent of Meeting immediately. Before entering the cloud of God's Presence on Mount Sinai, Moses needed six days of purification. He entered on the seventh day (the number seven represents sacred perfection). However, it was not until the eighth day that Moses entered the Tent of Meeting, along with Aaron, who was to minister in the Tabernacle (Lev. 8:1, 23). For the man-made tent required a seven-day period of preparation before it could be sanctified on the eighth day (the number eight represents sanctity beyond perfection).[1]

The aim of the Exodus from Egypt was to have the Divine Presence abide in the midst of the Israelite camp by way of the Tabernacle, as stated in Ex. 29:46: "[God] brought them out from the land of Egypt that I might abide among them." Nahmanides' notes in his introduction to Exodus that causing this Divine Presence to abide in Israel was itself redemption. Therefore the Book of Exodus, which begins with the bondage in Egypt and concludes with the Divine Presence descending on the Tent of Meeting, is called the book of exile and redemption (*galut* and *ge'ulah*). In Nahmanides' words (introduction to his commentary on Exodus):

> The Book of Exodus deals with the first exile...and the redemption from it. This exile did not end until the Israelites returned to their place and to the level of their ancestors. When they left Egypt they were still considered exiles, even though they had left the house of bondage, for they were in a land not their own, lost in the wilderness. It was when they came to Mount Sinai and made the Tabernacle, when God caused His Presence to abide in their midst, that they returned to the level of their ancestors, for the Mystery of God now lay over their tents. That was the Divine Chariot, and only then could the people be considered redeemed.[2] Therefore this book concludes with the

---

[1] See Rashi, Rashbam and Nahmanides on Ex. 40:35.

[2] That is, the Camp of Israel was the "chariot" or dwelling-place of the *Shekhinah*, when the *Shekhinah* dwelled between the two cherubs on the ark.

completion of the Tabernacle and the Presence of God always filling it.

Sefer Vayikra – The Book of Leviticus

Parashat Vayikra

NASI – KING OR LEADER?

Rabbi Judah Zoldan
Midrashah for Women

THIS WEEK'S READING mentions various types of sacrifices, including a sacrifice offered "where a chieftain incurs guilt" (Lev. 4:22). Who is this chieftain who must bring such an offering?[1]

The Hebrew word used here, *nasi*, is a general descriptive word referring to anyone who is elevated (Heb. *nissa*) above the people due to his status, function, or office. This term appears frequently in the Bible and may denote various positions.

Ephron is called *nesi Elohim*, the elect of God (Gen. 23:6). Likewise, Ishmael had twelve chieftains (Gen. 25:16); Shechem son of Hamor is called "chief of the country" (Gen. 34:2); there are twelve chieftains of the tribes (Num. 1:16). The twelve spies are also called chieftains, although they are not necessarily chieftains of the tribes (Num. 13:2). Even the half-tribe has a chieftain (Num. 34:23). The two-hundred and fifty men who offered incense in Korah's dispute were chieftains (Num. 16:2). King David is called *nasi*, "a ruler among them" (Ez. 34:24), as is his son Solomon (I Kings 11:34). Sheshbazzar was *nasi*, "prince" of Judah (Ezra 1:8), and the anointed king was called *nasi*, "prince" (Ezek. 48:22).

Towards the end of the Second Temple Period and thereafter, men who were authorized to give instruction about Jewish practice, the heads of the Sanhedrin, and the leaders of the Jewish community in the Land of

---

[1] See further R. Yehudah Shaviv, "'Al Mosad ha-Nesi'ut," *Shema'tin* 129–130 (1997), pp. 17–23.

Israel, were also called *nasi*. As Maimonides wrote (*Hilkhot Sanhedrin* 1.3), "The wisest of them all shall be placed at their head. He is the head of the *yeshivah*, and he is the one whom the Sages call *nasi* everywhere."

The Mishnah (*Horayot* 3.3) interprets the verse "If a chieftain incurs guilt" as referring to the king: "Who is meant by *nasi*? The king, for it says in the next part of the verse, 'by doing any of the things forbidden by the commandment of the Lord his God' (Lev. 4:22) – a ruler above whom there is none but the Lord his God."

A similar interpretation is found in the *Sifra:*

> Could *nasi* mean a chieftain of one of the tribes, such as Nahshon? The Torah says: "By doing any of the things forbidden by the commandment of the Lord his God," and further on it is written, "That he may learn to revere the Lord his God" (Deut. 17:19). Just as the second verse refers to a ruler above whom there is none but the Lord his God, so too *nasi* here means someone above whom there is none but the Lord his God.

From the unique expression, "the Lord his God," which occurs both in *Parashat Vayikra* and in the passage about kings in Deuteronomy, the rabbis inferred that the term *nasi* here referred specifically to a king and not to any person who wields power. However, if this verse pertains specifically to a king, why doesn't the Torah say so explicitly, instead of forcing us to infer this from other passages?

R. Judah ha-Nasi, the editor of the Mishnah who lived after the destruction of the Temple and was not a king, asked about himself (*Horayot* 11b): "Whom am I like with regard to [the requirement to bring a sin offering consisting of] a male goat? Rabbi Hiyya answered: You have a rival in Babylonia." Rashi explains that Rabbi asked whether he would have to bring a male goat, as required of a king, had he sinned during Temple times. Thus, he sought to determine the exact halakhic definition of *nasi*. Rabbi Hiyya replied that the Exilarch in Babylonia had greater sovereignty than the *Nasi* in the land of Israel, implying that the Exilarch would have to bring such an offering if the Temple still stood.[2] This shows that these verses do not necessarily deal with kings alone, but also with the Exilarch and the patriarch in post-biblical times.

The sages apparently understood our verse as referring to the head of the Jewish government. Generally this was the king, and when Israel had a king, he, rather than the tribal chieftain, had to bring such an offering. But when there is no king, this offering is brought by the leader of the government, e.g., the Exilarch, as indicated above.

Ibn Ezra seems to adopt a similar approach in his commentary on this verse (Lev. 4:22). Ibn Ezra explains that *nasi* in our verse means head of a tribe or clan, and hence the highest governing authority in Israel – in the early Biblical period, the chieftain of the tribe or the head of the clan.[3] That is why the Torah says "if a chieftain incurs guilt," and not "if a king incurs guilt"; kings merely exemplify the highest governmental office in Israel.

---

[2] Following the interpretation of R. Abraham Borenstein, *Teshuvot Avnei Nezer, Yoreh De'ah* 313.11. His son, R. Samuel Borenstein (author of *Shem Mi-Shemuel*), agrees; see his gloss in *Teshuvot Avnei Nezer, Yoreh De'ah* 112.27.

[3] Cf. R. Isaac of Karlin, *Keren Orah, Hiddushim le-Massekhet Horayot* (repr. New York 1983) on *Horayot* 11b, s.v. *yakhol*, p. 224.

Parashat Tzav

THE PRIESTHOOD – PRIVILEGE AND OBLIGATION

Rachel Lifshitz
Petach Tikvah

PARASHAT TZAV PRESENTS numerous laws pertaining to the priests (*kohanim*). Aaron, the father of the priests, was granted a special privilege, as were all of his subsequent descendants. Anyone could become a great Jewish leader, but one could only become a priest if he had been born to a priestly family. On the other hand, if a priest was not learned, wise, or righteous, his priestly status was not affected. Similarly, a person's world view, leadership and organizational talent are not relevant to his priestly status.

The Talmud (*Yoma* 71b) relates that a high priest once came out of the Temple, and all the people followed him. When they saw Shemayah and Avtalyon coming, the people left the priest and followed Shemayah and Avtalyon, since they were sages. When Shemayah and Avtalyon came to take their leave of the high priest, he said to them, "May the sons of foreign folk come in peace." (Shemayah and Avtalyon were descended from proselytes, and the high priest was thus poking fun at them.) Shemayah and Avtalyon answered, "May the sons of foreign folk who act like Aaron come in peace, but the descendant of Aaron who does not act like Aaron should not come in peace" (for he had not followed Aaron's example of loving peace and pursuing peace). Shemayah and Avtalyon's criticism of the high priest here provides further confirmation that the high priests were not always distinguished spiritual figures, even though they ministered in an important religious office. The priestly laws accordingly reflect a unique notion of authority, established by Divine command and doubtless taking into advance consideration the possibility that not all priests will be paragons of virtue.

Another aspect of the priesthood which distinguishes it from ordinary leadership positions is that a priest cannot resign from the priesthood. Being a priest, like being a prophet, is not an elective position. Once one is born a priest (or appointed a prophet), he must submit to God's will and perform the unique mission assigned to him.

The priests ministered in a sacred atmosphere, and they performed their service to create that atmosphere. They were both emissaries and servants of the people, who achieved spiritual elevation by offering various types of sacrifices. It was the priests' duty to represent the people before God by performing the priestly service prescribed by Him. The people's survival thus rested to a large extent on these intermediaries and emissaries.

There is a price to being a priest: a mistake can cost him his life, as it is written: "You shall keep the Lord's charge, that you may not die" (Lev. 8:35). When the high priest entered the Holy of Holies on the Day of Atonement, the people waited with bated breath: Would he emerge alive? Aaron and his descendants were privileged, but the privilege was accompanied by demands and potential danger.

Membership in the priesthood also entails waiving certain things. There are restrictions as to whom priests may marry; a priest may not marry a divorcee, a convert, or a woman who had had conjugal relations with someone she is not permitted to marry. Likewise, priests generally may not defile themselves through contact with a corpse, and the high priest may not defile himself even for his father or mother, "for he bears the distinction of the anointing oil of his God" (Lev. 21:11–12).

The priests, like the Levites, had no fixed tribal inheritance in the land of Israel. The priests received their share of the various sacrifices and priestly gifts, as stated in Num. 18:8: "I hereby give you charge of My gifts, all the sacred donations of the Israelites." The privilege of being a priest had various costs, one of which was dependence on the offerings brought by their fellow Jews. This reflects the dependence of the Jews and the priests on one another – one who ministers in sacred service depends on the people, just as they depend upon him.

Parashat Shemini

TRADITION, TRADITION!

Dr. Zohar Amar

Department of Land of Israel Studies

THE TORAH PERMITS us to eat a wide variety of animals and provides us with specific indicators by which they can be identified. Among these animals are mammals, fish, fowl and various grasshoppers. The Torah's list includes wild as well as domesticated animals (Lev. 11; Deut. 14). Rather than name all the permitted fowl, the Torah lists only the exceptions, meaning that "countless birds" remain permissible for eating (*Hullin* 63b), except for the twenty-four impure birds that are expressly forbidden. Moreover, the phrase "of every variety" (Lev. 11:22) indicates that the Torah is not dealing with specific breeds, but with broad categories of animals that share certain similarities of form or behavior.[1] Thus, the array of kosher animals available to our ancestors was rich and varied.

What has happened since? Over the years, the accepted identification of most of these varieties has been lost and the identity of many animals has become doubtful. Consequently, the choice of kosher meat available to us has become far more limited than that available to our ancestors.

---

[1] Maimonides, *Hilkhot Ma'akhalot Asurot* 1.8. See also M. Kislev, "'Ekronot ha-Miyyun li-Kevutzot shel Ba'alei Hayyim ba-Torah ve-Hadgamatam be-Shemonah ha-Sheratzim," *Halamish* 7 (1989), pp. 27–40; idem, "Behinat ha-Zihuyyim shel 'Aseret Minei Ma'alei ha-Gerah ha-Tehorim 'Al Pi ha-Taxonomiah," *Sinai* 125 (2000), pp. 216–225.

The Tradition of Identification

While many of the animal names and indicators of kashrut are explicitly mentioned in the Torah, what might have been obvious to the Israelites when they received the Torah was no longer so to later generations. Even when the Torah was given, it was necessary to unequivocally identify the animals mentioned, since not everyone was equally familiar with all these animals. Based on the Torah's words (Lev. 11:2), "These are the creatures that you may eat," the Rabbis concluded that God had conveyed the tradition to Moses in concrete fashion: "We learn from this that God took hold of each and every variety and showed it to Moses, saying to him, This you may eat, and this you may not eat" (*Hullin* 42a). Moses passed the tradition on to the Israelites in similar fashion: "These are the creatures that you may eat." From this, we learn that Moses too took hold of each creature and showed it to the Israelites, saying to them, "This you may eat, and this you may not eat. The following you shall abominate among the birds. These you shall abominate and these you shall not abominate. The following shall make you unclean; these are unclean, and these are clean" (*Sifra Shemini*, 2).

Later, identifying the names of the animals became problematic because of the absence of a continuous and reliable tradition of identification. The absence of such a tradition is due to events that befell the Jewish people: the exile from their land and their dispersion throughout the world, and the many years that have elapsed between antiquity and the present. This is compounded by the fact that some Jews arrived in places where certain animals that had been common in the biblical lands were not part of the local fauna or were not generally eaten there for cultural reasons.[2] Furthermore, the identification of animals by name alone is not always reliable, since names can change from place to place.

There are, broadly speaking, two approaches to the identification of the animals and plants mentioned in ancient sources. The first is the traditional approach, which is accepted in Jewish halakhah and traditional

---

[2] On the absence of a tradition of eating grasshoppers in Europe, see Zohar Amar, "Ha-Arbeh va-Akhilato be-Masoret Yisrael," Proceedings of the Bar-Ilan Conference (November 4, 1999), pp. 11–12.

exegesis. Scholars such as Rav Saadiah Gaon, Rashi, and Maimonides, who served as models for later commentators, generally derived their interpretations from the traditions of Jewish study current in their time and locale, and sometimes from independent analyses that gave rise to original interpretations.

The second approach to identification is the "scientific approach," which developed in recent generations in accordance with scientific method. This approach is, of course, based on an analysis of the sources themselves, but it also incorporates research from a number of other fields: linguistics, comparisons with the Apocrypha and Pseudepigrapha, archaeology, zoology, and other disciplines.[3]

The identifications suggested for animals according to both approaches, whether traditional or scientific, are not sufficient to qualify animals as permissible for eating even when the identification is almost definite. Other fundamental conditions must be satisfied as well, namely, recognizing the animals, their names, and signs, as determined by the Rabbis.[4] Another necessary condition is the existence of a "tradition." According to most halakhic authorities, this is essential for birds; as Rabbi Isaac said, "Birds are eaten by tradition" (*Hullin* 63b). As for animals, it follows from Maimonides (*Hilkhot Ma'akhalot Asurot*, 1.8) that recognizing them suffices. However, some Ashkenazic halakhic authorities have ruled that these animals also require a tradition.[5]

Halakhic Tradition

As indicated, in order to give binding halakhic force to a suggested identification, an additional fundamental requirement must be satisfied, namely, "tradition." This is not a marginal folkloristic matter; it is a fundamental halakhic principle. "Tradition" in this sense of the word

---

[3] The characteristics of the various methods of identification are illustrated in my "Zihui Minei Sheretz ha-'Of Bi-Re'i ha-Masoret ve-ha-Madda," *BDD* 11.

[4] Maimonides, *Hilkhot Ma'akhalot Asurot* 1.15; *Shulhan Arukh, Yoreh De'ah* 82.2.

[5] Especially Hazon Ish. See the discussion of A. Hamami, "Ha-Giraffa – Kashruto la-Akhilah," *Tehumin* 20 (2000), pp. 91–92; A. Z. Zivotofsky, "Kashrut of Exotic Animals: The Buffalo," *The Journal of Halacha and Contemporary Society* 38 (1999), pp. 117–128.

requires at least two essential conditions. The first is an ancient, reliable and authorized source for the tradition. The second is proper preservation to safeguard the tradition. These two conditions do not always coincide, and sometimes certain traditions, important as they may be, ceased to exist in certain communities for various reasons – for example, after the community lost contact with an important ancient center of Jewish study, or because of cultural and geographical circumstances. A halakhically acceptable tradition can only be received from reliable sources, meaning God-fearing people who possess a living and active tradition, in accordance with the Talmudic principle: "A hunter may be relied upon when he says, 'This bird is kosher; my rabbi has informed me'" (*Hullin* 63b).

Later generations relied primarily upon rabbis and ritual slaughterers (*shohatim*) who had traditions that had been passed on to them throughout the generations from one individual to the next and maintained through actual practice. They had authentic, precise and reliable information, since by its very nature halakhic tradition cannot rely on conjecture, but must be based on unequivocal identification, transmitted through an unbroken chain and remaining unchanged for centuries. The reliability of this tradition is absolute, since Jews throughout the Diaspora were known for their strict adherence to the dietary laws. In fact, it was precisely this extreme strictness that sometimes caused traditions that had ceased to be active to lose their validity.

The Importance of Preserving the Tradition in Our Day

An active tradition regarding the kashrut of a wide variety of animals existed from antiquity until recent times. Generally speaking, most members of traditional society were poor, and they took maximum advantage of potential benefits that could be derived from the world of nature. Therefore, it is not at all surprising that in many countries, especially in times of drought or famine, Jews ate locusts, small songbirds, or wild animals that were still readily available, such as gazelles. In fact, it is the relative prosperity in which we live and the impact of Western culture that have caused certain traditions to be lost and many others to be in danger of disappearing. Therefore, it is our duty to document these traditions and preserve them for the sake of future generations. These traditions can be received only from the "older generation," who are still in possession of an ancient and vibrant heritage – an "Oral Law," as it were. The order of the day is to commit these traditions to writing as clearly as possible and in accordance with scientific criteria, and to document them visually. This will assist in the preservation of the tradition and thus enable later generations to have a continuous tradition regarding the kashrut of various animals.

The Project for Preservation of the Tradition

As indicated, a tradition of kashrut existed in the past for a large number of animals. The tradition regarding many of these animals was lost, according to some rabbinical authorities, beyond retrieval. For example, there is no active tradition regarding the kashrut of giraffes, which according to some commentators are thought to be the biblical *zemer*.[6] Hence, one of our goals in preserving the tradition is to establish a preliminary list of animals that (a) clearly display signs of kashrut; (b) have an active tradition, supported by numerous sources, of being eaten in recent times; and (c) have reliable informants who can confirm and transmit the tradition.

The list includes some "high risk" animals, meaning animals which, in our opinion, are in the greatest danger of losing their kashrut tradition. Although the list includes domesticated animals such as the guinea hen, we decided to focus on non-domesticated animals such as the sparrow, partridge and gazelle. Another category includes animals that people have attempted to raise in captivity and market with kashrut certification, although such certification is questioned, e.g., quail, pheasant and deer.

In preparing the list we availed ourselves of relatively recent halakhic literature containing information about various species of kosher animals,[7]

---

[6] See Hamami, ibid., n. 10. R. Joseph Kafih ruled that the giraffe is kosher, and that no tradition is required to eat it. See my "Several Principles of R. Joseph Kafih's System of Identifying Plants and Realia," R. *Yosef Kafih Memorial Volume* (Tel Aviv 2001), pp. 68–73 (in Hebrew); A. Zivotofsky and A. Greenspan, "On the Kashrut of Pheasants," ibid., pp. 107–116.

[7] For example, R. Chaim Yosef David Azulai, *Mahazik Berakhah le-Yoreh De'ah*; Y. M. Cohen, *Zivhei Kohen* (Leghorn 1832); A. Ben-David, *Sihat Hullin* (Jerusalem 1997). Many other responsa collections, especially by *posekim* from Northern Africa, contain information that has not yet been fully utilized.

the important study by Y. M. Loewinger,[8] and additional primary sources culled from various informants, which may be decisive in determining the kashrut of animals according to Jewish tradition.

We modeled this project on the comprehensive interdisciplinary study recently conducted on the tradition among Yemenite and some North-African Jews to eat locusts, a study in which testimony was gathered from hundreds of informants. Among those interviewed were Jews who had immigrated to Israel from Yemen several years ago and who identified live locusts shown them with great certainty, even explaining how these creatures were eaten.[9]

Some Names of Specific Animals

* Only common names of species are listed

Hebrew name today	Scientific name	English	German	Arabic
Tzvi	*Gazella*	Gazelle	Pracht	A'zal, T'bi
Ayal	*Cervus, Capreolus*	Deer, Roe deer	Hirsch	Ayyal, Yahmor
Yahmor	*Dama Dama*	Fallow Deer	-------	Yahmor, Ayal, Adam
Dror	*Passer*	Sparrow	Sperling	A'tzpor
Hoglah	*Alectoris*	Partridge	Steinhuhn	Hajl
Slav	*Coturnix*	Quail	Wachtel	Slawi, Smani
Peniniyah	*Numida*	Guinea-fowl	Perlhuhn	Djaj Habshi, Harziyyah, Bar Elabid
Pasyon	*Phasianus*	Pheasant	Fasan	Tedraj, Deraj

[8] Y. M. Loewinger, *Mazon Kasher Min he-Hai* (Jerusalem 1980).

[9] H. Seri and Z. Amar, "The Kashrut of Locusts," *Tehumin* 19 (1999), pp. 283–299. The complete study will be published by Bar Ilan University.

Conclusion

In the final analysis, the validity of the traditions that we obtain depends on *posekim* confirming their accuracy. The validity of these traditions may differ from one animal to another, depending on the source of the tradition (land of origin) and its quality (degree of reliability, identity of the transmitter and the circle to which he belongs). In addition, it must be recalled that the system of *kashrut* in Israel and the Diaspora is not monolithic, but lies in the hands of various groups and authorities. In practice, even the Israeli Rabbinate governs various local authorities which lack uniformity in the level of *kashrut*, the differences depending first and foremost on the approach of each individual *kashrut* authority.

Therefore, we would like to initially document existing traditions before they disappear and to create a database for those wishing to preserve them. If this project succeeds, it might be possible to establish an authorized body, accepted by most religious circles, that would will be able to coordinate the various *kashrut* authorities and set standards and a system of accepted rules, so that everyone will be able to eat the animals permitted by his or her tradition.

Parashat Tazria

IN THE PRESENCE OF GOD

Dr. Rivka Raviv
Department of Talmud

MOST OF THE PURITY LAWS in the Torah are found in *Parashot Shemini*, *Tazria* and *Metzora*. These laws are surrounded by the account of the death of Aaron's two sons on the day when the Tabernacle was erected (Lev. 9–10) and the commandments given "after the death of Aaron's two sons" (Lev. 16:1), which seek to teach us that "[Aaron] is not to come at will into the Sanctuary" (Lev. 16:2). What is the significance of the location of the rules about purity at precisely this point?

Maimonides, in his *Guide for the Perplexed*, 3.47, explains the reason for these laws:

> The entire aim was to inspire awe in those who turned to the Temple, that they should be fearful when they see it, as it is written, "You shall...venerate My sanctuary" (Lev. 19:30, 26:2). When a person frequents a place, its impact on his soul diminishes, and he is gradually less awed by it...Since the objective was to maintain this sense of awe, the Almighty cautioned those who are unclean against entering the Sanctuary by stipulating many sorts of uncleanness, to the extent that hardly a person turns out to be clean, save for a very few.

Accordingly, the goal of constructing the Tabernacle was to afford men the religious experience of drawing close to God, Who dwells therein. To prevent the experience from losing its impact, the Torah made it impossible to enter the Temple at all times by establishing numerous sorts of impurity.

These laws are arranged as follows. First we find the laws of animal impurity, viz., the list of non-kosher animals (Lev. 11). These are followed by impurity among humans, namely, the impurity of a woman after childbirth (ch. 12), passages about leprosy (ch. 13–14), male impurity resulting from various discharges (15:1–18), and finally uncleanness of women during menstruation and discharge (15:19–33). The following questions accordingly arise: (1) Why do the laws of animal impurity precede the laws about human impurity? (2) Why are the laws of a woman after childbirth, whose blood renders her unclean, discussed separately from the laws of menstrual impurity?

The Rabbis suggested that the order of these laws reflects the order of creation. Thus, *Leviticus Rabbah* 14.1 (ed. Margaliyot, p. 299) states:

> R. Simlai said: Just as man's creation followed that of domesticated animals, wild beasts and birds, so too the instructions concerning him follow those of domesticated animals, wild beasts and birds. For it is written: "These are the instructions concerning animals" (Lev. 11:46), and then "When a woman gives birth" (Lev. 12:2).

Rabbenu Bahya continued this line of thought, noting another reflection of Creation in the fact that the passages in *Parashat Tazria* dealing with the impurity of humans begin with the impurity of a woman at childbirth. The analogy to Genesis can also clarify another difficulty in the text – why the passage about a woman giving birth is followed by the commandment to circumcise the child (Lev. 12:2–3).[1]

Several explanations have been offered as to why the Torah's discussion of childbirth impurity appears separately from its discussion of menstrual impurity. The Midrash suggests that there is a causal connection between birth impurity and leprosy, which is discussed immediately thereafter in the Torah (see Lev. 12–13): "Who caused the newborn to

---

[1] Rabbenu Bahya, *Be'ur 'Al ha-Torah* (Jerusalem 1977), 2.468.

come out with leprosy? His mother, who was not mindful of the laws of menstruation."[2] Or, put differently, "What has one thing to do with the other? God said: I told you to bring an offering when giving birth, and you did not do so. By your life, I shall force you to come before the priest [to bring the offering of the leper]."[3]

Ibn Ezra, Abarbanel and R. David Zvi Hoffmann suggested that the arrangement of these laws reflects the chronology of human life: the first thing that happens to a person is his birth, and hence the laws of human impurity begin with the impurity of a woman at childbirth. Other reasons for this arrangement have been suggested, including the idea that the most severe, i.e., lengthy, form of uncleanness is presented first. The Torah stipulates a protracted period of uncleanness for a woman after childbirth (40 or 80 days), which prevents her from entering the Temple; by contrast, the purification period for most other types of unclean people is at most seven days. It has also been suggested that birth is discussed first because it is a joyful occasion, in contrast to most of the other types of impurity described later on, which are associated with infirmity or disease.[4]

We would like to suggest another explanation for the justaposition of the passage about animal impurity to the Torah's discussion of childbirth impurity, and of why the latter passage opens the Torah's discussion of human impurity. The laws in Lev. 11 and in Lev. 12 address two themes: human nutrition (animals permitted for food) and reproduction (the woman at childbirth and the newborn). These areas are fundamental to survival, and they are mentioned in *Parashat Bereshit* at the conclusion of the Torah's account of Creation: "God blessed them and God said to them, 'Be fertile and increase, fill the earth [=reproduction]...See, I give you every seed-bearing plant...they shall be yours for food [=nutrition]" (Gen. 1:28–

---

[2] *Leviticus Rabbah*, 15.5 (ed. Margaliyot, p. 331).

[3] Ibid. 15.6, p. 332.

[4] Both explanations are given by R. Elhanan Samet, "Tum'at ha-Yoledet u-Milah li-Shemonah," http://www.etzion.org.il/vbm/archive/5-parsha/27tazria.rtf. Samet notes that menstruation is also considered a sort of ailment, as indicated by the Torah's language in Lev. 15:33 ("menstrual infirmity"). However, his suggestion does not satisfactorily explain why the passage about impurity from seminal emission is included among the passages dealing with other infirmities, unless this passage is considered a sort of appendix to the passage on discharge.

29). After the Flood, God blessed Noah and his sons, saying, "Be fertile and increase and fill the earth." The text continues, "Every creature that lives shall be yours to eat...You must not, however, eat flesh with its lifeblood in it" (Gen. 9:1–4).

On the eighth day of the inauguration ceremonies for the Tabernacle, the Torah sought to establish new limitations concerning these two areas, nutrition and reproduction. The world had reached a new era, since the Divine Presence now abode in the Israelite encampment.[5]

Under these new circumstances, these fundamental aspects of life took on new dimensions. With sanctity came notions of uncleanness and purity. The impurity of certain animals goes back to the time of Noah (Gen. 7:8), but now the Israelites were given explicit commandments as to which animals were clean and which were unclean.[6] The restrictions concerning purity were established in light of the developments that mankind had experienced so far. Antediluvian man was only permitted to eat plants, while the descendants of Noah were permitted the flesh of all animals, and the Israelites were permitted to eat only certain animals. Similarly, the commandment of circumcision was mentioned in the passage about childbirth, since this commandment is associated with birth.

Observing the purity laws leads makes sanctity possible, which leads to closeness to God. The passage listing the clean and unclean animals concludes: "You shall sanctify yourselves and be holy, for I am holy. You shall not make yourselves unclean...you shall be holy, for I am holy" (Lev. 11:44–45). Refraining from proximity to or contact with holy things while in a state of uncleanness is essential to avert the dangers of such contact: "You shall put the Israelites on guard against their uncleanness, lest they die through their uncleanness by defiling My Tabernacle which is among them" (Lev. 15:31).

---

[5] See *Bemidbar Rabbah* 12.6: "Rav said: Something which had not existed since Creation until that moment was brought into being on that day. From Creation until that time the Divine Presence had not dwelled in earthly realms; this only happened after the construction of the Tabernacle. Therefore it is written *va-yehi* ("and it was"), to indicate that something new had been created."

[6] See R. David Zvi Hoffmann's introduction to his commentary on Leviticus ch. 11, p. 218.

The following passages about leprosy and discharge impurity can be understood similarly. According to the rabbis, the physical disorders associated with these forms of impurity reflected Divine warning or punishment.[7] Such warnings and punishments show that God's presence in the Israelite camp reflects His providence in human affairs. Such providence can prove challenging, as proven by the story of Aaron's two sons, who died "when they drew too close to the presence of the Lord" (Lev. 16:1).[8] Indeed, earlier God had warned Moses, "If I were to go in your midst for one moment, I would destroy you" (Ex. 33:5).

In conclusion, the passages about the laws of purity and impurity can be seen as reflecting the development of a new reality characterized by increasing closeness between God and men. On the one hand, this closeness made it necessary to take precautions and to establish new restrictions on human behavior, so as to avoid the dangers it entailed. On the other hand, the most basic and essential events of human life, eating and reproduction, took on new and greater significance, as they acquired more profound meaning than ordinary physical acts.

---

[7] On leprosy as a sign of warning, see *Leviticus Rabbah* 14.34 (ed. Margaliyot, p. 381). On leprosy and discharge as punishment for sin, see ibid. 18.2, p. 400, and 18.3, p. 404.

[8] Note too that there are several stories in the Bible dealing with the leprosy of important people who were close to God, such as Moses (Ex. 4:6), Miriam (Num. 11:9), Elijah's servant Gehazi (II Kings 5:27), and King Uzziah of Judah, when he entered the Temple to burn incense (II Chr. 26:19).

Parashat Metzora

BIRTH, PURITY, AND IMPURITY

Rabbi Yuval Cherlow
Midrashah for Women

Eʀʟʏ Jᴇᴡɪsʜ ᴇxᴇɢᴇᴛᴇs took great pains to translate the concepts of purity (*taharah*) and impurity (*tum'ah*) into humanly comprehensible terms, since striving to understand the Torah was one of the fundamentals of Torah study in their view. Their recognition that the Torah contains commandments that we must accept even if we do not understand them (*mitzvot shim'iyot*) did not curtail their efforts, since there are relatively few commandments of this sort. Moreover, many of these obscure commandments have broad foundations in the world of rational thought, and only some of the laws that are derived from these commandments are inexplicable. Some of the sages' efforts were directed at matters of purity and impurity – a field of inquiry occupying extensive tracts of the Written and Oral Law. Among the better-known rational explanations is the one provided by Maimonides in his *Guide for the Perplexed*, 3.47:

> All this is reason to keep one's distance from the Temple, not setting foot there at any time. It is known that "a person should not enter the sacred precinct to worship, even if he is pure, until he has ritually immersed himself." These actions ensure that we always have a sense of awe, and the effort involved leads to the desired sense of submission. The greater the impurity, the more difficult and longer the process of purification.

Note also the earlier explanation given by R. Saadiah Gaon (*Sefer Ha-Emunot ve-ha-De'ot*, 3.2):

> Among the advantages of the laws of purity and impurity are that a person humbles himself in his own eyes, so prayer becomes dearer to him after a hiatus of several days, as sacred things are more highly regarded after a period of abstinence, and so a person is given to a sense of awe.

Yet R. Saadiah wrote elsewhere (ibid. 6.4) that the laws of purity and impurity have their foundation in statutes (*hukkim*, i.e., laws not given to our comprehension):

> As for keeping distance from things unclean and impure, we say...that the human body has no impurity in it, but is entirely pure, *for impurity is not something tangible or something our intelligence demands.* Rather, the Torah demands it. The Torah declares impure some of our human vitality after it has issued from the body, but does not declare it impure when it is in the body. But if someone were to lay down commandments for us that were devised of his own mind and impose strange things on us, we would not accept them.

One of the rational explanations for the laws of purity and impurity is found in the writings of R. Judah Halevi, despite his basic position that the concepts of the Torah cannot be translated into human rationality. This viewpoint is illustrated by the parable of the fool and the physician that appears at the beginning of the *Kuzari* (1.79), where the Lawgiver is compared to a physician, and the person who thinks that he can comprehend the foundations of the Torah through his own intellect is compared to a fool. This is not merely a declarative position taken by R. Judah Halevi; rather, this approach is reflected in his interpretation of the reasons for the commandments. Whenever R. Judah Halevi attempts to explain the reason for a particular commandment, he adds certain reservations – for example, in his treatment of the laws of sacrifice (2.26):

181

I do not, by any means, assert that the service was instituted in the order expounded by me, since it *entailed something more secret and higher.*

In his treatment of the laws of purity and impurity, R. Judah Halevi also added reservations, as noted here, before entering a deeper discussion of purity and impurity:

> The Rabbi: I told you that there is no comparison to be made between our intelligence and the Divine Influence, and it is proper that we leave the cause of these important things unexamined. *I take, however, the liberty of stating – though not with absolute uncertainty – that leprosy and issue are occasionally the consequence of contamination by corpses.* A dead body represents the highest degree of malignancy, and a leprous limb is as if dead. It is the same with lost sperm, because it had been endowed with the living power, capable of engendering a human being. Its loss, therefore, forms a contrast to the living and breathing.

This is not merely a question of interpretation. Indeed, R. Judah Halevi claims that it has empirical support (ibid.):

> From experience it is clear that the touch of the unclean causes such fine things as pearls and wine to deteriorate. Most of us are affected by the proximity of dead bodies and graves, and feel depressed when we find ourselves in a house in which there is a corpse. Coarser types remain untouched.

Even if we find it difficult to accept this as a valid empirical claim, the spiritual aspect of distancing oneself from death serves as a very significant rationale for the concept of purity and impurity. This explanation accounts for many commandments in which the Torah cautions us against contact of any kind with the dead: One may not summon the dead or practice necromancy, etc. The Torah reveals itself to be a Torah of life which seeks to reject the natural inclination, common in other religions, to stay away from the living and connect with the dead.

This natural inclination stems from the constant aspiration to connect to the sublime and the transcendent. A dead person could be perceived as a tool for forming such a connection, since on the one hand he is here in this world, yet on the other hand his soul has returned to its source.

Thus, the prohibitions regarding purity and impurity keep human beings distant from contact with death. This explanation is logical and can certainly also be applied to impurity that issues from the human body: menstrual impurity stems from non-fertilization, and the same holds true of the impurity of male discharge. Even the impurity of the leper becomes quite comprehensible, for in the story of Miriam's leprosy, the Torah itself attests that the leper was thought of as dead. However, the laws pertaining to women's impurity after childbirth, with which this week's reading begins, might appear to contradict this explanation, since birth and the impurity of a woman after birth are diametrically opposed to death.

This difficulty can be explained as follows: life and death are inextricably interwoven. In a world that is entirely good, there is no death, but neither is there life (as we know it). The Torah teaches us that light and shadow depend on and are inseparable from one another. The story of a person's death is also the story of his life, for as soon as a person enters the cycle of life, death awaits. This idea can be found in the writings of the rabbis (*Genesis Rabbah* 9:10): "And behold, it was very good (Gen. 1:31) – that is the angel of death."

Thus, the constant attempt to keep away from death and the fact that the Torah is a Torah of life do not contradict the profound recognition that death is bound up with our existence from the moment we come into being, an idea that is expressed in the impurity of a woman after childbirth. It is hard to find a more precise description of the life cycle in which we find ourselves, when the moment of bringing new life into the world and rejuvenating the Jewish people also requires us to acknowledge the existence of death in the world and at the same time to cling to life.

Parashat Aharei Mot

"A WOMAN COURTS A MAN" – MNEMONIC DEVICES FOR TORAH READING

Dr. Yosef Ofer
Department of Bible

IT IS WELL KNOWN that reading the Torah from a Torah scroll is no easy task. A Torah scroll contains only the consonantal text of the Torah, without vowels or cantillation marks, so the reader must learn both the pronunciation of the words and the traditional chanting of each verse by heart. While some verses in the Torah are textually similar, they might be vocalized or chanted differently. Hence the reader might easily confuse such a verse with another verse that closely resembles it. This similarity of verses is likely to trip up even the most experienced reader. Little wonder that throughout the generations Torah readers have attempted to develop mnemonic devices to help them distinguish between similar forms and verses. Such techniques have been listed in Massoretic notes, and some of them are particularly clever and intellectually challenging.

In this week's reading, two verses which are relatively close to one another contain the words *nefesh* (life), *basar* (flesh) and *dam* (blood):

> For the life of the flesh is in the blood, and I have assigned it to you for making expiation for your lives upon the altar; it is the blood, as life, that effects expiation (17:11).
>
> For the life of all flesh – its blood is its life. So I say to the Israelite people: You shall not partake of the blood of any flesh, for the life of all flesh is its blood. Anyone who partakes of it shall be cut off (17:14).

The similarity of so many of the words makes these verses particularly difficult for the reader. The letters *heh-vav-alef*, which can mean "he" or "she," occur four times here, and the reader needs to know whether to read the word as *hu* (masculine) or *hi* (feminine). This is no trifling matter, since as Rashi notes, "Blood (*dam*) and flesh (*basar*) are masculine words, and life (*nefesh*) is feminine." The structure of the sentences is far from simple, making identification of the subject in each sentence quite difficult.

The Massorah Magna in the Leningrad codex notes in this regard: "Two verses regarding this matter are deceptive. The first has *hi* followed by *hu*; the second has *hu* followed by *hi*. Thus we find that the feminine surrounds the masculine."

The wording of the mnemonic "The feminine surrounds the masculine" comes from a verse in Jeremiah ("A woman courts a man," Jer. 31:21). Here it means that of the four occurrences, the two "inner" ones are read *hu* (masculine), while the two "outer" ones, which surround the two occurrences of *hu*, are read *hi* (feminine).

This mnemonic device proved quite successful and was also included in the Massorah Magna of *Mikra'ot Gedolot*, as well as in Hizkuni's commentary (written by the thirteenth-century rabbi, R. Hezekiah b. Manoah) on this chapter. The mnemonic device is short, making it easy to remember while reading.

Other Massoretic notes attempted to cope with the far more complicated challenge of describing all occurrences of *hi-hu* in Leviticus.[1] While such a Massoretic note can be helpful to scribes and those vocalizing the text, it is too long and convoluted to be of use to the Torah reader.

Hizkuni's commentary on this week's reading mentions another mnemonic device, also related to the way to read *heh-vav-alef*. We quote the commentary on Lev. 18:22–23: "'It is an abhorrence' *[to'evah hi]* with a *hirik*, as the neighboring word indicates *[yaggid 'alav re'o]*, both being in the feminine; and 'it is perversion' *[tevel hu]* with a *shuruk*, as the neighboring

---

[1] See the note in the Massorah Magna printed in *Mikra'ot Gedolot* on Lev. 2:15. For parallel sources and further discussion, see C. D. Ginzburg, *Ha-Masorah 'al-Pi Kitvei Yad 'Attikim* (London 1885), 5.89.

word indicates." Here, too, the mnemonic device or sign comes from a verse in Job (36:33): *Yaggid 'alav re'o*. In the context there the verse means "Its noise tells of Him," but here it means that the gender of the adjoining word (*re'o*, its friend) indicates how the word *heh-vav-alef* should be read.[2]

Hizkuni mentions many such mnemonic devices, only some of them known to us from the Massorah. Another two mnemonic devices, this time for verses in *Parashat Aharei Mot*, will be discussed here:

Lev. 16:31: "'It shall be a Sabbath of complete rest for you,' written with a *yod* [=*hi*], and in *Parashat Emor* (Lev. 23:32), with a *vav* [=*hu*]. Both are read according to their orthography, and the mnemonic sign is "*va-tokhal hi ve-hu*" ("and she and he...had food," I Kings 17:15).

The following example deals with two similar verses which, though not located close to one another, are phrased similarly and deal with the same subject – the Day of Atonement as a day of complete rest and fasting: "*Shabbat shabbaton hi/hu lakhem ve'initem et nafshoteikhem.*" Two mnemonic devices were offered the reader here. The first is quite simple: Read the text as written, for in the first case the word in question is spelled *hi* and in the second, *hu*. The second device is a verse in which the word *hi* (according to the *keri*, the tradition of how the text is to be read) precedes the word *hu*.

Lev. 16:20-21 provides another example: "'The live goat shall be brought forward' – in the first instance 'live' is read with a *segol* under the *heh*, and a *kamatz* under the *het* [*he-hoy* in Ashkenazic pronunciation], and the second with a *patah* under both the *heh* and under the *het* [*ha-hay* in Ashkenazic pronunciation], and the device for remembering this is *he-harim*." The question is which of these verses should be read "*ha-sa'ir he-hay*" and which "*ha-sa'ir ha-hoy*." Hizkuni does not mention the vocalization of the *het*, but only the vowel under the *heh* (which is a consequence of the change in the vowel under the *het*). Evidently, he did not distinguish between the pronunciation of a *kamatz* and a *pattah*, as we know was the case in pre-Ashkenazi pronunciation. The mnemonic device suggested here is the word *he-harim*, in which the first *heh* is vocalized with a *segol* (e) and the following one with the vowel "a." This device also attests to its author

---

[2] This is a mnemonic device and not a grammatical argument, since the subject of the sentence is the act of copulation.

being unaware of a distinction in pronunciation between *kamatz* and *pattah*, since a *heh* with a *kamatz* is used to remember a *heh* with a *pattah*.[3] In other words, this device was devised by a Sephardic Jew who pronounced the word as *he-harim*, not *he-horim*.

Another mnemonic device for this week's reading appears in the Massorah Parva of *Mikra'ot Gedolot* on Lev. 18:23: "*Tevel*, with the stress on the penultimate syllable, and the mnemonic device is *ha-aretz mi-tahat* (on the earth beneath)." This device is explained as follows: "The two occurrences of *tevel* [with a *segol* under the *taf* and *bet*, in this verse and in 20:12, below] refer to adultery and illicit sexual practices, and are pronounced with the stress on the penultimate syllable...but *tevel*, with a *tzere* under the *taf* and the *bet*, whose meaning is *eretz* (=earth), is beneath, i.e., is pronounced with the stress on the last syllable" (R. Joseph ben R. David Heilbrun, *Mevin Hidot – Perush 'al ha-Massorah* [Amsterdam 1865]).

These are but a few of the many mnemonic devices that have been utilized from the time of the Massoretes until our day. These devices, or *simanim*, are delightful, clever and even amusing. At the same time, they are helpful to the Torah reader, for "knowledge of the Torah is only acquired through *simanim*" (*'Eruvin* 54b).

---

[3] The last two devices (*va-tohal hi ve-hu* and *he-harim*) are mentioned in a Massoretic note cited by Ginzburg, 6.285. Hizkuni might have based his comments on such a note. Nevertheless, it is uncharacteristic of the Tiberian Massorah to fail to distinguish between *kamatz* and *pattah*.

Parashat Aharei Mot-Kedoshim

THE LAW OF THE SCAPEGOAT[1]

Dr. Alexander Klein
Department of Mathematics

PARASHAT AHAREI MOT PRESENTS the laws concerning the male goat that is sent off to the wilderness to expiate our sins (Lev. 16:6–30):

> And Aaron shall present the bullock of the sin offering which is for himself and make atonement for himself and for his household. He shall take the two goats and set them before the Lord at the door of the tent of meeting. And Aaron shall cast lots upon the two goats: one lot for the Lord, and the other lot for *'azazel*...But the goat on which the lot fell for *'azazel* shall be set alive before the Lord to make atonement over him, to send him away for *'azazel* into the wilderness...And it shall be a statute forever unto you: in the seventh month, on the tenth day of the month...For on this day shall atonement be made for you to cleanse you; from all your sins shall you be clean before the Lord.

In *Hilkhot 'Avodat Yom Ha-Kippurim* (3.1–7), Maimonides ruled:

> There are two lots: On one is written "to the Lord," and on the other, "to *'azazel*." Both goats are made to stand facing westward,

---

[1] Much of this article is based on joint study with my friend Dr. Yitzhak Isaac. See idem and Alexander Klein, *Be-Nivhei ha-Teshuvah, Be'ur le-Hilkhot Teshuvah la-Rambam* (Jerusalem 1997), pp. 21–22.

their hindquarters facing east, and the High Priest comes there with the prefect on his right and the chief of the weekly guard on his left, and both goats in front of him, one to his right and the other to his left. He mixes the lots, and takes one in each hand for the two goats...He then places the lots on each, the one in his right hand on the goat to the right, and the one in his left hand on the one to the left...and he ties a strip of crimson wool weighing two *selas* on the head of the scapegoat and stands it over against the departure gate, and on the one to be slaughtered round its throat, and he slaughters his sin offering of a bullock...Then he sends off the live goat with a person appointed to lead him into the wilderness...How did he do it? He would split the strip of crimson on his horns, tying half to a rock and half between his two horns, and then he would shove it back behind him so that it rolled over the edge and fell. By the time it was half way down the mountain, its limbs would be torn apart.

Two major questions arise regarding the laws of the scapegoat:

1. Why are the goat for the Lord and the goat for *'azazel* opposed, as it were, to one other? Is it conceivable that the goat for *'azazel* is not also for God? A literal reading of the text might seem to imply a duality of the Deity!

2. Why is the scapegoat thrown off the cliff, instead of being slaughtered like all other offerings?

Maimonides held that the scapegoat is an offering to God, and since it is "atonement for all of Israel," the High Priest, as the representative of the entire people of Israel, was responsible for dealing with it. By virtue of a seemingly incomprehensible decree of the Torah,[2] it "atones for all transgressions in the Torah." In his *Guide for the Perplexed* (3.46) Maimonides explained why this sacrifice differs from all other offerings:

---

[2] According to Maimonides at the end of *Hilkhot Me'ilah*, the commandment of the scapegoat is a *hok*, i.e., a commandment whose rationale is unknown. Nevertheless, this did not prevent Maimonides from suggesting an explanation; see Isadore Twersky, *Introduction to the Code of Maimonides* (New Haven 1980), pp. 407–418.

> It bears all the sins, and therefore is not sent to be slaughtered, burned, or made into an offering. Rather, it is sent away as far as possible, by sending it off to *eretz gezerah*, a desolate wilderness. No one actually believes that sins are like weights that can be transferred from the back of one being to another. Rather all these acts are but symbols to impress the soul so that it be moved to repent. That is, we have cleansed ourselves of all our previous deeds, casting them off and rejecting them utterly.

In other words, this offering is so heavily loaded down with sin that it is not proper to offer it in the Temple. It must rather be offered using a symbolic act that will deeply impress our consciousness. It is utterly banished so that we rid ourselves of it as if we wished to distance ourselves from and rid ourselves of all our sins.

Some[3] have understood from Maimonides' remarks in his *Guide for the Perplexed* that the scapegoat is not killed, but only sent to the wilderness, contrary to what he wrote in *Hilkhot 'Avodat Yom Ha-Kippurim* (3.7). In his philosophical work, Maimonides paid close attention to the details of the commandment of the scapegoat, explaining the ideas underlying it, just as he did with all other commandments. "Sending away as utterly as possible" was translated by halakhic authorities into killing the scapegoat by pushing it over a cliff.

It is notable that Maimonides did not explain the law of the scapegoat as a sublimation of pagan practices, which was his explanation for sacrificial worship in general.[4] However, there is extensive evidence that this was what many primitive cultures did, as described by Fraser.[5] Evidently, Maimonides was not aware of these practices.

Ibn Ezra offered a different interpretation from Maimonides. In his commentary on Lev. 16:8 he cites R. Samuel ben Hofni Gaon, who held that the scapegoat was also a sacrifice to God. However, Ibn Ezra rejected

---

[3] Yaakov Loewinger, *Ha-Rambam ke-Philosoph u-ke-Posek* (Jerusalem 1992), p. 180.

[4] See *Guide for the Perplexed*, 3.32.

[5] James George Frazer, *The Golden Bough, A Study in Magic and Religion*, VI: *The Scapegoat* (London 1925).

this interpretation because the scapegoat was not slaughtered and offered on the altar. Ibn Ezra concluded that the entire matter is mystic and beyond his ability to understand. As he puts it:

> R. Samuel said, "Even though [the Torah] says that the goat to be given as a sin offering is for the Lord, the scapegoat is also for the Lord." This is not necessarily so, for the scapegoat is not a sacrifice, since it is not slaughtered. If you could understand the occult reference behind *'azazel*, you would know its secret and the secret of its name, for there are similar occurrences in the Torah. I shall reveal some of the mystery by way of intimation – when you are thirty-three you shall know it.

Nahmanides, following Ibn Ezra, wrote on the same verse:

> Ibn Ezra typically obscures the matter, but I, being more loquacious, shall reveal the secret, which has already been revealed by the Rabbis in many sources...It is explicitly stated in *Pirkei R. Eliezer Ha-Gadol* (ch. 46) that it was customary to bribe Samael (Satan) on the Day of Atonement so that he not annul [the Jews'] sacrificial offering, as it is written: "One lot for the Lord and one lot for *'azazel*." The lot for the Lord went to the burnt offering, and the lot for *'azazel* to the goat sin offering which bore all the sins of Israel, as it is written, "The goat shall carry on it all their iniquities." Seeing that they bore no iniquities on the Day of Atonement, Samael would say to the Holy One, blessed be He: Lord of the Universe, You have one people on Earth who are like the ministering angels in Heaven...And God would hear the testimony against Israel from the prosecuting angel...
>
> Herein lies the secret of the matter; for the people would serve "other gods," the angels, offering them sacrifices as a sweet savor to them...Now the Torah absolutely forbade accepting the angels as deities and worshipping them in any way; but God commanded that on the Day of Atonement we send a goat off to the

wilderness to the minister who rules (*sar ha-moshel*) over wastelands – and that is what befits him, since from his strength there comes destruction and desolation...

Now the intention in our sending away the goat was not that it should be a sacrifice from us to him [Satan], Heaven forbid. Rather, our intention is to obey the will of our Creator, who commanded us to do so...Indeed, Ibn Ezra hinted that you will understand this secret when you come to the verse, "that they may offer their sacrifices no more to the goat-demons" (*se'irim*, Lev. 17:7).[6]

Thus we see that according to Nahmanides, the scapegoat served as a bribe to Satan to keep him from annulling the offering of the Israelites. Moreover, Nahmanides maintained that in so doing we were actually performing the will of God, Who cares for the livelihood of all His servants, including Satan, who represents the force of evil in the world.

A talmudic text seems to support Nahmanides' approach; thus we read in *Hullin* 109b:

Yalta once said to R. Nahman, Observe that for everything that the Torah has forbidden us, it has permitted us an equivalent: It has forbidden us blood, but has permitted us liver; it has forbidden us intercourse during menstruation, but it has permitted us the blood of purification (relations after childbirth); it has forbidden us the fat of cattle, but it has permitted us the fat of wild beasts...I wish to eat milk and meat; [where is its equivalent?]" Thereupon R. Nahman said to the butchers, Give her roasted udders.

According to Maharsha, this text implies that one should not attempt to explain God's commandments, which are divine decrees, since any logical explanation may turn out to be incorrect. For every forbidden action

---

[6] This verse appears thirty-three verses after the verse "Aaron shall place lots upon the two goats, one lot for the Lord and the other lot for *'azazel*."

has a parallel action that is permitted and even positively commanded. The same applies to the scapegoat: Although it may appear to be pagan worship, it is nevertheless a commandment of the Torah.[7]

R. Joseph Dov Soloveitchik[8] commented on Nahmanides: "This is appalling. Heaven forbid! How can Nahmanides have said such a thing? Offering a goat to Satan is pagan worship! This is a truly alarming interpretation."

R. Soloveitchik continued with an attempt to explain Nahmanides in a way that he could accept. It appears, however, that instead of trying to understand Nahmanides in terms of the latter's *Weltanschauung*, which included cosmic forces endowed with will and free choice, he analyzed Nahmanides through Maimonides' eyes. The impact of the Kabbalah on Nahmanides' world view is well known,[9] and his commentary on our question is in line with the Zohar's theory of the *Sitra Ahra*, the forces of "the other camp" or Satan.[10]

In contrast to Nahmanides, Maimonides held that aside from man and God, there is no other independent force with the power of choice. Anyone who addresses such forces through ritual acts or any mode of entreaty not only engages in pagan worship, but also shows that he is totally misguided, since in Maimonides' opinion such forces do not exist. In *Hilkhot 'Avodah Zarah* (1.1–2) Maimonides explained how human beings began to make such mistakes, leading them to say, "This form brings good or evil, and so should be worshipped and feared." In *Hilkhot Teshuvah* (3.7), he stated that whoever falls into error and "worships stars or fortunes other than God in order to be an intercessor between him and the Lord of the universe...is a heretic."

---

[7] See Yehudah Nahshoni, *Hagut be-Parshiyyot Ha-Torah* (Bnei Berak 1989), p. 475.

[8] R. Joseph Dov Soloveitchik, *'Al Ha-Teshuvah* (Jerusalem 1975), p. 287.

[9] Mordechai Margaliyot, "R. Moshe b. R. Nahman," in *Encyclopedia le-Toledot Gedolei Yisrael* (Tel Aviv 1973), wrote: "Prof. Scholem has shown that Nahmanides was a kabbalist who embraced mysticism with all his soul and viewed the Kabbalah as the crowning glory of faith. In all his work, and especially as an exegete of the Torah, he constantly alluded to the world of the esoteric."

[10] This does not necessarily imply that Ibn Ezra shared the same world view as Nahmanides. For the Zohar's view on this issue, see Yeshayahu Tishbi, *Mishnat ha-Zohar* (Jerusalem 1971), pp. 280–281.

Another explanation of Ibn Ezra's obscure remarks has been offered by R. Isaac Mehler in his *'Ezra le-Havin*.[11]

> "The secret is after the word *'azazel*" (so Ibn Ezra on Lev. 16:8) – the next word [in the Torah] is "into the wilderness" (*ha-midbarah*). This word is superfluous, since they were in the wilderness at that time. Most likely, the word *'azazel* was added later by scribes in the Land of Israel..."Thirty-three" [referring to what Ibn Ezra wrote: "I will reveal the secret when you will reach thirty-three"] – this hints to the conclusion of the thirty-third chapter of Deuteronomy, where the text [34:1] begins, "Moses went up from the plains of Moav...and died there...Never again did there arise in Israel a prophet like Moses," which surely was not written by Moses himself. [So too the word *'azazel* here was added after the time of Moses.]

Thus, R. Mehler did not understand Ibn Ezra as commenting on the scapegoat, but on the word *'azazel*. According to R. Mehler, Ibn Ezra was explaining that there was a later addition to the text. However, R. Mehler subsequently rejected the boldness of his own suggestion:

> In my preface I made it clear that I am only explicating the words of the rabbi [Ibn Ezra], but I in no way concur with these things, that in truth did not come from the rabbi's mouth.[12]

Rabbi Shlomo Aviner, inspired by Rav Kook's *Orot ha-Teshuvah*, has offered an original explanation of the significance of the two male goats:[13]

---

[11] Tel Aviv, undated, p. 96.

[12] It is not clear what he meant by the words "that in truth did not come from the rabbi's mouth." Nevertheless, his reservations did not prevent Rabbi Yehudah Gershuni from writing: "I have noted in *'Ezra le-Havin*, a book printed with rabbinical endorsement, an interpretation that shocks the mind." Again, it is not clear whether this was indeed Ibn Ezra's view. Cf. Barukh Spinoza, *Tractatus Theologico-Politicus* (Jerusalem 1989), pp. 95–96.

[13] R. Shlomo Aviner, *Tal Hermon* (Jerusalem 1985), pp. 184–185.

Human beings are responsible for making amends for their sins and for doing everything that they can to improve. However, they are not responsible for the existence of evil in the world. God assumes responsibility for the evil resulting from the Divine act of creation, insofar as He is also the creator of woe (see Is. 45:7). Thus, responsibility for evil is divided between God, Who created evil, and human beings. After human beings do their utmost to amend evil, the remaining responsibility for delivering the world from evil rests on God. The two male goats in the ritual of the Day of Atonement denote this dual responsibility, divided between God and Israel: One goat is for God, to atone for our share of the responsibility, and that is the goat which serves as a sin-offering of repentance, and the other goat is for *'azazel*, for the forces of evil, as if to atone for God, who created evil. That goat "carries our iniquities to a deserted land," for our sins are not only the results of our deeds, but also a product of the force of evil in the world, the force of wilderness, emptiness, desolation and destruction, and it is this force that bears part of the responsibility.

Thus Rabbi Aviner's explanation resembles Maimonides' in that he maintains that the rite of sending off the scapegoat should be viewed symbolically, its objective being to express and remind us of a basic principle. According to Maimonides, the scapegoat rite signifies distancing ourselves from any contact with our sins, and according to Rabbi Aviner, it serves as a reminder that evil exists in the world, that it is a product of God's creation of the world, and that we must come to terms with this as part of reality.

BETWEEN HOLY AND HOLY: ON THE RELATIONSHIP BETWEEN *AHAREI MOT* AND *KEDOSHIM*

Rabbi Abraham Walfish
Department of Talmud

TRYING TO UNDERSTAND the arrangement of the laws that appear in the readings of *Aharei Mot* and *Kedoshim* raises many difficult questions. However, clarifying these questions will give us a better idea of the structure of the entire book of Leviticus.

In fact, if we investigate the larger structure of Leviticus, we will immediately see the difficulties inherent in the position of *Parashat Aharei Mot* within this book. R. David Zvi Hoffmann, in the preface to his commentary on Leviticus, explains the structure of Leviticus in light of a verse which preceded the theophany at Mount Sinai (Ex. 19:6): "You shall be to Me a *kingdom of priests* and *a holy nation.*" This verse indicates that Leviticus begin with *Sefer Kohanim*, or the Priestly Code (chapters 1–15).[1] He explains the aim of this book as follows: "After the Israelites were commanded in Exodus 25, 'Let them make Me a sanctuary that I may dwell among them'...and after the account of the fulfillment of this command and of God appearing in His glory in the Holy of Holies, the Israelites were

---

[1] See pp. 10–11 of Hoffmann's introduction, and cf. Nahmanides' remarks in his introduction, which begins with an analysis similar to that of Rabbi Hoffmann, although Nahmanides goes on to say that "most of this book deals with sacrifices," a statement that leads him to interpret the arrangement of many chapters of Leviticus in a rather far-fetched manner. According to Hoffmann, chapters 16–17 also belong to the *Sefer Kohanim*, and chapter 18 to the Book of Holiness. I prefer to view the Book of Holiness as beginning with the command, "You shall be holy" (19:2). Later on I will discuss the location of chapters 16–17.

finally called upon [in Leviticus] to aspire to commune with God in His sanctuary, and to distance themselves from everything that the Divine Presence finds abhorrent."

This *Sefer Kohanim* can be divided into two parts. The first part (Lev. 1–10) deals with sacrifice, and "imposes on Israel the duty of being steadfast to God...atoning by means of sacrifice for the breach in the covenant with God caused by sinning." The second part (Lev. 11–15) deals with purity and impurity, since "in order to safeguard and maintain God's dwelling amidst Israel and to keep away all impurity...all those who are in a state of impurity must keep their distance from His dwelling and from His sacrifices and must observe the laws of purity."

The Torah the continues with the second half of Leviticus, which reflects the second concept mentioned in the aforementioned verse from Exodus, that the Jews must be "a holy nation." This section of Leviticus is thus called "The Holiness Code" (chapters 19–27), and it seeks to make the members of the "holy people" able to "excel in greater sanctity."

The first two parts of the first section in Leviticus, the *Sefer Kohanim*, treat holiness as a ritual concept. Holiness is tied to the Divine Presence dwelling among the people and the ways in which the Divine Presence can be approached and retained in the Jews' midst. The Book of Holiness, on the other hand, extends the concept of holiness, treating it more abstractly and spiritually. Here, beginning with *Parashat Kedoshim*, holiness (*kedushah*) finds expression in the sanctification of those things which ordinary people, not priests, do in their daily lives.

A striking feature of this overall analysis of Leviticus is that the content of *Parashat Aharei Mot* (chapters 16–18) does not appear to fit the structure of the book. The three chapters in this week's reading deal with three subjects which belong neither to the part preceding them, nor to the section following them. Chapter 16 deals with the sacrificial worship on the Day of Atonement, chapter 17 with the laws of eating and offering sacrifices, and chapter 18 primarily with forbidden relationships (*'arayot*). Chapters 16 and 17, which deal with the sacrifices of the Day of Atonement and where and how to slaughter animals, could ostensibly be viewed as an appendix to the first part of the first section of Leviticus, which dealt with sacrifice, but the inclusion of this appendix in its present position is perplexing.

Leaving aside our "macro" view of the arrangement of Leviticus, the problematic location of *Parashat Aharei Mot* is actually evident on the "micro" level from the first verse of our reading, and it has been discussed at length by commentators from the Midrash to the present day. How is one to understand the opening words, "The Lord spoke to Moses *after the death of the two sons of Aaron*," considering that so much text has intervened between the account of the death of Nadab and Abihu in *Parashat Shemini* (10:1–2) and this week's reading?

Some commentators[2] suggest that this week's reading was spoken a long while after the death of Nadab and Abihu, not immediately thereafter, relying on the remarks of R. Elazar ben Azariah in Sifra that the connection between the deaths of Aaron's sons and the Yom Kippur ritual in chapter 16 is based on the similarity with regard to the subject matter, not the chronology: "'Tell your brother Aaron that he is not to come'...so that he does not die as his sons did" (Rashi). Other commentators[3] took the opening verse at face value, suggesting that the commandments about sacrificial worship on the Day of Atonement were given immediately after the death of Nadab and Abihu.[4] In their opinion, the intervening material (the end of *Parashat Shemini* and the readings of *Tazria* and *Metzora*) was included there because "the Torah first noted the commandments God gave all of Israel against ritual defilement (unclean foods, leprosy, etc.), and then it included the commandments about ritual defilement which apply to the individual [Aaron the High Priest]" (Nahmanides). Nahmanides' comment provides a possible explanation for the position of chapter 16, but not for chapters 17 and 18.

---

[2] Rashi, R. Joseph Bekhor Shor, and Hizkuni. Ibn Ezra should also be interpreted this way.

[3] See Nahmanides, R. David Zvi Hoffmann, and such modern commentators as Menahem Bulle in *Da'at Mikra* and Jacob Milgrom in the *Anchor Bible*.

[4] Cf. Nahmanides: "The text would mean that God said to Moses: 'After the two sons of Aaron died when they drew too close to the presence of the Lord, tell Aaron not to come at will into the Sanctuary, lest he die.'"

The key to understanding the arrangement of these chapters, in light of our view of the greater structure of Leviticus given above, lies in perceiving them as transitional chapters between the "Priestly Code" and the "Holiness Code." As we shall see below, this week's reading sets us at a major crossroads in the saga of Israel's redemption.

The nature of chapters 16–18 as transitional chapters can be seen in the fact that these chapters use the terminology characteristic of the Book of the Priests, albeit in a sense closer to that the Book of Holiness. This warrants further explanation:

1. Chapter 16, the description of the Yom Kippur ritual, serves as an appendix not only to the section on sacrifice, but also to the part about purity and impurity, since the purpose of the offerings discussed here is to atone (*le-khapper*)[5] and to purify (*le-taher*): "Thus he shall purge (*ve-khipper*) the Sanctuary of the uncleanness and transgression of the Israelites, whatever their sins" (Lev. 16:16); "For on this day atonement shall be made for you (*yekhapper*) to cleanse you (*le-taher*) of all your sins; you shall be clean before the Lord" (16:30). In the first verse these words are used in their ritual sense, i.e., purifying the Tabernacle from the uncleanness that adhered to it,[6] but in the second verse the words "you shall be clean" have a broader, metaphorical significance: to purify oneself of the impurity of sin. Note that this verse is the cornerstone of our Yom Kippur prayers and the concept of *teshuvah* or repentance.

2. Chapter 17 also combines appendices concerning sacrifice – the slaughter of animals for food, the prohibition against eating blood, and the requirement that blood be covered – with additional laws on uncleanness (e.g. of dead animals). Nevertheless, while this terminology is similar to the language found in the *Sefer Kohanim*, our chapter adopts a somewhat different perspective on matters. While the first half of Leviticus deals with the question of how to worship God by offering sacrifices, chapter 17 begins from the opposite point of view: "If anyone of the house of Israel

---

[5] The root *k-p-r* (atone or purge) is used in both the sections on sacrifice (1:4, 4:20, 26, 31 etc.) and on purity (14:20, 21, 29, 31, etc.)

[6] Cf. Jacob Milgrom in the *Anchor Bible*, p. 254 ff., and his response to the criticism of Noam Zohar in *JBL* 109 (1990), pp. 111–113.

slaughters an ox or sheep or goat in the camp…and does not bring it to the entrance of the Tent of Meeting to present it as an offering to the Lord, before the Lord's Tabernacle, bloodguilt shall be imputed to that man: he has shed blood; that man shall be cut off from among his people." According to the plain sense of this text (see Nahmanides on Lev. 17:2–3), this passage deals with a person who slaughters an animal with the intention of eating it, not in order to worship God. The Torah teaches us here that as long as the children of Israel are encamped around the Tabernacle,[7] they may eat meat only if the animal is slaughtered as a sacrifice of *shelamim*. Thus, the Torah instructs us regarding how the sanctity of the Tabernacle can be brought into the individual's private kitchen, and this is the principal goal of most of the laws in this chapter (except for verses 6–8).

3. Chapter 18 contains mostly laws about illicit sexual relationships. The close connection between this chapter and the second half of Leviticus is strongly felt in the clear parallels between the punishments mentioned at the end of *Parashat Kedoshim* (chapter 20) and the list of prohibitions in this chapter. In addition, chapter 18 employs language characteristic of the Book of Holiness, for example, the repeated use of formulas such as "I am the Lord" and "I the Lord am your God." Nevertheless, this chapter is also tied to the *Sefer Kohanim*. As Nahmanides noted in his preface to Leviticus: "It follows that He warned about illicit relationships, because such relations cause uncleanness (*tum'ah*) and transgressing them brings defilement, causing the Divine Presence to withdraw and leading to exile." Nahmanides' remarks here allude to verses 24–30, which sum up the prohibitions in this chapter with the warning that violating them will cause the land to spew them out for defiling it. This chapter uses the term defilement (*tum'ah*) in a broad and abstract sense, as befits the transitional chapters of *Aharei Mot*.

To sum up: *Parashat Aharei Mot* is situated at the transitional point between the ritual concept of sanctity pertaining to the Tabernacle, in the *Sefer Kohanim*, and the abstract and spiritual concept of holiness in one's

---

[7] I.e., until they enter the land and its boundaries are extended, as described in Deut. 12:20–28.

daily life, in the Book of Holiness. In the three chapters comprising the Sabbath reading, the Torah shows how to extend these formal concepts about the sanctity of the Sanctuary and apply them to each and every individual's private existence. In this way, *Parashat Aharei Mot* provides a fitting introduction to the commandment, "You shall be holy" (Lev. 19:2), which begins the Book of Holiness.

Parashat Aharei Mot can be seen as transitional in another sense as well, which finds expression in the introduction to its last section (18:3): "You shall not copy the practices of the land of Egypt where you dwelt, or of the land of Canaan to which I am taking you, nor shall you follow their laws." Egypt and the land of Canaan appear only rarely in the *Sefer Kohanim*,[8] but they play an important role in the Book of Holiness.[9] Here, in chapter 18, both countries appear together as nations whose practices and laws we are forbidden to follow. Support can be found for Rashi's suggestion that these two nations symbolize the depths of moral depravity, especially with regard to sexual relations. Moreover, the language of the verse hints at another reason for coupling Egypt with Canaan in this context. Egypt represents the Israelites' past ("where you dwelt"), and Canaan represents its future ("to which I am taking you"). More than any other nation, these two nations are likely to have an impact on the character and values of the people of Israel. God warns His people to sever themselves totally from the values characterizing the people from which Israel was recently delivered, and not to adopt the laws and ways of the people in whose midst they are going to live.

In the wilderness, the Israelites were suspended between two cultures, and God commanded them to maintain their spiritual independence with respect to both. Severing themselves from the laws of Egypt marks the culmination of the process of redeeming the people from Egypt, and keeping their distance from the laws of Canaan marks the beginning of the people's preparing to enter the land. As Nahmanides explained in his

---

[8] Each appears only once: Egypt, 11:45; Canaan, 14:34.

[9] The land of Egypt is mentioned 10 times from chapter 19 onward, and in the Holiness Code there are many commandments relating to the land of Israel, e.g., *'orlah,* the *'omer,* the sabbatical year and the jubilee year.

introduction to Exodus, redemption from Egypt was complete only when God's Presence dwelled in their midst (see the end of Exodus). The *Sefer Kohanim* describes the consequences of God's dwelling amidst the people and thereby completing their spiritual redemption. This notion is summed up in the commandment that opens chapter 18: to keep far from the practices of the land of Egypt. By freeing themselves of these ways, which cause spiritual defilement and remove God's Presence, the people complete their spiritual redemption from Egypt and become a "kingdom of priests," worthy of God dwelling in their midst.

The last part of Leviticus is addressed to a people who had achieved complete redemption and the unique status of God's servants. At this point the servants of God were called to attain the level of a "holy people," worthy of settling the land promised to the descendants of the patriarchs. In the Book of Holiness, the sanctity of the people of Israel is associated with the sanctity of the land of Israel. Note, for example, how the commandment concerning the jubilee associates the liberation of slaves with freeing lands ("each of you shall return to his holding," 25:13). The people are God's ("For they are My servants, whom I freed from the land of Egypt," 25:42), as is the land ("for the land is Mine," 25:23). Therefore, no member of the Israelite people may sell either himself or his land in perpetuity, but only until the jubilee. This section of Leviticus is preceded by chapter 18, which contains the commandment not to follow the laws of the land of Canaan. Observing the laws of illicit relationships guarantees preservation of the sanctity of the individual and of the land, so they will not be defiled and so the people will not be spit out.

The two parts of Leviticus thus symbolize the stages in the spiritual development of the people of Israel. The transition from leaving Egypt to preparation to enter the land is accompanied by a change in emphasis, from the sanctity of the Divine Presence, in whose presence Man dwells, to the inner sanctity of the person himself. The sanctity of the Divine Presence finds expression in a tremendously powerful religious experience, with the concomitant danger of coming too close (Nadab and Abihu), and of transgressing in ways that cause defilement and remove the Divine Presence from our midst. On the other hand, obeying the command "You shall be holy" does not involve any powerful experience. It is a quiet, ongoing sanctity that finds expression in the person's daily life and deeds. At the juncture of these two worlds are the chapters comprising *Aharei Mot*, which combine these two worlds of holiness. The God who reveals Himself to man through cloud and fire is the same God Who dwells in the depths of each person's soul.

Parashat Emor

THE SABBATH AND THE HOLY DAYS

Prof. Shubert Spero

Department of Basic Jewish Studies

THE LORD SPOKE TO MOSES, saying: Speak to the Israelite people and say to them: These are My fixed times, the fixed times of the Lord, which you shall proclaim as sacred occasions. On six days work may be done, but on the seventh day there shall be a sabbath of complete rest, a sacred occasion. You shall do no work; it shall be a sabbath of the Lord throughout your settlements. These are the set times of the Lord, the sacred occasions, which you shall celebrate each at its appointed time (Lev. 23:1–4).

Rashi asks (v. 3):

> What has the Sabbath to do with the festivals? It is to teach us that whoever profanes the fixed times is considered as if he has profaned the Sabbath, and whoever observes the fixed times is considered as if he has observed the Sabbath.

Were it not for the repetition in v. 4 of the words "These are the set times (*mo'adei*) of the Lord," one might argue that the words "These are...the fixed times (*mo'adei*) of the Lord" (v. 2) refers to the Sabbath, mentioned in the next verse, as Ibn Ezra and Hizkuni maintained. After all, the term *mo'ed* denotes a specific place (e.g. the Tent of Meeting, *ohel mo'ed*) or a specific time, as in the phrase, "I will return to you at the time (*la-mo'ed*) next year" (Gen. 18:14). Hence the term *mo'ed* can denote the Sabbath, like its companion term, "sacred occasions," *mikra'ei kodesh,* which according to Nahmanides in his commentary on these verses means a day on which "every one is called to gather together to sanctify it, for Israel are commanded to gather together in the House of God on the days of *mo'ed* to publicly sanctify the day through prayer, praising the Lord, wearing clean garments and making it a day of feasting."

In its narrowest sense, however, the word *mo'ed* refers only to specific days associated with particular customs that are repeated in a yearly cycle; hence this term does not apply to the Sabbath and New Moon. There are only seven days in the year that can be called *mo'ed*: the first and seventh days of Passover, Shavuot, Yom Kippur, Rosh Hashanah, and the first and eighth days of Sukkot.

The prominent features of the Sabbath that set it apart from the days of *mo'ed* are:

1. The sanctity of the Sabbath is fixed and has existed since time immemorial, as this day was sanctified by God himself. By contrast, the sanctity of the *mo'adim* stems from the sanctity of Israel, since the day of the *mo'ed* depends on the number of days in the month, which in turn depends on the Jewish court determining exactly when the New Moon falls (see *Pesahim* 107a).

2. On the Sabbath all work is prohibited, as it is written, "You shall do no work" (Lev. 23:3). However, on the days of *mo'ed* it is forbidden to "work at your occupations" (v. 7), and therefore work necessary for preparing food is permitted (see *Pesahim* 68b).

Accordingly, it is not clear why, after declaring its intention to list the days of *mo'ed*, the Torah pauses to mention the commandment of the Sabbath, which is not included in the term *mo'ed*; indeed, as a result of this seeming interruption, the Torah had to repeat the statement, "These are the set times of the Lord."

There are two ways to account for the juxtaposition of dissimilar subjects or subjects which at first glance might appear similar but in fact are very different. Such juxtaposition might have been intended to make the weaker subject more prominent, by comparing it to the stronger one with which it is juxtaposed. Alternatively, such juxtaposition might have been intended to stress the uniqueness of the stronger subject, so that it does not become blurred as a result of the natural tendency to equate it with the weaker concept. Rashi favored the first option, writing: "To teach you that whoever profanes the days of *moed* is considered as if he had profaned the Sabbath." Nahmanides, on the other hand, chose the second option: "The first statement deals with the days of *mo'ed*. However, the Sabbath was mentioned to indicate that it does not follow the laws of *mo'ed*: when the Sabbath falls on a *mo'ed* the laws of the Sabbath are not suspended so as to permit preparation of food." In other words, when a holiday falls on the Sabbath, one should not make the mistake of thinking that the permission to prepare food on the holiday overrules the prohibition against doing "any work" on the Sabbath.

I would like to suggest another explanation for mentioning the Sabbath in the context of the days of *mo'ed*. Following Nahmanides, I believe that the comparison was intended to reinforce the greater importance of the Sabbath over that of the holidays by giving precedence to the Sabbath, which finds expression in the fact that the Sabbath is mentioned before the holidays in other passages as well (Ex. 23:12, Num. 28:9, but see also Ex. 34:21; see Nahmanides and Sforno on the latter verse).

The juxtaposition underscores the radical difference between the Sabbath and the holidays in terms of the general orientation of each, as well as in terms of the relationship of one to the other. The origins of the holidays reflect the history of the people of Israel and are directed at the Jewish community. However, the origins of the Sabbath are rooted in the mysteries of the universe; the Sabbath is directed at all of mankind. Therefore, in a certain sense it might be said that the Sabbath is the ultimate objective of the holidays.

My teacher, Rabbi Shraga Feivel Mendlovitz (the head of Yeshiva Torah Vodaath in New York) used to explain this metaphorically: The function of the days of *mo'ed* is to train and educate the individual to be a Jew, through the correspondence between the historical experience and consciousness of God that finds expression in the days of *mo'ed*. These holidays clarify to us God's role in the history of the nation (Passover, Shavuot, and Sukkot), the connection between the individual and his Maker

(Rosh Hashanah, Yom Kippur), and the place of Divine Providence in the ecological life of the soil (spring, harvest time, the gathering of the fruits). As a responsible partner to the Covenant and a member of the house of Israel, by observing the days of *mo'ed*, the individual "finishes his studies and receives his degree." Only then does he begin his most professional work, namely, to observe the Sabbath.

The prohibition against doing any work on the Sabbath is not simply a stricter version of the prohibition against "working at your occupations" on the days of *mo'ed*; rather, these commandments are fundamentally different. Maimonides wrote that abstaining from work on the seventh day is an affirmative commandment, as it is written, "On the seventh day you shall cease from labor" (*Hilkhot Shabbat* 1.1). As R. Joseph Dov Soloveitchik explained, "The Sabbath is not about forbidding us to do work; it is an affirmative commandment that we cease from work...the main thing is to declare the Sabbath as testimony, 'a sign for all times'" (*Ha-Adam ve-'Olamo*, pp. 244–245). The basic obligation that the people of Israel took upon themselves as a nation "in all your dwelling-places," as part of their covenant with God, is to attest through their total devotion to the Sabbath rest, even under the most difficult circumstances, that the One God of Abraham, Isaac and Jacob, who gave us the Torah, is the Creator and Ruler of the universe. Rashi interpreted the verse, "Speak to the people of Israel and say: Nevertheless, you must keep My Sabbaths, for this is a sign between Me and you throughout the ages, that you may know (*la-da'at*) that I the Lord have consecrated you" (Ex. 31:13), as follows: "*la-da'at* – [not "that *you* may know" but] that the nations of the world may know through it [the Sabbath]." The word *le-'olam* in the verse "It shall be a sign for all time (*le-'olam*) between Me and the people of Israel" (v. 17), according to Rashi, can be rendered as "for all inhabitants of the Earth." Israel is to keep the Sabbath as a sign between God and Israel, and the nations of the world will thereby come to acknowledge God's actions in nature.

Once we recognize the fundamental difference between the Sabbath and the days of *mo'ed*, we are in a better position to understand several of the unique characteristics of the Sabbath:

1. The Sabbath is the only ritual that is included in the Ten Commandments, since it is one of the basic objectives of the covenant.

2. Due to its great importance, the punishment for violating the Sabbath is very strict: "He who profanes it shall be put to death" (Ex. 31:14). Because the Sabbath is a sign of the Covenant and is testimony to the rest of the world, violating it publicly is considered an extremely serious sin.

3. Even though there is no historical connection between the people of Israel and the Sabbath, "Sabbath rest" was given to Israel as a pleasure, not just as an obligation. The Sages call the Sabbath a "fine gift," given to Israel as an expression of God's love for His people. This is the reason that the word *be-ahavah*, "lovingly," is added to the prayers recited on the Sabbath.

What does the Sabbath have to do with the days of *mo'ed*? It is to remind us that all the holidays, with all of their symbolic richness and the great impact they have on our lives, are only a preparatory step for making the people Israel worthy witnesses: when they keep the Sabbath, they bear witness that God, who is One, made heaven and earth.

Parashat Emor

"HE BLASPHEMED GOD"

Professor Haim Genizi
Department of General History

AND THE SON of an Israelite woman, whose father was an Egyptian, went out among the children of Israel; and the son of the Israelite woman and a man of Israel fought together in the camp. And the son of the Israelite woman blasphemed the Name, and cursed; and he was brought before Moses. And his mother's name was Shelomith, the daughter of Dibri, of the tribe of Dan (Lev. 24:10-11).

The wording of the first verse appears problematic. Seemingly, the order of the words ought to have been as follows: "The son of an Israelite woman came out (*va-yetze*) among the Israelites, and he was the son of an Egyptian man."[1] Various exegetes have commented on this verse, attempting to explain from where this man came out and what his sin was.[2]

---

[1] Note how this difficulty is solved in the new JPS translation (*The Torah: New Translation of the Holy Scriptures*, 2d ed. [Philadelphia 1962], p. 227): "There came out among the Israelites one whose mother was Israelite and whose father was Egyptian; and a fight broke out in the camp between the half-Israelite and a certain Israelite. The son of the Israelite woman pronounced the Name in blasphemy, and he was brought to Moses – now his mother's name was Shelomith daughter of Dibri of the tribe of Dan." See also R. Aryeh Kaplan, *The Living Torah* (New York and Jerusalem 1981), p. 365: "The son of an Israelite woman and an Egyptian man went out among the Israelites."

[2] See the commentary of R. Samson Raphael Hirsch on Lev. 24:11: "At that time she was the only woman in Israel who had committed a transgression...She went astray with a non-Jewish man, and consequently the seed of that crime was implanted among

Ibn Ezra, adhering to the plain meaning of the text, wrote that he "came out" of his tent. Nahmanides took the same approach, and Rabbi David Zvi Hoffmann, in his commentary on Leviticus, followed Ibn Ezra, providing substantiation for his view from Num. 16:27 and from Est. 4:1, "He went through the city." Hoffmann nevertheless disagrees with Nahmanides' view that "among the children of Israel" refers to the man's location; according to Hoffmann, "among the children of Israel" means that he cursed in public, in the presence of the people.[3]

Unlike Ibn Ezra and Nahmanides, Rashi followed the Midrash. He chose three different interpretations from Midrash Tanhuma (*Emor* 23) and Sifra (*Emor* 235):

> "The son of an Israelite woman...went out." From where did he come out? R. Levi said, From his world. R. Berakhyah said, From the previous passage: He came to mock and said in wonderment, "It is written, 'He shall arrange them [=the twelve loaves placed on the table in the Sanctuary once a week] every Sabbath day" (Lev. 23:8). Kings eat fresh hot bread every day. Must [God] eat cold bread nine days old?!"
>
> In a *baraita* we learn: He came out of Moses' court, which had ruled against him. He had come to pitch his tent in the encampment of Dan, and they asked him, "What is your business here?" He answered, "I am from the Danites." They said, "It is written (Num. 2:2), 'Each with his standard, under the banners of their father's house.'"[4] So he took his case to Moses' court, where the court ruled against him. [Thereupon] he stood up and cursed.

---

the Jews. The mother, Shelomit, is seen as the primary cause of the terrible sin committed by the son." *Da'at Mikra* takes the same line, interpreting "the son of an Egyptian man" as follows: "His education by an Egyptian father and his mother's dubious loyalty to the Israelites – she had apparently married an Egyptian man while still in Egypt – were what caused him to commit the crime." See also Nechama Leibowitz, *Iyyunim Hadashim be-Sefer Vayikra* (Jerusalem 1984), pp. 378–389.

[3] R. David Zvi Hoffmann, *Sefer Vayikra* (Jerusalem 1954), 2.213.

[4] Since his father was an Egyptian, he had no right to pitch his tent among the tribe of Dan.

Here we shall try to explain Rashi's interpretation. In asking, "From where did he come out?" Rashi intended to reject the possibility that the blasphemer had emerged from a physical location in the camp, since all the Israelites were in the camp, and there would be no point in relating this information. As Malbim (*Vayikra*, §335) observed:

> One might be tempted to interpret the phrase "There came out...among the Israelites" in the same way as "He went through the city" (Est. 4:1) [the same verb and preposition, *va-yetze...betokh*, appear in both]. But in fact this expression [*va-yetze...betokh benei yisrael*] would have to mean "someone who comes out and goes from person to person and from place to place." Additionally, why would it denote something that was permitted? Therefore, the words, "There came out among the Israelites and...a fight broke out in the camp" were unnecessary.

The views that Rashi cites indicate that he was interested in the cause of the argument, not its location. He wants to know why one of the parties was led to blaspheme God when the argument here took place between two individuals.

The first opinion Rashi cites is that of R. Levi, who said, "He went out of his world," an explanation that Bible commentators found difficult to understand.[5] Nechama Leibowitz maintained that R. Levi was not trying to explain what led the person to commit such a terrible transgression; rather, he sought to explain the act itself. However, it seems to us that R. Levi, like R. Berakhyah and the *baraita* (the two other interpretations cited by Rashi),

---

[5] Nechama Leibowitz (above, n. 2), p. 382 cites four views about this. Rabbenu Bahya believed that every person is a world unto himself, and consequently the man who cursed "came out of himself," i.e., departed from his true nature. Rabbi Samuel Jaffe Ashkenazi explained that the blasphemer "left the world of supreme wisdom that dwelt among them, and that was his world." R. Issachar Ber, the author of *Mattenot Kehunah*, maintained that the man "turned aside and distanced himself from other men," and R. David Luria (Radal), like Ashkenazi, wrote that the man "came out of his world, which is the stronghold of God." See also *Siftei Hakhamim* on Lev. 24:10: "He went out of his world."

was in fact addressing the question of what caused the son of the Israelite woman to commit so egregious a sin as to curse God.

Perhaps the expression "he came out of his world" means that the man acted out of character and lost his senses, deviating from his normal behavior to the extreme. It is not unknown for a person in the midst of an intense argument to lose self-control. Indeed, great anger and strife can even cause temporary loss of sanity. While the claim of temporary insanity is often made – and sometimes accepted – in modern courts of law, the Torah decrees that the man who cursed God should be stoned. Losing control and even temporary insanity are not considered acceptable defenses here, for the Torah demands that we curb our impulses. We must never allow ourselves to reach such a state. This is why the man who cursed God was sentenced to death.

Thus, R. Levi held that losing one's senses and stepping beyond accepted bounds can lead one to curse God. The difficulty with this explanation is that it does not relate specifically to the case discussed here, but could apply to any transgression. As Resh Lakish said, "A person does not commit a transgression unless a spirit of folly has overcome him."[6] Perhaps Rashi found this explanation inadequate precisely for this reason, and hence he cited two additional opinions to supplement it.

The second interpretation presented by Rashi is that of R. Berakhyah, whose interpretation is based on the juxtaposition of this episode with the discussion of the showbread that immediately precedes it. The Midrash asks: "From where did he emerge? From the previous passage. For it is said...'He shall arrange them before the Lord regularly every Sabbath day.' He said, 'It is the custom of kings to eat fresh hot bread every day. Is He to eat cold bread?'" Note that when Rashi cited this homily, he altered the wording of the *Tanhuma*, adding the word *ligleg*, "he came to mock."

According to Rashi's understanding, R. Berakhyah believed that it was the man's scorn that caused him to commit such an extreme act. Lack of faith and refusal to accept the logic of the Torah's commandments provide

---

[6] *Sotah* 3a. Perhaps R. Levi's interpretation is based on the juxtaposition of the passages (*semikhut*), since the previous passage ends with the words *hok 'olam* ("a law for all time," Lev. 24:9). See *Siftei Hakhamim*, s.v. *me-'olamo yatza*.

the wicked with a pretext for being scornful, as with Korah's mockery of the laws of *tzitzit*.[7] The sinner mentioned in our reading ridiculed things that others held sacred, and his seeming concern for the honor of the King of Kings, lest He "eat nine-day-old cold bread," in contrast to human kings, who eat fresh bread daily, is an indication of his cynicism and wickedness, since God does not "eat" the showbread. Furthermore, the showbread, which was made of unleavened bread a handbreadth thick, surely did not dry out very quickly. Thus, scorn for the Torah's commandments – laws which we do not always fully understand – and the mockery of matters that others hold sacred, can lead to blasphemy.

Rashi, however, was not entirely satisfied with this explanation, even though it was based on the juxtaposition of texts, since our verse, according to this interpretation, did not refer to the other verses about the man who cursed God. Hence Rashi included another midrash, from *Sifra* (*Emor* 235): "He came out of Moses' court, which had found against him."

It should be recalled that the man who cursed was the son of an Egyptian father and a Jewish mother, "Shelomit daughter of Divri of the tribe of Dan." Since nationality, according to the *halakhah*, follows the mother, this man was halakhically considered an Israelite,[8] and as such he was obligated to fulfill all the commandments of the Torah; if he transgressed any of them, he would be punished. Since all the Torah's injunctions applied to him, he wished to belong to the Israelites, and since he was associated with the Israelites through his mother, who was from the tribe of Dan, he sought to pitch his tent in Dan's encampment. But the Danites would not let him join them: "'What is your business here?' they asked. He answered, 'I am born of a Danite woman.' They said, 'It is written, Each with his standard, under the banners of their fathers' house'" (Num. 2:2). Although nationality was determined by the mother, tribal encampment was determined by the father. The son of the Israelite woman

---

[7] See Rashi on Num. 16:1, s.v. *ve-Datan va-Aviram*.

[8] R. Samson Raphael Hirsch remarked, "Since there was some doubt as to whether the status of people born before the giving of the Torah followed the mother, Rashi commented on the words, 'Among the children of Israel' – this indicates that he had converted."

found himself in an impossible situation: Although he bore all the obligations of an Israelite, he was denied the privileges of living within Israelite society. Where could he go – to the mixed multitude of Egyptians, where his father dwelt and where he could live free of the burden of the Torah's commandments? In despair, he turned to the highest authority – to Moses' court of justice. But, to his great disappointment, the court found him bound by the Torah's commandments. This man suffered real injury at the hands of the law, and so he asked himself what sort of law this was that considered him bound by all the obligations but not entitled to any of the privileges? He concluded that there was no justice in this law, and since the law was not just, the Lawgiver – God – must be unjust too.

This, in the view of the *baraita*, is what caused the son of the Israelite woman to curse God. It was neither loss of control in a fight nor scorn for the Torah's commandments, but rather pain over the injustice of the Torah's laws, as he perceived things. The *baraita's* interpretation provides a rational explanation for the factors that might cause someone to overstep his bounds and commit such a grave act.[9] Nevertheless, God commanded: "Take the blasphemer outside the camp, and...let the whole community stone him" (Lev. 24:14). The hardship the blasphemer faced was not taken into consideration, since the law serves to protect the majority. In every society there will always be a small minority that suffers because of the law. But if as a result, the minority breaks the law and blasphemes the lawgiver, no society could survive. Every social framework is based on a system of laws that regulate relations among the majority in the society. If a minority is hurt, it must try to find ways to change and improve the law.

The Torah wants to teach us that an individual's suffering does not entitle him to express his protest by cursing God. That is not how to amend the law. There are other ways, as in the case of the daughters of Zelofehad, who, faced with a similarly unjust situation, approached Moses and successfully petitioned for their inheritance rights (Num. 27:1–11).

---

[9] This homily suggests that the Sages may have felt uncomfortable about the fact that no solution was found for the grievance of the son of the Israelite woman, who had been injured by the law.

The *baraita's* interpretation provides a more appropriate explanation than the two preceding ones insofar as it refers back to explicit remarks made in the episode it seeks to explain. As Rashi pointed out in his commentary on Lev. 24:10, the confrontation in the camp concerned affairs related to the camp itself: the right to pitch one's tent in Dan's encampment.

Thus, we see that Rashi presented three views on the question of what led the son of the Israelite woman to curse God. The first interpretation, based on R. Levi's view, was too general and too far from the text. The second interpretation, based on R. Berakhyah's view, was closer to the text insofar as it referred back to the previous passage about the showbread. But only the third interpretation, that of the *baraita*, referred specifically to the subject of the altercation that led to the blasphemy. By presenting these three interpretations in succession, Rashi demonstrated systematic refinement of his interpretation of the biblical text.

Parashat Behar

RENEWAL IN THE SABBATH YEAR

Dr. Yaakov Charlap
Department of Talmud

PARASHAT BEHAR (Lev. 25:2–5) presents the laws of the sabbatical year:

> When you enter the land that I give you, the land shall observe a sabbath of the Lord. Six years you may sow your field and six years you may prune your vineyard and gather in the yield. But in the seventh year, the land shall have a sabbath of complete rest, a sabbath of the Lord...it shall be a year of complete rest for the land.

The punishment for failure to observe the commandments of the sabbatical year appears later, in *Parashat Behukkotai* (Lev. 26:32–35):

> I will make the land desolate, so that your enemies who settle in it shall be appalled by it. And you I will scatter among the nations, and I will unsheathe the sword against you. Your land shall become a desolation and your cities a ruin. Then the land will make up for its sabbath years through the time that it is desolate and while you are in the land of your enemies; then the land will rest and make up for its sabbath years. Throughout the time that it is desolate, it shall observe the rest that it did not observe in your sabbath years while you were dwelling upon it.

Avot De-Rabbi Nathan (Version A, Ch. 38) remarks:

How do we know that exile comes to the world...because of the sabbath of the land? As it is written, "Then the land shall rest and make up for its sabbath years" (v. 34). God said to Israel: Since you have not given the land its rest, it shall take rest of you. As are the number of months that you do not give the land its rest, so shall it take its rest. Therefore it is written, "Then shall the land rest and make up for its sabbath years. Throughout the time that it is desolate, it shall observe the rest that it did not observe in your sabbath years while you were dwelling upon it."

The problematic nature of this commandment was observed long ago by R. Isaac Nafha, a second generation *amora* living in the land of Israel, as cited in *Tanhuma Vayikra*, 1:

"Bless the Lord, O His angels, mighty creatures who do His bidding, ever obedient to His bidding" (Ps. 103:20)...R. Isaac Nafha said: This refers to those who observe the laws of the sabbatical year. Why were they called mighty creatures? Because when they saw their fields abandoned, their trees untended, their fences breached, and their fruits being eaten, they repressed their evil inclination [to work the land and keep its produce] and said nothing; and our rabbis taught us that the mighty are those who repress their evil inclination.

The rationale for the sabbatical year, as presented in *Sanhedrin* 39a, in the name of R. Abbahu, is well known:

A disciple came and asked [R. Abbahu]: What is the rationale behind the commandment of the sabbatical year? He answered: God told the Israelites to sow six years but to rest on the seventh, so that they will know that the land belongs to God. However, they did not do so, but sinned and were exiled.

According to this text, the message of the commandment of the sabbatical year is that men are not the true owners of the land they possess; but rather that God is master of the land. In line with this explanation, we can understand why the punishment for violating this law is exile: The people failed to acknowledge God's ownership of the land, and God demonstrated His ownership by removing the people from the land, punishing them measure for measure.

Numerous other explanations of this commandment have been suggested over the generations. *Shem mi-Shemu'el* by R. Samuel of Sokhachov offers an original explanation based on a remark by the author of *Or Ha-Hayyim* on Gen. 2:3. When God created the world, "He did not create a force in the world with the strength to endure for more than six days, as it is written, 'In six days the Lord made heaven and earth' (Ex. 20:11). The forces of creation must be renewed every Sabbath."[1] *Shem mi-Shemu'el* carries this notion over to Lev. 25:2. There the Torah says, "When you enter the land that I assign (*ani noten*) to you." Now, the verb *noten* is in the present tense, meaning that the land of Israel is given anew to the people of Israel every seven years, since in the seventh year it reverts to God. When the sabbatical year is observed, the land is again given to Israel. As R. Samuel put it:

> It must be said that assigning the land of Israel to the people of Israel is like Creation in general: the land is given to them only for seven years, to work it, and then God gives it again for another seven years, to be worked and cared for. Therefore, in the seventh year, the land reverts to the One Who gave it, and all those who eat of its fruits partake of [His] lofty table...Therefore the introductory words "When you enter the land that I give you" are in the present tense, rather than in the past or future...to indicate that the act of giving you the land is continuous, not once for all time (*Behar*, ibid.).

---

[1] Cf. also *Or Ha-Hayyim* on Ex. 20:11, s.v. *'od yirtzeh*, as well as Onkelos and Nahmanides on this verse.

In other words, the connection between the people and the land is not static; it is dynamic, demanding constant renewal. The sabbatical year provides the opportunity to renew the bond between the people and their land. The additional implication of the comparison to Genesis is that God renews the strength of the land in the sabbatical year.

Maimonides mentions the notion of renewal in his *Guide for the Perplexed*, where he stresses the land's need for rest. In his opinion, letting a field lie fallow for a year improves the quality and quantity of its yield in subsequent years. Thus, Maimonides combines the agricultural advantage for the land with the benefit derived by the owner of the field (*Guide*, 3.39).

R. Isaac Arama (*Akedat Yitzhak*) and Don Isaac Abarbanel challenge this explanation of Maimonides. In their opinion, the severe consequences for failing to observe the commandment to let one's field rest is not consonant with this interpretation. If the commandment was intended to ensure the well-being of the owner of the field, then the owner who failed to observe the commandment would be causing himself harm. Why then would the Torah view this violation with such severity? As R. Isaac Arama explained (*'Akedat Yitzhak, Vayikra, Behar Sinai*, 69):

> Wonderful insight and revelation is provided by the fact that the Torah was so strict about this commandment. The Sages said that exile comes to the world because of [violation of] the sabbath of the land (*Avot*, 5). One wonders why the punishment for this sin should be so severe. If forcing the land to rest is for agricultural reasons, as is the practice of farmers to leave the land to lie fallow for several years in order to restore its strength and improve its yield, then it would suffice that...poor yields would be their punishment. Why then must they be exiled from the land in punishment for this sin?

Abarbanel raises yet another difficulty in connection with Maimonides' explanation, based on a different verse in *Parashat Behar* (Lev. 25:21): "I will ordain My blessing for you in the sixth year, so that it shall yield a crop sufficient for three years." If yield is improved as a result of letting the land lie fallow, how could this blessing come in the sixth year, before the land has had its rest? How would the land be able to yield the equivalent of three years of crops just before the sabbatical year? Hence, he concludes that the sabbatical year is rooted in spiritual concerns rather than agricultural advantages. Maimonides' argument is also rejected by R. Moses Alsheikh (in *Alsheikh 'Al Ha-Torah* ad loc.), on the grounds that giving this commandment at Mount Sinai and couching it in the terms of the land "having its sabbath" indicates that the commandment conveys a spiritual message rather than one of material advantage. In Alsheikh's opinion, even though Maimonides' explanation has some validity, the land of Israel itself does not need rest:

> For the land of Israel is not like other lands; its strength is not drained. Hence it is called a "land of milk and honey," for it flows with richness as a result of God's blessing...Therefore, say that it is not because of depletion of its strength that God commanded and ordained that we give it a sabbath.

In short, Maimonides' explanation of the commandment to let the land rest has been rejected by these commentators, whether due to problems raised by other relevant verses in the Torah or because of logical difficulties.

Alsheikh also notes another aspect of renewal of the land – renewal in the sense of added divine inspiration (see his commentary on Lev. 25 in *Derekh Ha-Shani*). He claims that during this year, God imbues the land of Israel with additional sanctity.

> If you ask how the sanctity of the land in that year finds expression...That sabbath is a sabbath of the Lord (*shabbat la-shem*), insofar as the experience it will have is from God, for He too has a part in the matter. It is a sort of primal sabbath of creation, in the same way that every person has an added spirituality from God. And God too has joy and rest, as is well known to those versed in mysticism.

Furthermore, it is the divine inspiration of this year that causes the high yield of the seventh year. That is why the produce of the seventh year is owned by no one and belongs to everyone, since it is not the product of the owner of the field. Contrariwise, whoever does not abstain from agricultural work in the seventh year prevents the divine abundance and blessing from descending to earth, and hence the great severity with which the Sages viewed the prohibition against farming in the seventh year.

The concept of renewing the human spirit and overcoming materialistic desires is discussed in R. Isaac Arama's *'Akedat Yitzḥak*, which discusses the duality of human beings, in that they consist of both matter and spirit. On the one hand, men have physical needs essential to living, and on the other hand, they have a soul with a propensity and need for spiritual accomplishments. R. Isaac Arama considered God's gift of the land of Israel to the people of Israel and His choice of the land of Israel as a lesson intended to teach us how to live. In order to attain the spiritual, man needs material possessions and economic independence, for without these things a person cannot devote himself to spiritual matters, since he would otherwise have to spend all his time struggling for a livelihood. But in order to prevent one from descending to purely physical pursuits, the Torah commanded us concerning the sabbatical year, ordering us to cease tilling the soil and to abandon the produce of our fields for all to take. Thus the Torah instructs us that man's main purpose is the pursuit of spiritual accomplishments, material concerns being but a vehicle to help us attain our true destiny:

> In truth it is but to address our souls, open our ears, and stir our hearts, providing great and numerous signs, opening blind eyes that are sunk deep in thoughts of our desires...that we should till the soil...For in the cycle of seven years of toil, the seventh being a sabbath year, He stirs our hearts and tells us that we were not sent here to be slaves, subjugated to the soil, but for quite a different and lofty purpose...as has been rightly explained in saying, "When you enter the land that I assign you, the land shall observe a sabbath of the Lord. Six years...But in the seventh year..." We did not enter the land in order to become slaves to it,

to work the soil so that we may derive benefit from it, like the other nations...To establish and reinforce this essential point, a great sign was written and given to those who work the land for six years and then let it rest, that they may know that a person does not attain greatness from the strength of the soil, but that their work is something from which one rests for the sake of God (ibid.).[2]

A person who observes this commandment and internalizes the message it conveys can be expected to act in an upright and moral way during the six years when he is engaged in material pursuits and commerce with others:

> Since honesty and all good traits in restraining desires and curtailing covetousness of worldly possessions follow from this, it is said in close proximity, "When you sell property to your neighbor...you shall not wrong one another," to indicate that this stems from the previous moral lesson. For of their own accord, by their honesty and kindness of heart, they will not wish to do wrong or take advantage, so that when they sell or purchase property, they, buyer and seller alike, will be careful not to take advantage, and they will take from one another only what is fair exchange (ibid., p. 148).[3]

---

[2] Abarbanel (*Nahalat Avot* 5.11) expresses reservations about R. Isaac Arama's approach, viewing the desire to stimulate spiritual renewal as merely a secondary aim of the commandment about the sabbatical year: "One of the rabbis of our times thought that the aim of this [commandment]...was to awaken our souls, and while this idea is fine in itself...there is no doubt that the Torah did not have this in mind as the goal of the commandment of the sabbatical year. For the divine commandments have their own intrinsic purpose, and any extension of them to matters of human behavior...is secondary...If this alone were the aim of the commandment of the sabbatical year...why did the *Tanna* state that exile results from violation of the commandment of the sabbatical year, without mentioning violation of the Sabbath or the jubilee year?"

[3] See R. Jonathan Eybeschuetz, *Urim ve-Tummim, Hoshen Mishpat*, 67.1, who also considered this commandment a way to encourage people to make do with a minimum of material possessions: "How great is this commandment and the idea behind it, that the Israelites know that our days are like a passing shadow over the land...and that the

This wary attitude towards worldliness and material pursuits also finds expression in R. Isaac Arama's commentary on Genesis ('*Akedat Yitzḥak*, §11, 103b), in connection with the question of why Abel's offering was accepted and Cain's rejected. Many interpretations have been offered in the Midrash and by biblical exegetes to explain this. R. Isaac Arama suggested that tilling the soil symbolizes a descent into the pursuit of material possessions, whereas shepherding symbolizes spirituality. The offerings that Cain and Abel brought represented what each believed was the ideal pursuit. Abel's offering was accepted while Cain's was not in order to teach us that acquiring material possessions should not be mankind's ultimate purpose.

This basic idea is further developed by Abarbanel in his comments on the sin of the generation of the Tower of Babel (Gen. 11). Abarbanel explains that the divine ideal is for human beings to make do with the natural things created by God for sustenance and to apply the greater part of their time and energy to spiritual pursuits, as symbolized by the shepherd who, following nature, herds his sheep. However, Adam, Cain and the generation of the Tower of Babel rejected this calling, drawn as they were to the all-consuming materialism of civilization, which leaves no time for spiritual endeavors. This ultimately also led to a quest for glory, leading to jealousy, theft and bloodshed.

When the Torah was given to the people of Israel, a lifestyle involving agriculture – the pursuit of the material – was not forbidden, since it was already deeply ingrained in human nature, and weaning humans from it would be exceedingly difficult. Hence we were commanded that when leading this sort of life, we should make every effort to behave morally.

It would appear that these commentators viewed a life of farming as less than ideal,[4] since it was likely to lead to the pursuit of materialism and

---

earth and all that it holds are the Lord's [see Ps. 24]. They should know that occupying oneself with the acquisition of possessions and amassing material things does not lead to human perfection – one knows not who will get them. For they will see that the sabbath of the land is a sabbath of the Lord, and that every person has an equal hold on the land on which God always keeps His eye."

[4] Different attitudes towards tilling the soil are found in rabbinic literature. Some rabbis took a negative attitude towards farming; for example, *Yevamot* 63a: "R. Eleazar

the acquisition of possessions. Accordingly, the commandment of the sabbatical year was viewed as a vehicle for improving the world and refining and renewing the spirit. The commandment of the sabbatical year, which enjoins us to cease tilling the soil and leave its fruit for the needy, was a corrective measure aimed at teaching us to aspire not to material possessions, but to spiritual assets, as our ideal.

---

said: There is no occupation more lowly than that of farming." Similarly *Sanhedrin* 58b: "Resh Lakish said: Why does the Torah say, 'He who tills his land shall have an abundance of food' (Prov. 12:11)? If a person turns himself into a slave, he will have an abundance of food; and if not, he will not have an abundance of food." Other sources, however, evince a more positive approach. For example, *Sifra Behar* 5: "How do we know that a person is not allowed to sell his field, put down his purse, and purchase an animal, tools, and a house unless he has become impoverished? As it is written, 'If your kinsman is in straits and has to sell'" Similarly in *Yevamot* 63a: "R. Eleazar said: A person who does not own land is not a person...R. Eleazar also said: Ultimately all craftsmen will stand on the soil." Cf. also *Genesis Rabbah* 39: "R. Levi said: When Abraham was traveling through Aram Naharayim and Aram Nahor, and he saw the people there eating and drinking and behaving wantonly, he said, 'Would that I have no part of this land.' But when he arrived at the Ladder of Tyre and saw the people there weeding at weeding time and hoeing at hoeing time, he said, 'Would that I have a part in this land!' So God said to him, 'To your offspring shall I give this land.'" For further discussion, see Hillel Zeitlin, *Sifran Shel Yehidim* (Jerusalem 1980), pp. 217–223.

Parashat Behukkotai

NOTES ON THE CONCEPT OF HOLINESS – *KADOSH, KEDUSHAH*

Prof. Dov Landau
Department of Hebrew Literature

THE ROOT *K-D-SH* occurs nineteen times in *Parashat Behukkotai*, the last portion of the book of Leviticus, which contains a total of 152 occurrences of this root. The Torah never explicitly defines the concept of *kedushah*, which is usually translated as "holiness" or "sanctity." Nevertheless, the use of this root has developed extensively, so that today we speak of making *kiddush* on wine, of reciting *kaddish* and the *kedushah* in the synagogue service, of performing the *kiddushin* marriage ceremony. We behave as if we understand the meaning of the root *k-d-sh,* which underlies all of these actions. We tend to forget that *kedushah* or holiness is a transcendental, divine concept, and therefore, like the concept of God, is beyond human comprehension.

The same may be said of the opposite of *kedushah*, the concept of *hullin* (the secular or profane). Similarly obscure are the concepts of *taharah* (ritual purity) and its opposite *tum'ah* (ritual impurity).

To help clarify this concept, let us examine the meaning of *kadosh* and *kedushah* as they appear in a sampling of some thirty verses from the Bible.

Kadosh is associated with loftiness, with being raised or exalted: "He who is high and lofty, dwells for eternity, whose name is holy [*kadosh*]" (Is. 57:15). Similarly, "You have lifted your eyes haughtily against the Holy One [*kedosh*] of Israel" (II Kings 19:22).

Kadosh is incomprehensible: "To whom, then, can you liken Me...says the Holy One" (Is. 40:25), and "A God dreaded in the great council of the holy ones" (Ps. 89:8).

Kadosh is awesome: "They praise Your name as great and awesome" (Ps. 99:3); "His name is holy and awesome" (Ps. 111:9).

Kadosh is fervent: "The Light of Israel will be fire and its Holy One flame" (Is. 10:17).

Kadosh is righteous: "The Holy God is sanctified by righteousness" (Is. 5:16).

Kadosh is God's chosen: "The one whom the Lord shall choose, he shall be holy" (Num. 16:7).

God is *kadosh*: "For I am holy" (Lev. 11:44; 19:2; 20:26; 21:8); "Holy, holy, holy is The Lord of Hosts!" (Is. 6:3); for "I am the Lord, the Holy One in Israel" (Ez. 39:7); "Through those that are near to Me will I be sanctified" (Lev. 10:3).

The Nazarite is *kadosh*: "Throughout his term as Nazarite he is consecrated [*kadosh*] to the Lord" (Num. 6:8).

The Israelites are *kedoshim*: "For you are a people consecrated [*kadosh*] to the Lord your God" (Deut. 7:6; 14:2; 14:21); "A kingdom of priests and a holy nation" (Ex. 19:6); "For I am the Lord that brought you out of the land of Egypt to be your God; you shall be holy, for I am holy" (Lev. 11:45).

The prophet is *kadosh*: "This is a holy man of God" (II Kings 4:9).

The Sabbath is *kedoshah*: "You shall call the Sabbath a delight, the Lord's holy day honored" (Is. 58:13); "Tomorrow is a day of rest, a holy sabbath of the Lord" (Ex. 16:23); "But on the seventh day there shall be a sabbath of complete rest, a sacred time" (Lev. 23:3).

The festivals are *kedoshim*: "These are the appointed times of the Lord, the sacred times" (Lev. 23:4).

The jubilee is *kadosh*: "For it is a jubilee; it shall be holy to you" (Lev. 25:12).

The sacrifices are *kedoshim*: "Afterward he may eat of the holy things" (Lev. 22:7); "He may eat of the food of his God, of the most holy as well as of the holy" (Lev. 21:22).

The heavens are *kedoshim*: "Look down from Your holy abode, from heaven" (Deut. 26:15).

Jerusalem is *kedoshah*: "Settle in the holy city of Jerusalem" (Neh. 11:1).

The Temple is *kadosh*: "And he shall make atonement for the most holy place" (Lev. 16:33); "I will bring them to My sacred mount" (Is. 56:7); "Heathens...defiled Your holy temple" (Ps. 79:1).

The Torah is *kedoshah*: "Her priests have violated My Torah; they have profaned what is sacred to Me" (Ezek. 22:26).

The six characteristics listed above reveal the principal elements of the holy: it is lofty, mysterious, awesome, fervent, righteous and chosen by God. The implication is that holiness entails an element of being separate from all other worldly things that fall into the realm of *hullin* – the secular or profane. An almost identical conclusion can be drawn from the second set of verses cited above, which refer to what is considered to have *kedushah*: God, the Nazarite, the prophet, the Sabbath, the festivals, the jubilee, and likewise the heavens, Jerusalem, the Temple and of course the Torah, are all elevated and separate from mundane existence. From among this list, God, the prophet and his word, and the heavens are concepts that are beyond human comprehension.

The best way of arriving at an understanding of *kedushah* might be by means of a dictionary definition of the term, but this is problematic, because many dictionaries are evasive when it comes to abstract concepts. Defining an object such as a chair presents no difficulty, for a chair belongs to the general category of furniture, within which its specific characteristics, details and purpose can be specified. But what is *kedushah*? What is its essence? What is the general category to which *kedushah* belongs, and what are its specific details? What are its uses? We shall attempt to present a theoretical analysis of the elements and characteristics of the concept of *kedushah*, based on the uses cited above.

1. *Kedushah* is constant, everlasting, almost eternal; it is very resistant to change and almost immutable. Many people with heightened religious sensibilities instinctively object to discussion of the "development of the halakhah," and some scholars even prefer to speak of the unfolding of the halakhah instead. Change is usually slow and limited. Many feel that change subverts the essence of holiness. This may be the reason that customs that are considered sacred are rarely abolished even when their justification is no longer valid. A sacred law is not like a secular law, which can be changed as needed.

2. That which is *kadosh* broadens and expands the scope of its applicability, force and validity – like our universe, which since the Big Bang has been expanding in all directions, reaching towards the infinite. Holiness embodies an aspiration to perfection, to do everything in the best possible way, seeking ever-stronger strictures. Those of us who occasionally mock these aspirations are actually moving away from the holy and moving dangerously closer to the secular.

3. *Kedushah* means having a sense of religiosity and immanent spirituality, of a total inner conviction that I sense the holy because I believe, and if I believe that means I exist. The converse is also true: if I exist, this forces me to believe and obliges me to aspire to sanctity, whereas if I do not believe and if there is no sanctity in me, my very existence is called into doubt. Mircea Eliade[1] shows that sanctified times, like sanctified places, break up the indifference and dull monotony of life and create units of unique, sanctified time and place, which give men a sense of spirituality and of sublime and awesome elevation.

Rudolf Otto[2] claims that the way we use the adjective "sacred" has been extended to apply to absolute good, morality, decency, uprightness and truth, which are essentially rational characteristics. In contrast, the original, primal meaning of "sacred" is a feeling that is utterly devoid of any theoretical-rational component, and is a category totally unique, something that words cannot define. It is a spiritual condition or state of mind that can neither be defined nor explained. At best, we can cause a person to recognize this spiritual condition or state of mind in himself. This is a human, spiritual state of festive elevation and exaltation, a sense of elation, of being connected to the sublime.

Otto explained that this special concept of sanctity, which he called "numinous," was not dependent on the good or the moral. Numinousness does not stem from a sense of fear, of awe-filled trembling, of dependence or absolute worthlessness, yet neither does it stem from absolute faith, overwhelming love or a sense of security or dedication. Numinousness or holiness is "creature-consciousness," says Otto, "the emotion of a creature,

---

[1] *The Sacred and the Profane* (New York 1959).

[2] Rudolf Otto, *The Idea of the Holy* (Oxford 1950).

submerged and overwhelmed by its own nothingness in contrast to that which is supreme above all creatures."[3]

Otto was aware of the shortcomings in his explanation of this concept and maintained that it does not contribute sufficiently to clarifying the conceptual-theoretical notion of sanctity that he wished to explain. Therefore, he also rejected part of the approach taken by William James,[4] accepting from him only the claim that religious experience or sanctity is a sense of an objective presence outside the self.

Clearly, the approach described here involves an extremely complex expression of this phenomenon, and may bear some resemblance to the approach taken by R. Isaac Arama regarding the necessity of the flood in preserving mankind's humanity. Immersed in the routine of daily life, the men of the generation of the flood ceased to feel any amazement at the newness and sanctity of the world, and only the complete eradication of everything that had been created could reinstate humanity's sense of wonder. Perhaps it is also similar to the distinction drawn between the Hebrew word *pahad* – the rational and concrete fear of an approaching calamity – and the word *yir'ah*, awe, which in addition to "fear" connotes a sense of elevation stemming from admiration and amazement.

Human wonderment is so important in Judaism that it is considered the characteristic that separates human beings from the rest of creation, the basis of human morality and of the cultural restraint of urges and desires. The first stage is amazement and questioning, the second is awe, the third is moral and cultural restraint, and the fourth is religious restraint – that is, sanctity. If the world loses its power to cause wonderment and amazement, if the human soul takes the world for granted and is governed by routine, then the motivation for moral development disappears and the world will be taken over by violence, theft and corruption, which can ultimately even lead to bloodshed. Apparently, this is how we should understand the words of the patriarch Abraham about Sarah on their way to the land of the Philistines: "Abraham said of Sarah his wife, 'She is my sister.' So King Abimelech of Gerar had Sarah brought to him...'What, then,' Abimelech

---

[3] Otto, p. 10.

[4] William James, *The Varieties of Religious Experience* (New York 1958).

demanded of Abraham, 'was your purpose in doing this thing?' 'I thought,' said Abraham, 'surely there is no fear of God in this place, and they will kill me because of my wife'" (Gen. 20:2, 10–11). This is what Abraham feared, knowing that the inhabitants of the land of Canaan at that time were people who lived their daily lives with indifference, without fear of God, exultation of the soul or a sense of the holy.

Sefer Bemidbar – The Book of Numbers

Parashat Bemidbar

INTRODUCTION TO THE BOOK OF NUMBERS

Dr. David Elgavish
Department of Bible

THE FIVE BOOKS OF THE TORAH are arranged in chronological and logical order. The stories about the Patriarchs are found in Genesis, while the stories about their descendants appear in the following books. In Genesis God makes two fundamental promises to the patriarchs: He will choose their descendants as His people, and He will give them the land of Canaan. Thus Abraham was told, "I will maintain My covenant between Me and you...to be God for you and for your future offspring. I give you...and your future offspring...all the land of Canaan as an everlasting possession" (Gen. 17:7–8).

The subsequent books of the Torah describe the fulfillment of these promises to later generations. Exodus and Leviticus describe the fulfillment of the first promise: God made a covenant with the people at Sinai and caused His presence to dwell among them in the Sanctuary, where they were given the laws of sacrifices and rules of holiness. The first chapters of the book of Numbers also deal with various aspects of the first promise – the procedures for transporting the Sanctuary and safeguarding it. This book then continues by discussing various laws and events associated with fulfillment of the second promise – taking possession of the land of Israel. Here the Torah describes the Israelites' journey through the wilderness of Sinai[1] to the plains of Moab and the conquests of Moses and the Israelites

---

[1] In contrast to modern usage, where the term "Sinai desert" refers to the entire Sinai peninsula, the biblical "wilderness of Sinai" *(midbar Sinai)* included only a small part of

on the eastern side of the Jordan. This part of the book prepares us for the book of Deuteronomy, which consists of the speeches made by Moses in the plains of Moab before the Israelites entered the western part of the land of Israel.

The Structure of the Book of Numbers

Numbers is divided into three parts. The first part deals with the period spent in the wilderness of Sinai (chapters 1–10), the second part with the Israelites' travels from the wilderness of Sinai to Kadesh Barnea (11–20:13), and the third part with the Israelites' travels from Kadesh Barnea to the plains of Moab (20:14–36:13).

These three parts differ not only in geographical focus, but also in content and style. The first part describes the structure of the Israelite camp and how the Israelites were supposed to travel through the desert. This part of the book contains no stories. The second part, by contrast, is extremely dynamic and presents a series of seven narratives about the Israelites' complaints to God and Moses. The transition from the second part to the third part describes the deaths of Miriam and Aaron and God's decree that Moses would not enter the land of Israel; by relating the death of these leaders, the Torah takes leave of the generation of the Exodus and moves on to their children. The third part opens with the journey from Kadesh Barnea toward the land of Israel and recounts the Israelites' victory over the Canaanites of Arad, marking the transition to the younger generation which will enter the land of Israel and conquer it.

Our division of the book of Numbers finds support in the rabbinic dictum that the passage beginning with the words "When the Ark set out" and concluding with the words "Israel's myriads of thousands" (10:35–36) constitutes a separate biblical book (*Shabbat* 116a): this passage concludes the first section of our suggested division.

---

this region. Menashe Harel, *Masʿei Sinai* (Tel Aviv 1969), pp. 206–207, identifies the biblical wilderness of Sinai as the northeastern coast of the Suez Gulf, while Yehudah Elitzur and Yehudah Kiel locate it in the southern part of the Sinai peninsula; see their *Atlas Daʿat Mikra* (Jerusalem 1993), pp. 100–101.

Numbers: Contents and Characteristics

The Hebrew name for the book of Numbers is *Bemidbar* ("in the wilderness"), a name which is most appropriate in light of the book's content.

The first part of the book deals with the procedures for transporting the Sanctuary, rebuilding it after traveling through the desert and safeguarding its sanctity. Therefore these chapters include laws pertaining to the priests and general sanctity laws, e.g., the law that unclean people must be sent out of the camp (5:1–4). Likewise, this part of the book describes the ritual performed when a woman is suspected of adultery (5:11–31) and the Nazirite ritual (6:1–21), both of which require priestly participation, as well as the the priestly blessing (6:22–27).

The second part of Numbers, as indicated, deals with inheritance of the land of Israel. Thus, this part of the book relates the incident of the spies, as well as various laws that pertain specifically to the land of Israel, such as the laws of meal-offerings (*minhah*), drink-offerings (*nesakhim*), and *hallah* (15:1–21). Likewise, this part of the book contains accounts of the people's complaints, indicating that they were not yet worthy of inheriting the land. Only in the third part of the book do we read of their battles and early conquests on their way to conquering the land of Israel.

This Week's Reading: The Structure of the Israelite Camp

At the center of this week's Torah portion we find instructions for the arrangement of the Israelite camp around the Sanctuary. The leaders of the people, Moses and Aaron, encamped at the entrance to the Sanctuary, while the three Levite families encamped on the remaining three sides. Thus, the Sanctuary was surrounded by a square which was surrounded by yet another square, where the other tribes encamped. The Levites served, as it were, as a buffer between the Sanctuary and the Israelites.

This arrangement was of fundamental importance, for God's revelation at Mount Sinai continued at the Tent of Assembly (*ohel mo'ed*, identical to the Sanctuary). Thus, the giving of the Torah did not cease at Sinai, since God continued to teach Moses from the Tent of Assembly. Accordingly, Nahmanides explains in his introduction to the book of

Numbers that guarding the sanctity of the Tent of Assembly paralleled guarding the sanctity of Mount Sinai in the book of Exodus.

The German-Jewish Bible commentator Benno Jacob[2] added that the Tent of Assembly was important not only as a place where the Torah was given, but also as a dwelling place for God. God, as it were, folded up the heavens and brought them down to earth so that His Presence (*Shekhinah*) could dwell among human beings. Hence the Levites were chosen for service of the Sanctuary, since they were not tainted by the sin of the Golden Calf, which took place after the giving of the Torah on Mount Sinai. Likewise, strict rules were given to ensure the proper organization and sanctity of the camp, so that the people should be worthy of God's Presence.

The organization of the Israelite camp also had functional importance – first and foremost, from a military perspective. Likewise, it helped to free them of the habits of slavery which they had acquired in Egypt and to train them to act like a free people, accepting duty and discipline. Living in the wilderness, which might have led to laxness and even mutiny, instead became a positive factor (so S. D. Luzzatto in his commentary on Num. 1:3). In addition, the census of the people, whereby everyone aged twenty and above who was fit to fight was counted, helped to prepare the people for the war to conquer the land of Israel (so Rashbam in his commentary on Num. 1:2).

The Timetable of the Book of Numbers

The first part of the book describes the initial journey of the Israelites in the wilderness as they marched confidently toward the land of Israel, before they were condemned to wander around it for forty years. This section opens with a date, "On the first day of the second month in the second year of their exodus from the land of Egypt" (1:1), and it concludes with another date, "In the second year, in the second month, on the twentieth of the month" (10:11). These verses mark the boundaries of the first part of the book, indicating that it deals with the events that took place

---

[2] Benno Jacob, *The Second Book of the Bible, Exodus,* trans. Walter Jacob (Hoboken, New Jersey 1992), pp. 758–759.

within a period of nineteen days. From this perspective, chapters 7–9 are not really relevant, as they discuss the first month of the second year (7:1; 9:1, 15), and thus precede the section in which they appear by about a month.

The third section parallels the first. Once again the people are described as moving towards the land of Israel. By now, however, the generation of the Exodus has died in the wilderness, and it is their children who are on the march. The time covered by this part of the book is the fortieth year after the Israelites left Egypt (20:28; 33:38)

The second section of the book is not dated. Only one of the incidents included in this part of the book, the episode of the spies, can be dated with certainty, since it was this sin which resulted in a forty-year delay being imposed on the people (14:34). We may therefore conclude that thirty-eight years of the sojourn in the wilderness are not discussed by the Torah. Apparently, the aim of the book of Numbers was to describe the progress toward realization of the promise made to the Patriarchs. Hence the Torah describes the milestones on the way toward conquest of the land of Israel, but it does not discuss the thirty-eight years in the wilderness, when no significant progress was made toward this goal.

Parashat Naso

The Priestly Blessing and Social Harmony

Aryeh Arazi

The Martin Szusz Department of Land of Israel Studies

In *Parashat Naso*, the priests are commanded to bless the people of Israel (Num. 6:23): "Speak to Aaron and his sons, Thus shall you bless the people of Israel." The priests pronounced the benediction, but at the end God says (v. 27), "Thus they shall put My name on the people of Israel, and I will bless them."[1] The blessing is God's; the priests do not give their own blessing. Rather, they recite precisely the text that is spoken to them, so that they serve merely as the vehicle through which God's blessing is conveyed to the people.

In his commentary on this verse, R. Samson Raphael Hirsch noted:

> It is not the priests who bless the people of Israel. Under no circumstances do the words that they utter have the force of a blessing...Their role is to place the name of God on the people of Israel, so that the people of Israel shall be a vehicle for the Divine presence.

Why then were the priests chosen for this task? After all, God could have blessed Israel directly! This question is addressed in *Sefer Ha-Hinukh* (378):

---

[1] In *Hullin* 49a we find a dispute between R. Ishmael and R. Akiva as to whether God blesses the priests or the people of Israel.

> For God, in His great beneficence, sought to bless His people through His servants who abide constantly in the House of the Lord, whose every thought is directed to His worship, whose souls are bound in awe of Him all day, that the blessing may come upon His people through their merits.

Malbim took a similar approach, explaining that the recipients of God's abundance are not always capable of absorbing it because of their level of spirituality. Therefore God chose to transmit His divine abundance "by means of Godly people who are servants of the Lord, that they may open the channels of blessing through their deeds, prayers and benedictions, bringing this blessing upon the people. Thus He chose the sons of Aaron, who in their sacred service are close to the Lord."[2]

In light of these explanations, we should inquire whether today's priests are at the spiritual level depicted by *Sefer Ha-Hinukh* or in Malbim's commentary.

Regretfully, the answer is no.[3] Priests today are no different from the rest of the Jewish people in terms of their religious-spiritual level or their occupations and vocations. If we ask whether this affects their ability to bless the people or the congregation's ability to receive the blessing, we find ourselves facing a complex question that has no simple answer. The Talmud Yerushalmi says: "How do we know that a member of the Jewish people whom the priests bless may not say: 'So-and-so is involved in illicit sexual relations and bloodshed, and yet he blesses me!' God said: Who is it that blesses you? Is it not I, as it is said, 'And I shall bless them'?" (*Yerushalmi Gittin* 5:8). It would appear from this passage that the spiritual level of the priest has no bearing on the blessing.

But matters are not so simple. First, the discussion in the Talmud Yerushalmi deals with a priest who repented. Moreover, the Babylonian Talmud says, "R. Yohanan said: A priest who has killed another person

---

[2] Malbim on Num. 6:22.

[3] See Eyal Dodson, "Ha-Kehunah be-Yisrael le-Doroteha, mi-Ye'ud ve-'Erekh le-Ibbud ha-Derekh," *Talelei Orot* 9 (2000), pp. 169–193.

may not recite the priestly blessing."[4] Indeed, the question of whether a sinful priest may recite the priestly blessings might depend upon the dispute as to whether halakhic conclusions can be based on rationales, explicit or putative, for the commandments (ta'amei ha-mitzvot).[5] Surely, those who maintain that halakhic conclusions can be drawn from the assumed reasons for the Torah's commandments would conclude that the inferior spiritual state of today's priests, which in no way resembles the description of the priests in Sefer Ha-Hinukh or Malbim, must affect the very spiritual process that should occur during the priestly blessing.

One solution to this problem, albeit a partial one, can be found in the concluding words of the benediction recited by the priests before they pronounce the priestly blessing, "Blessed are You...who commanded us to bless His people Israel with love." This benediction originates in the Talmud: "What is the benediction? Rabbi Zera quoted Rav Hisda, who said: 'Who has sanctified us with the sanctity of Aaron and has commanded us to bless His people Israel with love'" (Sotah 39a). From where did the Sages infer the imperative of this act being performed "with love," since this was explicitly commanded of them? In his commentary on R. Sa'adiah Gaon's Sefer Ha-Mitzvot,[6] R. Yeruham Perla notes that the Talmud (Sotah 39b) says, and this view is accepted by modern halakhists (Mishnah Berurah 128.10), that the words "thus shall you bless" imply that the blessing is to be delivered face to face, which is an indication of love and affection; cf. the way the cherubim in the Sanctuary faced one another ("When the people of Israel obey God's will, the cherubim face one another, like a male and a female," Bava Batra 99b).

---

[4] Berakhot 32b; see also Torah Temimah on Numbers 6:27 (159).

[5] See the dispute between R. Simeon b. Yohai and R. Judah in Bava Metzia 115a and Sanhedrin 21a, and the subsequent dispute among medieval halakhists, e.g., Maimonides, Hilkhot Malveh ve-Loveh, 3.5 and Tur Hoshen Mishpat, 97.14. To cite one concrete example, the Torah states, "You shall not take a widow's garment in pawn" (Deut. 24:17). R. Simeon b. Yohai explains that the reason for this commandment is that taking the widow's garment will cause her financial harm. Accordingly, this verse refers solely to poor widows; however, it would be permissible to take the garment of a wealthy widow in pawn. By contrast, R. Judah maintains that the reason for this law is unknown, and hence this commandment applies to all widows, rich or poor. See also Encyclopedia Talmudit, 20.568–595.

[6] Sefer Ha-Mitzvot le-Rav Sa'adiah Gaon, Mitzvat 'Aseh, 16.

This relationship of love demanded of the priests when they bless the people is not a one-sided relationship that the priests alone must adopt towards the people whom they bless; rather, it is a mutual condition that should prevail between the priests and the community as well as among the members of the community themselves. R. Samson Raphael Hirsch[7] explained that the priests serve as emissaries of the public, and when the priests give their blessing, it is as if the entire community is standing and directing its heart toward a state of love. In the words of R. Hirsch:

> Thus, the priests who pronounce the blessing are altogether passive...They give the blessing only when called upon to do so by the congregation, and they recite only the blessing that is read out to them on behalf of the congregation. In truth, it is the congregation that draws upon itself the blessing that comes from the mouths of the priests at the Lord's command.

In his *Nefesh ha-Hayyim*, Rabbi Chaim of Volozhin noted that God wished to give men all the blessings in the world, but for men to enjoy the divine abundance showered on them they must be worthy of such blessing. Accordingly, only when there is harmony and love in the community – when this act is carried out "with love" – can the community be worthy of enjoying the divine abundance of the priestly blessing. This approach, according to which God's "ability" to determine what happens on earth depends on our behavior, is further strengthened by the words of R. Hanina Bar Pappa in the Talmud, that "whoever benefits from the things of this world without a blessing is like one who steals from God and the Jewish people" (*Berakhot* 35b). Seemingly – and this may be the plain meaning of this statement – if a person eats food which is not his before he has blessed God for it, he is stealing. Rashi, however, did not understand the Talmud this way, for he commented: "He has stolen God's blessing from Him." This was further elaborated upon by Rabbi A. Kahn,[8] based on

---

[7] In his commentary on Num. 6:23.

[8] http://aish.com/torahportion/moray/Divine_Abundance.asp

an idea suggested by Rabbi Chaim of Volozhin,[9] that it is not the food that is stolen from God, but the blessing. God created the world as a system in which humans can develop a relationship with Him, as a result of which divine abundance is given to the world, blessing it with the Divine presence. Refraining from reciting a blessing before eating creates a distance between man and God, preventing Divine abundance from being bestowed on the earth, thus stealing God's blessing by preventing it from being bestowed on the Jewish people.

Thus, we discover how important, even essential, love is to the priestly blessing. Only when the community and society function in harmony and love can the priests function effectively as the link through which the community receives the Divine blessing. This notion finds concrete expression in the halakhic principle[10] that a priest may not recite the priestly blessing if he does not love his congregation (or if they do not love him).

In conclusion, we may inquire if and how one can attain the degree of love that maximizes the application of the priestly blessing for every community. The best way to attain this appears to be the development of mutual respect, tolerance and openness, making it possible to maintain a pluralistic exchange of views among all members of a community. Likewise, assistance should be extended to the weaker members of the community, to provide them with both financial and moral support. This will enable the priestly blessing to be realized in its entirety: "May God bless you and protect you. May His face shine upon you and give you favor. May God lift His face toward you and grant you peace."

---

[9] *Nefesh ha-Hayyim*, 2.4.

[10] *Shulhan 'Arukh, Orah Hayyim* 128.11, *Ba'er Hetev* §20.

Parashat Beha'alotekha

MOSES AND HOVAV: THE ART OF CONVINCING

Prof. Amos Frisch
Department of Bible

PARASHAT BEHA'ALOTEKHA PRESENTS the brief but enigmatic story of Moses' invitation to Hovav to "accompany us" (Num. 10:29–32). Aside from the baffling question of Hovav's identity, with which we shall not deal at present,[1] several other questions arise:

1. Why did Moses want Hovav to join them? Did the Israelites, led by God, need a human guide as well?

2. Hovav declined the offer (v. 30) and Moses repeated his invitation that he join them (vv. 31–32); is there any difference between the second request and the first (v. 29)?

3. Hovav's response to the second request is not given. What did he answer? Did he comply with Moses' request in the end, or did he stand firm in his refusal?

4. How does this story fit into the context of the narrative, as it appears after the description of the arrangement of the various tribes when journeying through the desert (10:11–28) and before the report on the journey from the mountain of God (10:33–34)?

The purpose of asking Hovav to come along is ostensibly explained in Moses' request: "You know where we should camp in the wilderness and you can serve as our eyes" (v. 31). As Jacob Licht states in his commentary,

---

[1] See Jacob Milgrom, *Numbers, The JPS Torah Commentary* (Philadelphia 1990), p. 78; T. R. Ashley, *The Book of Numbers* (Grand Rapids 1993), pp. 195–197.

"According to the plain sense of the text, Moses sought human leadership in addition to divine leadership, and this was difficult for the Jews of antiquity to accept. This is why the ancient translations did not render this verse according to its plain sense."[2] But what they concealed the eminent exegete Nahmanides stated outright: "Since you know the wilderness, you will be like eyes for us in conquering the lands, and you can show us the route we ought to take" (see also R. Naftali Zvi Yehudah Berlin's commentary ad loc.). Yet the question remains why Moses wished to add human leadership to divine leadership. Furthermore, if Hovav did not comply with the request (see question 3 above), what alternative action was taken?

The key to understanding the story can be found in a close reading of the text, with careful attention paid to phrases that are repeated as well and to the significance of variations in the repetitions.

Two roots are repeated numerous times this story, and they may be viewed as key words, or what Martin Buber termed "leading words": *t-o-v* / *y-t-v* (in the forms *ve-hetavnu*, *ha-tov*, *yetiv* and *hetavnu*, i.e., "we will be generous with you," "we will extend to you the same bounty that the Lord grants us") and *h-l-kh* (to go; *lekha ittanu*, *lo elekh*, *elekh*, *ki telekh*, "come with us," "I will not go," "I will return," "if you come"). These words express the gist of the story: the beneficence promised to Hovav if he goes with the Israelites.

Moreover, the root *h-l-kh*, which is used by both speakers, Moses and Hovav, underscores their differences. To Moses' request, "Come with us and we will be generous with you," Hovav responds, "I will not go, but I will return to my native land." This is a declaration of loyalty to his native land,[3] but Moses considers this abandonment: "Please do not leave us

---

[2] J. Licht, *Perush 'Al Sefer Bamidbar*, 1 (Jerusalem 1985), p. 162.

[3] Contrast the commandment given to Abraham to cut off all ties with his family and home: "Go forth from your native land and from your father's house" (Gen. 12:1), and cf. Boaz's description of Ruth's conduct: "You left your father and mother and the land of your birth and came to a people you had not known before" (Ruth 2:11).

(10:31)," [4] and similarly he reiterates his promise to Hovav: "So if you come with us…"

In contrast to the verb *h-l-kh*, which pertains only to Hovav's actions, the verb *t-o-v* / *y-t-v* is associated with God's deeds (as the subject of the verb), Israel (as the object and subject), and Hovav (only as the object, the recipient of the good), yet in all five instances it is used only by Moses. It is worth paying close attention to the fine differences in the way it occurs. In his first appeal to Hovav, Moses says: "Come with us and we will be generous with you (*ve-hetavnu lakh*), for the Lord has promised to be generous (*dibber tov*) to Israel" (10:29). In Moses' second appeal he says, "So if you come with us, we will extend the same bounty that the Lord grants us" (*ha-tov asher yetiv…ve-hetavnu lakh*, 10:32).

The promise to be generous (*ve-hetavnu lakh*) appears in both requests, but in different contexts. In the first request this promise appears at the outset, with no further details given, followed by the explanation, "For the Lord has promised to be generous to Israel" – the Lord has been good to us, and you can share part of that bounty. However, the second request, where the phrase appears at the end, speaks of equality: the same bounty that the Lord gives us we shall give you. Thus, after Hovav's initial refusal, Moses tries to persuade him both by more sweeping promises and by defining Yitro's refusal as abandonment.

Having noted these differences in Moses' two requests, we could say that the reason suggested for Hovav accompanying them – "you can be our eyes" – which appears only in the second request, is also part of Moses' attempt to sway Hovav. The differences between the arguments are explained clearly by R. Samson Raphael Hirsch:

> In the previous verses the request was claimed to be for Hovav's benefit [="you will be rewarded"]…Therefore Moses reiterated his request, explaining it in greater detail: Please do not leave us; your

---

[4] Yehudah Shaviv, "'Iyyun bi-Te'arav Shel Yitro – Signon Mikra," *Beit Mikra* 35 (1990), p. 89, perceptively noted that the name used to refer to this man reflects the vacillations over his affiliation: "Hovav son of Re'uel the Midianite, Moses' father-in-law" – on the one hand he was the son of Re'uel and a Midianite, but on the other hand he was related by marriage to Moses' family.

presence benefits us...I appeal to you...because you are expert on the terrain in the places where we will camp.

According to this explanation, it seems that Moses never intended to use Hovav's services as a guide, but asked him to join the Israelites out of personal and family loyalty. Only when his first request was turned down did Moses suggest a new argument, focusing on the benefit the people could derive from Hovav's presence among them. Thus, the mention of guidance can be interpreted not as reflecting a real need, but as a rhetorical device intended to persuade Hovav, after Moses had failed to convince him with the offer of personal benefit to Hovav.[5] The fact that Moses emphasized the importance of guiding the people, an argument for the general welfare, reflects high estimation of Hovav.

As stated, Hovav's response is not given in the Torah, nor does the Torah tell us that he joined the people. Quite the contrary, we are immediately told about the people setting forth on its journey with the Ark of the Covenant leading and guiding them; hence one might conclude that Hovav did not join the journeying tribes. At the same time, we are not told explicitly that he returned to his land. In view of our suggestion that the proposal to guide is a rhetorical device, the use of the Ark as guide should not be viewed as an alternative to Hovav's guidance; rather, this was the plan from the outset.

Commentators differ in their views about Hovav's response. Nahmanides, for instance, believes that Hovav eventually complied. However, Abarbanel and Sforno suggest that he did not agree to journey with the Israelites, although his sons joined Israel, and thus we hear elsewhere of descendants of Moses' father-in-law belonging to the Israelite

---

[5] Cf. R. Levi ben Gershom (Ralbag), *Perushei ha-Torah le-Rabbenu Levi ben Gershom*, ed. Y. Levy, 4 (Jerusalem 1998), p. 37: "Moses' words seemed to indicate that Israel needed Yitro...but Moses said this out of modesty, since Yitro was not truly needed for this." Rabbenu Bahya ben Asher too asked what need they had of Yitro, but he explained matters somewhat differently: Moses invited him "to encourage those of little faith among them," i.e., to address a psychological need of some of the people.

people (Jud. 1:16; 4:11).[6] Perhaps Hovav himself joined the Israelites at a later stage.

We can learn something about Hovav's role as a guide from the surrounding context and from two other leading words in our passage. In the description of the people's journeys through the wilderness in the book of Numbers, emphasis is placed on God's role in guiding His people.[7] The roots *n-s-'* ("set out") and *h-n-h* ("encamped") are repeated numerous times in the passages that precede our story. For example, "At a command of the Lord the Israelites broke camp, and at a command of the Lord they made camp" (9:18); "They remained encamped at a command of the Lord, and broke camp at a command of the Lord" (9:20, 23); "However long the cloud lingered...the Israelites remained encamped and did not set out" (9:22); "The divisions encamped on the east shall move forward" (10:5).

Not long before the conversation between Moses and Hovav, we are told about the Israelites breaking camp: "They marched from the mountain of the Lord a distance of three days. The Ark of the Covenant of the Lord traveled in front of them on that three days' journey to seek out a resting place for them" (v. 33). Thus both verbs, *h-n-h* and *n-s-'*, appear side by side once again. The Torah's description concludes with the ceremonious song that accompanies the ark's traveling: "When the ark was to set out (*bi-nesoa'*), Moses would say: Advance, O Lord...And when it halted (*u-ve-nuho*), he would say: Return, O Lord, to Israel's myriads of thousands!" (10:35–36).

Thus, this attempt to include Hovav in the group that was journeying is located within the broader context of breaking camp and encamping. Lest one receive the mistaken impression that his leadership was necessary, the text emphasizes that it is God's providence that guided the people

---

[6] Perhaps Saul's words to the Kenites during the war against Amalek, "For you showed kindness to all the Israelites when they left Egypt" (I Sam. 15:6), allude to Hovav's guiding the people in the wilderness.

[7] Yehiel Moskowitz, *Bemidbar, Da'at Mikra* (Jerusalem 1988), p. 103, sees this passage as a single comprehensive unit which he calls "the journeys of Israel" (9:15–36). See also Licht (above n. 2), who finds three distinct literary units: the description of the cloud (9:15–23), the law of the trumpets (10:1–10), and the journey from Sinai (10:11–36). Elsewhere (p. 1) he, too, notes the importance of these texts for the Israelites' journeys.

throughout their wanderings in the wilderness. Even the use of the word *menuhah* in verse 33 – "The Ark of the Covenant of the Lord traveled...to seek out a resting-place *(menuhah)* for them" – suggests the superiority of Divine guidance to human scouts. Not content with providing the people with a place to encamp, God even found them a place of repose.[8]

---

[8] The significance of the word *menuhah* may be inferred from comparison with a similar statement by Moses where he used the word *hanayah* ("encamping") rather than *menuhah*. See Deut. 1:33: "Who goes before you on your journeys to scout the place where you are to *encamp*."

Parashat Shelah

THE ORDER OF THE LIST OF SPIES

Menahem Ben-Yashar
Department of Bible

WHO WERE THE SPIES that Moses sent to scout the land of Canaan (Num. 13:1–16)? Seemingly, they were "leaders of the Israelites," as they are referred to in Num. 3. They are also called "each one a prince (*nasi*) among them" (v. 2). But were they indeed tribal princes? The list that appears in Num. 1–2 as well as the account of offerings made by the princes in ch. 7 present different sets of names, and these lists were made but a few months before the spies were dispatched. Abarbanel's hypothesis that all the princes died in the plague at Kivrot Ha-Ta'avah (11:33–34) is unlikely. And it is equally unlikely that tribal elders would be selected for as dangerous and secret a mission such as spying. Yet that was indeed what happened: The spies were selected from among the leaders of the Israelites. They were important personages, trusted and accepted by the public, but not necessarily the tribal princes.

To understand the reference to princes here, let us consider the rendition of our passage in Targum Yonatan. There the words "each one a prince among them" (*kol nasi bahem*) are rendered as "from before each prince among them." As Hizkuni already understood, this meant that the spies were sent as agents of the princes. In other words, when we read, "Send one man from each of their ancestral tribes," we must ask who is doing the sending. The end of the verse provides the answer: "All the princes among them." The prince of each tribe knew who in his tribe was best qualified to be trusted with such a mission. Therefore, it was the princes who chose the representative of each tribe to be sent on this reconnoitering mission.

Moses is indeed instructed in the beginning of v. 2 to "send men," and it is Moses who sends them: "So Moses...sent them out" (13:3). However, at the end of that same verse, in accordance with the Targum we cited, we see that it is the princes who send the scouts. This implies duplication of authority, which does not bode well. Hence God's words to Moses emphasize *shelah lekha* – "Send for yourself," i.e., see to it that this mission comes entirely from you. Even if the princes select the spies, Moses is to be the sole source of authority.

In the final analysis this is not what happened. When the spies returned they came "to Moses and Aaron and the whole congregation of the children of Israel...and they made their report to them and to the whole congregation" (v. 26). The initiative and the command slipped out of Moses' hands, passing to the "whole congregation." They wanted to plan a war and wage it democratically, and the ensuing results are revealed in the next part of this week's reading.

Several commentators have remarked on the order in which the spies are listed.[1] The lists of the tribes in the Torah are arranged according to a variety of principles. The princes through whom the land is to be apportioned in *Parashat Mas'ei* (Num. 34:19–28) are listed according to the geographical arrangement of the tribal apportionments, and so are the tribes in Moses' blessing (Deut. 33:7–25). The tribal princes at the beginning of Numbers are listed according to the matriarchs, Jacob's wives. In the actual census of the tribes (Num. 1:20–43), the order is changed slightly to fit the division of the twelve tribes into four banners or camps, three tribes per banner, as they encamped around the Tabernacle at the center (ch. 2), in fulfillment of the words "that I may dwell among them" (Ex. 25:8). Later, in Num. 26:5–51, as the tribes were about to enter Canaan, the tribes are listed in the second census in the same way, albeit with a few minor differences.[2]

---

[1] See M. Cohen, "Yahad Shivtei Yisra'el," *Sedeh Hemed* 40 (1997), pp. 9–29.

[2] There the banner of Reuven is mentioned first, perhaps because the Torah wanted to return to the natural genealogical ordering before the Israelites entered Canaan and

The list of the spies by tribe in this week's reading deviates from the order of all these other listings and does not readily reflect any systematic arrangement. Nahmanides despaired of finding any tribal order here and wrote that the spies were appointed according to their personal importance. Sforno, who often concurred with Nahmanides, also assumed that personal criteria were the determining factor here, although he maintains that the spies' importance was not the determining factor; otherwise, Joshua son of Nun ought to have been appointed head of the delegation, since he was Moses' attendant, later his deputy and ultimately his successor. Similarly, Caleb ben Yefuneh ought to have been appointed Joshua's deputy since he too was righteous and was eventually appointed prince of the tribe of Judah (34:19). These arguments led Sforno to suggest that the spies were appointed by age. This appears to be a solution of last resort, since nowhere in the Bible do we see people arranged by age.[3]

The views of these two commentators seems to be contradicted by the fact that the first four names in the list of spies are arranged genealogically: all of these men were descended from Leah and are listed in order of birth. Likewise, the last four spies were all representatives of the tribes descended from Jacob's concubines. This might be reasonable in terms of Nahmanides' theory, as the social status of the tribes descended from the concubines was presumably lower than that of the tribes descended from his regular wives. However, this does not explain the order of all the spies. Also, it is clearly not coincidental that both the first four spies and the last four spies are listed in genealogical order. Hence, we still have to seek the basis of the arrangement of the list of spies.

Abarbanel also sought to account for the arrangement of the list of tribes here. He explains that Reuven, the eldest tribe, was listed first along with Shimon, his second in command, who followed him in the banner of Reuven. The remaining banners appear in similar fashion: the leader of the

---

divided the land among the tribes. Likewise, the tribe of Manasseh, Joseph's older son, is mentioned before Ephraim.

[3] The ages of Moses and Aaron are an exception (Ex. 7:6), as they were listed for the sake of the chronology of the Israelites' sojourn in Egypt. Another exception is the age of the prophet-priest Ezekiel (Ezek. 1:1), who began to prophesy at age 30, the age when a priest enters service (Num. 4:3).

banner of Judah, followed by the second in that camp, Issachar; then the leader of the third banner, Ephraim, and with him "the most respected of those under his banner, namely, Benjamin." Following him come the remaining sons of the matriarchs – Zevulun and Manasseh – and at the end, the tribes descended from the concubines.[4]

The strength of Abarbanel's argument lies in his arranging the tribes by their banners. Yet therein also lies its weakness, since this arrangement lacks consistency. Thus, in the order of the camps, as in the offerings of the princes according to that order (Num. 7), Reuven, the firstborn (who was stripped of his status of firstborn; see Gen. 49:3–4 and I Chr. 5:1–2) is not listed as the first banner, but is superseded by the banner of Judah. Moreover, the second in command under the banner of Ephraim is his brother Manasseh, not Benjamin. Furthermore, if the banners were the determining factor, why weren't all three tribes under each banner listed together? Why list only two tribes, leaving out the third, to be listed at the end?

Therefore, it seems we must seek the answer in yet another tribal criterion: the order in which the matriarchs, Jacob's wives, bore their sons, as related in Gen. 29–30, with two minor reservations: (1) here too the wives, Leah and Rachel, precede the concubines, Bilhah and Zilpah; (2) as with the order of the banners, the tribe of Levi is absent, since they do not go out to war or receive a contiguous apportionment of land in Israel. To maintain the pattern of twelve tribes, Joseph is split into two tribes, Ephraim and Manasseh.[5]

This is the resulting order: In her first round of births, Leah gave birth to four sons (Gen. 29:31–35), Reuven, Shimon, Levi and Judah. Since, as we have observed, Levi is not listed here, the group of four is completed with Leah's next son, Issachar. The matriarch Rachel bore two sons, Joseph and Benjamin, and they are listed next. Joseph, whose offspring was split into two tribes, is represented here by Ephraim, whom Jacob chose as Joseph's preferred son. After them, the Torah completes the list with the

---

[4] This view is shared by M. Cohen (above, n. 1), pp. 12–13.

[5] The reckoning of the tribes is detailed in Josh. 14:1–4.

two other tribes descended from the matriarchs – Zevulun, Leah's offspring, and Manasseh, Rachel's offspring.

This arrangement explains a puzzling phrase in the list, according to which Manasseh is mentioned as being "from the tribe of Joseph, namely, the tribe of Manasseh" (13:11), without a parallel formulation for his brother, Ephraim. In all the other listings of the tribes, the heading "the sons of Joseph" precedes the two secondary tribes together (as in Num. 1:32: "Of the descendants of Joseph: of the descendants of Ephraim...of the descendants of Manasseh"; cf. Num. 34:23). In one list this phrase even appears twice, at both the beginning and end: "The sons of Joseph were Manasseh and Ephraim, by their families" (Num. 26:28); "Those are the families of Manasseh...These are the descendants of Ephraim by their families...Those are the descendants of Joseph by their families" (Num. 26:34–37). Why then did the Torah mention "the tribe of Joseph" here only in reference to Manasseh? According to the order that we have suggested, the reason is as follows: Joseph, represented by Ephraim, had already been mentioned above with the sons of Rachel. One person remained to be mentioned from the "tribe of Joseph," and he was "from the tribe of Manasseh." That person is added here.

As for the order of the concubines' sons, Abarbanel's view – that the order of the banners was the determining factor – seems likely. Since each banner included three tribes, and the concubines had a total of four sons, Gad, the oldest son of Leah's maidservant Zilpah, is included in the banner of Leah's sons. Leading the banner of the concubines' sons was the second oldest – Dan, son of Rachel's maidservant Bilhah. They were followed by the tribes in the same order of priority: Asher, the second son of Zilpah, Leah's maidservant, and Naphtali, the second son of Bilhah, Rachel's maidservant.

Similarly with regard to the order of the banners: in the list of spies, all four tribes of the concubines were listed together, with the first three listed as in their banner – Dan, Asher, Naphtali. This is appropriate, since Dan was the firstborn of all the concubines' sons. Gad, who in the order of the banners was added to the sons of the primary wives, is demoted to the end of the list here. Thus, the criterion that gave Gad an advantage in the order of the banners caused him a disadvantage in the order of the spies.

The groupings in the listing of the spies turn out to be chiastic, as is frequently the case with orderings in the Torah. There are two groupings, one at the beginning and one at the end, each consisting of four elements – first the four sons of Leah, and last, the four sons of the concubines. In the middle are two additional groupings, each consisting of two elements – first, Rachel's son, and next, the sons remaining from the primary wives. Thus, in the end, we see that there is a definite order and that the sequence in the Torah is deliberate.

Parashat Korah

A PORTION IN THE LORD, A PORTION IN THE LAND

Rabbi Yisrael Samet
Midrashah for Women

KORAH'S "PARTY," the group that challenged Moses and Aaron, consisted of several factions. While all complained about Moses and Aaron setting themselves above the community, each group in Korah's following apparently had its own set of grievances. Datan and Aviram complained that Moses had taken the children of Israel out of a perfectly good land, Egypt, without bringing them to another land.[1] The words of the 250 princes of this group are not cited in the Torah independently of the claims of the group as a whole, so we can only infer their arguments based on the test proposed by Moses: the offering of incense. Since the Torah is exceedingly strict about the burning of "alien incense,"[2] offering incense here is a way of determining who is holy and "whom the Lord chooses" (Num. 16:5), i.e., who is worthy of the priesthood. Thus, we may infer that the 250 men wished to be priests.[3] Datan and Aviram were not included in

---

[1] So according to Nahmanides. According to Ibn Ezra (on 16:1), all the members of Korah's following complained about the rights of the firstborns being taken away, while Datan and Aviram, the sons of Reuven, also complained that the rights of the firstborn had been taken from Reuven and given to Joseph (see I Chr. 5:1–2). This interpretation is somewhat problematic, since Datan and Aviram did not refer to the rights of the firstborn in their arguments.

[2] Ex. 30:9: "You shall not offer alien incense on it." See also Ex. 30:37–38, Lev. 10:1, and parallels.

[3] See Deut. 18:5: "For the Lord your God has chosen him"; Deut. 21:5: "The priests, the sons of Levi, shall come forward, for the Lord your God has chosen them to minister to Him." See also Num. 17:20. According to the interpretations of Ibn Ezra and Nahmanides, the 250 princes were firstborns who were accustomed to offering

the test of offering incense because they did not seek the priesthood.[4] Thus, we see that one part of Korah's following desired land, and the other, the priesthood.[5]

Nor was the punishment meted out to the different groups identical: one group was incinerated while offering the incense, while the other was swallowed up by the earth. The punishment directly reflected the substance of the complaints: those who challenged Aaron's priesthood died while attempting to offer incense like priests, whereas those who complained about not yet being brought into the Land of Israel did not live to inherit the earth, but were instead swallowed up by it.[6]

As stated, Korah's following consisted of several factions, each of which made a variety of claims, and each of which was punished in accordance with its complaint. The question we want to explore here is whether the various groups shared a common ideological denominator, or whether they all banded together solely for the sake of challenging Moses and Aaron, each for its own reasons.

The Torah associates the factions who followed Korah in its descriptions of their punishments. Though different punishments were meted out to each group, the Torah uses words associated with eating or consuming for both. In the case of Datan and Aviram we are told, "The

---

sacrifices, and they accordingly objected to the priesthood being taken from the firstborn and given to the priests. See also R. Naftali Zvi Yehudah Berlin's *Ha'amek Davar* on this week's reading, according to whom the 250 princes were motivated by love of God.

[4] See Nahmanides on Num. 16:16, who suggests that when Moses realized what Datan and Aviram meant, he decreed that they should die a terrible death and removed them from the incense test that was given to Korah's following. However, according to our analysis here, the incense test was inappropriate from the outset for Datan and Aviram.

[5] The text does not specifically mention Korah's own claims or those of the other Levites with him (see Moses' remarks to Korah in Num. 16:8–10). However, we may infer from Moses' reply that the Levites wished to share in the priesthood. The rabbis suggested that Korah wanted to rule; see Rashi on 16:1: "What induced Korah to quarrel with Moses? He was jealous of Elitzafan ben Uziel, whom Moses had appointed leader."

[6] Exactly what punishment was meted out to Korah is not fully clear from this week's reading. The Torah states (Num. 26:10): "The earth opened its mouth and swallowed them up with Korah," and some rabbis explain that Korah was among the people swallowed and burned, while others disagree. See *Sanhedrin* 110a.

earth opened its mouth and swallowed them up" (Num. 16:32). Similarly, in the punishment of the 250 princes, "Fire went forth from the Lord and consumed them" (Num. 16:35). Furthermore, the Torah stresses that both penalties were extraordinary happenings wrought by God. In the case of Datan and Aviram, Moses says, "But if the Lord creates something new and the earth opens its mouth" (Num. 16:30), and in describing the punishment of those who offered incense, the Torah says, "Fire went forth from the Lord" (Num. 16:35).

Another theme associating the two factions emerges from the laws concerning gifts to the priests and Levites, the *terumot* and *ma'asrot* mentioned at the end of our reading: "And the Lord said to Aaron: You shall, however, have no territorial share among them or own any portion in their midst; I am your portion and your share among the Israelites" (Num. 18:20). This principle is reiterated in connection with the gifts to the Levites: "And to the Levites I hereby give all the tithes in Israel as their share...But they shall have no territorial share among the Israelites, for it is the tithes set aside by the Israelites...that I give to the Levites as their share. Therefore I have said concerning them: They shall have no territorial share among the Israelites" (vv. 21–24).

Why was this collection of laws about tithes included immediately after the story of Korah and his factions? The Torah chose to define the gifts given the priests and Levites as their "share," drawing a clear parallel between their share and the Israelites' inheritance (*nahalah*) in the land. The words used by the Torah in connection with the priests and Levites recall the words uttered by Datan and Aviram: "Even if you had brought us to a land flowing with milk and honey and given us possession of fields and vineyards (*nahalat sadeh va-kerem*)" (Num. 16:14).

The theme of the gifts given to the priests and Levites is also related to the controversy of Korah and his following. On the one hand, these commandments bolster the position of the priests and Levites, which had been challenged by Korah and his following.[7] On the other hand, these

---

[7] "Because Korah came and challenged Aaron's right to the priesthood, the Torah gave him twenty-four priestly gifts as an everlasting covenant. Therefore this passage was included here" (Rashi on Num. 18:8).

commandments show that the rights of the priests and Levites were not based on power and supremacy, since the priests and Levites had no portion in the land. This comparison indicates that the Torah sought to associate the rights of the priests and Levites with the issue of inheriting the land, which figured prominently in the arguments of Datan and Aviram. Thus, a connection emerges between the claims to priesthood made by the 250 princes and the claims to the land made by Datan and Aviram.

To appreciate this connection, we must understand the relationship between the role of the priests and Levites and the role of the Israelites. When the Israelites enter the land, each person will be obliged to dwell in his tribal inheritance: "The Israelite tribes shall remain bound each to its portion" (Num. 36:9). The "portions" of the priests and Levites are the gifts given to the priests and Levites, the "portion" given the priests being greater than that given to the Levites. The Levites are given the tithes of the Israelites as their portion, whereas the priests are told, "I am your portion and your share," which Nahmanides interprets as meaning, "At My table shall you eat." The priests, as God's servants, are permanent residents in His house and eat, as it were, at His table.[8]

The principle that God's dwelling is also that of the priests explains the test of the staffs that appears in this week's reading (17:16–24). This test proved that Aaron had been chosen for the priesthood by virtue of the fact that of all the princes' staffs, his was the only one that blossomed and produced fruit. This proved that the Tent of Meeting was the place for Aaron to flourish: "I am your portion and your share." It should be added that the sanctity of the priests serving in the Temple and the sanctity of the Israelites receiving a portion in the land are interrelated. The sanctity of the priests and Levites emanates "from among the Israelites" (Num. 8:16) and expresses the sanctity of the entire people, which was "a kingdom of priests and a holy nation" (Ex. 19:6). Just as Israel cannot not be without priests who will express the holiness of the people, so too the priests cannot be without the body of Israel from which they were "separated" to serve (18:6). Even the Sanctuary is not a place for the Divine spirit to dwell away

---

[8] "The priests were awarded [the right to] eat at God's table" (*Betzah* 21a).

from the people, as it is written, "Let them make Me a sanctuary that I may dwell among them" (Ex. 25:8).

In the wilderness, a temporary state of affairs developed, which differed from what would prevail in the Land of Israel. The people as a whole had not yet received their portions, but the priests were already serving in their office. In the previous week's reading, it was decreed that the Israelites would remain in the wilderness for forty years. The positions taken by Korah and his following were influenced by this unnatural situation.

We return to the connection between the punishments and the factions comprising Korah's following: Korah's adherents were swallowed up precisely because of what they desired. We may infer from this that their sin, too, lay in their having been engulfed by their desire. In the wilderness all the Israelites were like priests, insofar as they had no portion in the land and their sustenance was provided miraculously.[9] The Israelites should have learned from this that "man does not live on bread alone, but man may live on anything that the Lord decrees" (Deut. 8:3). The 250 princes who desired the priesthood sought to perpetuate this state of affairs. Perhaps they understood that the Israelites would not live on miracles forever, but would some day settle on their own land; however, they believed that anyone who so desired could abandon his portion of land and become a priest, the Lord becoming his portion.[10] This group aspired to be part of the priesthood, which was denied a share in the land, and did not want the usual portion. They were consumed by fire to teach us that a priesthood that is not integrally bound up with the people who receive a portion in the land cannot maintain itself in this world and is destined to be consumed by Divine fire.

The other group in Korah's following wanted to receive a portion in the land of Israel and did not consider the existence of the Israelites in the wilderness as a genuine national entity. In this group's view, the essential condition for the existence of the nation was that it possess its own land;

---

[9] See *Mekhilta De-Rabbi Ishmael, Beshallah*.

[10] This aspiration was later realized by King Jeroboam ben Nevat of Israel, who "ordained as priests of the shrines any who so desired" (I Kings 13:33).

they held in contempt the spiritual development associated with the priesthood which had already been conferred upon the Israelites. For them, the priesthood was but an added embellishment, superfluous to the nation's existence. The fact that Datan and Aviram were swallowed up by the earth indicates that land without the holiness of the priesthood is destined to descend into the netherworld.

While different claims were made by the members of Korah's following, these claims nevertheless shared a common denominator. The argument made by Korah and his following that "all the community are holy, all of them," did not reflect national unity, but rather the opposite. It evinced an approach in which each individual sought to fulfill whatever role he personally desired, without taking into account that his individual role is part of a broader superstructure. Thus, this week's reading teaches us that the Israelites' *nahalot* or "portions" differed one from another: for some their portion was the priesthood, and for others it was a portion of the land. Only when there is a cohesive bond and unity among all the separate parts of the nation can the House of Israel be fully established.

Parashat Korah

ON CONTROVERSY

Prof. Hannah Kasher
Department of Philosophy

GREAT IS PEACE; despicable is controversy. How so? A city in which there is controversy will come to ruin. The Sages said, "Controversy in a city leads to bloodshed"...A home in which there is controversy will come to ruin...The Sages said, "Controversy in a court leads to the destruction of the world" (*Derekh Eretz* 7.37).

Seemingly all would agree that wisdom, industriousness and peace are commendable qualities. Yet we can find words of praise for the opposite of each of these qualities. Centuries ago, Erasmus won fame for his *Encomium Moriae* ("In Praise of Folly"); several decades ago, Bertrand Russell wrote *In Praise of Idleness*, and today we find discussions extolling the advantages of controversy, presenting it as the lifeblood of human society everywhere. Some have even gone so far as to say that Judaism is typified by controversy.

The latter argument was presented in the fourteenth century, albeit disapprovingly, by the exegete R. Joseph ibn Caspi, who ascribed significance to the fact that Peleg (which in Hebrew means "faction" or "division" as well as "stream" or "brook"), son of Ever (Gen. 11:17), is mentioned as one of the ancestors of the Hebrews:

But we are still the descendants of Peleg, all of us: quarrelsome, contentious and dissident. It is this trait that led to the destruction of our Temple, and yet it continues.[1]

Notwithstanding the many sayings of the Sages condemning controversy, we can also find remarks that find merit in it. One such adage is found in *Avot* 5.17:

Every controversy that is for God's sake shall endure (Heb. *sofah le-hitkayyem*), but one that is not for the sake of God shall not endure. Which controversy was for the sake of God? This was the controversy of Hillel and Shammai. And which was not for the sake of God? Such was the controversy of Korah and his faction.

It need not be assumed that this remark was intended to promote controversy in Israel. This remark is one of four statements in Mishnah *Avot* that deal with actions carried out "for God's sake."[2] Thus, taken in context, the basic point of this remark was to distinguish between two things: something that might appear negative but in certain circumstances could have lasting value, and something that is indeed negative and is destined to pass from the world. The underlying motive or purpose – that a controversy was "for God's sake" – was the criterion for this distinction. The controversy of Korah and his faction is an example of a controversy that was wholly negative, whereas the controversy between Hillel and Shammai had lasting value.

The claim that there is a direct relationship between the nature of a controversy's motives ("for the sake of God") and its ability to endure ("shall in the end endure") is questionable both factually and theoretically.

---

[1] R. Joseph ibn Caspi, *Matzref Le-Kesef* (Cracow 1906), p. 43.

[2] "Let all who labor with the congregation labor with them for the sake of Heaven" (2.2), "May all your deeds be for the sake of Heaven" (2.12), "Every assembly that is for the sake of Heaven shall endure in the end" (4.11), "Every controversy that is for God's sake will endure in the end" (5.17). The term *le-shem shamayim* can be interpreted as "for the glory of God," or, perhaps, as "not driven by a passion to prevail over the other side." See also Maimonides' commentary ad loc.: "If someone argues not from a lesser motive, but to seek the truth, his words will endure, and they will not die."

The factual basis for this claim is refuted by the fact that the controversy between Hillel and Shammai was transient: this controversy was terminated by the ruling that in all cases of disagreement, Hillel's view was to be accepted (see Rashbatz, *Magen Avot*, on this Mishnah). This would appear to prove that even a controversy for the sake of God does not ultimately endure. The theoretical argument against this statement in Mishnah *Avot* is that the motives of a controversy are irrelevant to its permanence. In any controversy, only one of the parties is correct, so it is fitting that the controversy should end with the law being decided according to the view of that party (R. Isaac Arama, *'Akedat Yitzhak*, 78).

In the wake of these arguments, other interpretations of the expression *sofah le-hitkayem* have been offered. Some maintain that these words refer not to the argument enduring, but rather to the parties to the argument enduring: they will enjoy long life, in contrast to the untimely demise of Korah and his followers (see R. Jonah Gerondi's commentary ad loc.), or they will merit eternal life. Another interpretation views the word *sof* in this expression as synonymous with "end-purpose" or "goal," meaning that some sort of reward befitting the true objectives of those arguing for God's sake is promised. According to this interpretation, the Mishnaic promise is realized when the truth of the issue becomes evident (see R. Obadiah of Bertinoro's commentary on our Mishnah and Rashbatz, *Magen Avot* ad loc.).

The Sages' remark about the endurance of arguments made for the sake of God presents yet another difficulty. The dispute between Shammai and Hillel and their schools is presented as a model of a worthy controversy. Indeed, it is well attested in rabbinic sources (see e.g. *Yevamot* 14b) that the halakhic differences between the two sages did not harm the personal relations between them, and that "they treated one another with friendship and affection." However, even this model controversy came under attack, with both its causes and consequences being criticized: "When insufficiently trained disciples of Shammai and Hillel proliferated, controversy became rife in Israel, and it was as if the Torah had become two Torahs" (*Sanhedrin* 88b). The scope of the controversy was attributed to insufficient diligence on the part of those involved – they were "insufficiently trained." Also, the fact that this controversy endured –

endurance is interpreted in Ethics of the Fathers as the reward for those who participated – is presented here as an obstacle to proper Jewish life, for "it was as if the Torah had become two Torahs." Moreover, the description in *Yevamot* of the friendship and affection between Hillel and Shammai is incompatible with the general state of relations between the schools of Shammai and Hillel, as evinced by the description in the Talmud Yerushalmi (*Shabbat* 1.3) of a violent conflict between the rival groups:

> The disciples of the school of Shammai stood below, slaughtering the disciples of the school of Hillel. Six of them ascended, while the rest threatened them with swords and spears.

Thus, we see that even a polemic between Tannaim, which originated as an argument for the sake of God, eventually developed into violent civil strife.

Those who speak in praise of controversy sometimes also cite another statement that seemingly supports controversy: "These and those are the words of the living God" (*'Eruvin* 13b, *Gittin* 6b). However, the original context of this statement does not necessarily prove that controversy is intrinsically desirable. The expression "the words of the living God" is apparently intended to underscore the fact that viewpoints which are rejected may also have great value, due to their motivation, subject, authors, or content, but this does not prove that controversy is inherently desirable. It is often argued in support of controversy that it lends suitable expression to the plurality of people's views and ways of life. One can indeed picture groups that behave differently while living together harmoniously.

So how can arguments be resolved? It seems that the more significant the controversial issue is, the more essential and pressing it is to terminate the controversy. Thus, the controversy about the date of the new month was ended unequivocally when R. Joshua expressed his submission by coming to Rabban Gamaliel with his staff and his money in hand "on the day when the Day of Atonement occurred according to his reckoning" (Mishnah *Rosh Hashanah* 2.9). This was vital because a uniform calendar of festivals, holidays and fast days is one of the most important elements of a united people.

Pluralism is most likely to exist precisely where it is not crucial that the parties who hold the different views cooperate. A controversy over beliefs that do not elicit practical application can endure, as Maimonides pointed out in his commentary on the Mishnah:

> In any controversy between Sages that does not involve practical application, but only a statement of opinion, it is not necessary to rule in accordance with one of them (commentary on *Sanhedrin* 10.3; see also ibid. *Sotah* 3.3, *Shevu'ot* 1.4, and *Iggeret Tehiyyat ha-Metim*, 2).

It is notable, however, that Maimonides made this claim about tolerance only regarding issues that were not of fundamental importance in his view. He made this claim with regard to the following questions: Did a particular group of sinful people from biblical times have a share in the world to come? How is innocence established by the water used in the rite of the *sotah*? Should the narrative of the valley of dry bones in Ezekiel be understood as an allegory? Indeed, Maimonides ruled explicitly that there is a halakhic obligation to accept certain positions about subjects that he considered essential tenets of the faith. As we know, even this attempt to create uniformity in matters of faith encountered difficulty, as attested by the prolonged debate among Jewish philosophers over the existence and essence of certain articles of faith in Judaism.[3]

But even the claim that a controversy without practical implications can continue undisturbed and unresolved is not without problems. Some people are unwilling to accept the legitimacy of ideological deviation from their own opinions, whether due to a paternalistic approach that seeks to impose its own views, a lack of tolerance of other views, or the fear that even a controversy over something that is purely a matter of opinion can threaten the well-being of society. Ironically, sometimes controversies that are purely theoretical are resolved without coercion, when in the course of time the truth comes to light.

---

[3] For a comprehensive discussion see Menahem Kellner, *Torat ha-'Ikkarim ba-Philosophiyah ha-Yehudit bi-Yemei ha-Beinayim* (Jerusalem 1991).

Regarding the natural tendency to become involved in controversy, which begins with the inclination of human beings to hold different views, but which may end in tragedy, it is appropriate to conclude with the remarks of R. Yehezkel Landau, author of *Teshuvot Noda' bi-Yehudah* (*Yoreh De'ah*, 1):

> Please heed my advice and make room for peace. For there is nothing worse than discord. These days, controversies for the sake of God are rarely found, and Satan rejoices. So I implore you, make peace, and may He who makes peace on high bless his people Israel with peace.

Parashat Hukkat

WAS OG JUST A TALL TALE?

Dr. Admiel Kosman
Naftal-Yaffe Department of Talmud

THE ISRAELITES' VICTORY over King Og of Bashan is first mentioned in the Torah in this week's reading (Num. 21:33–35):

> They marched on and went up the road to Bashan, and King Og of Bashan with all his people came out to Edrei to engage them in battle. But the Lord said to Moses, "Do not fear him, for I shall deliver him and all his people and his land into your hands. You shall do to him as you did to King Sihon of the Amorites who dwelt in Heshbon." They smote him, his sons, and all his people, until no remnant was left of him, and they took possession of his country.

In a previous article,[1] I discussed the legends that appear in the Talmud and various other sources about Og's fantastic size. This article discusses the interpretation of these astonishing legends by medieval scholars. First, let us consider briefly the story related in a *baraita* in *Berakhot* 54a:

> The rabbis taught: A person who sees straits in the ocean, the fords of the Jordan, the fords of the Arnon, the meteoric rocks on the slopes of Beit Horon, *the rock that King Og of Bashan wanted*

---

[1] Bar-Ilan *Daf Shevu'i*, No. 353.

to throw on the Israelites, the stone upon which Moses sat when Joshua fought Amalek, Lot's wife, the wall of Jericho that was swallowed up where it stood – for all these he should give praise and thanksgiving to God.[2]

The ensuing Talmudic discussion of this *baraita* (ibid. 54b) describes the encounter between Og and the Israelites as follows:[3]

> Og said: "How large is the Israelite camp? Three parasangs [about 12 miles]. I shall uproot a mountain of three parasangs and throw it on them and kill them." He uprooted a mountain of three parasangs and placed it on his head. But God set grasshoppers upon it, and they burrowed a hole in the mountain and it fell around his neck. He tried to pull it off his head, but his teeth stuck out to the right and left, and he could not tear it off. This is what the Torah meant [by the verse] "You break the teeth of the wicked" (Ps. 3:8), as Resh Lakish explained. For R. Shimon ben Lakish said: What does "You break (*shibbarta*) the teeth of the wicked" mean? Do not read it as *shibbarta*, but as *shirbavta*, "you entangled." How tall was Moses? Ten cubits. He grabbed hold of an axe ten cubits long, leapt ten cubits, struck Og in the ankle and killed him.[4]

The fantastic figure of Og as presented in these legends made medieval commentators rather uneasy. For example, in *Hiddushei ha-Ge'onim*[5] we read: "This remark is bizarre and farfetched, inconceivable and

---

[2] This ruling is accepted in *Shulhan Arukh, Orah Hayyim*, 218.1.

[3] This story has no parallels in tannaitic literature or in the Talmud Yerushalmi.

[4] See further on this story Louis Ginzberg, *Legends of the Jews*, 6 (New York 1946), p. 120, n. 695, and Avigdor Shinan, *Targum va-Aggadah Bo* (Jerusalem 1993), p. 172. For the three parasangs mentioned here, see Rashi's commentary ad loc., s.v. *mahaneh Yisra'el*, which refers to the statements of Rabbah bar bar Hannah in *'Eruvin* 55a. Perhaps there is a connection between the hyperbolic statements there and our story here (see below, n. 6).

[5] Printed in *Ein Ya'akov* on *Berakhot* 54a, s.v. *even*.

very discomfiting." Therefore many commentators interpreted these legends symbolically, removing them from their fantastic, hyperbolic context.[6] These interpretations not only served those within the Jewish community who found the legends problematic, but also helped defend the Jewish position in disputations with Christians about the status of the Talmud.

One interpretative trend stressed that the legends of the Talmud should not be considered authoritative. For example, Ibn Ezra, in his commentary on Deut. 3:11, writes that according to the plain sense of the text, we should take the biblical report of the size of Og's bed[7] as an indication that he was twice as tall as a normal person, but no more: "'By a man's forearm' – meaning by the standard cubit. This means that [Og] was twice the size [of a normal person], but it does not make sense that the Torah meant that he was twice the size when measured by his own forearm,[8] for what would the Torah mean [by this]? Moreover, in that case, he would bear no resemblance to a human being."

Maimonides (1135–1204) wrote in similar vein in his *Guide for the Perplexed*, 2:47:[9]

> Regarding what the Torah says about Og's bedstead, "His bedstead, a bedstead of iron" – a person's bedstead is not the same size as the person, since it is not like a garment that one wears. Rather, a bedstead is always larger than the person who

---

[6] On hyperbole in rabbinic literature, see M. B. Lerner, "Ha-Guzma Etzel Hazal," *Mahanayim* 79 (1963), pp. 68–73; Dina Stein, "Devarim she-Ro'im mi-Sham Lo Ro'im mi-Kan: 'Iyyun be-Bava Batra 73a–75b," *Mehkerei Yerushalayim be-Sifrut Ivrit* 17 (1999), pp. 9–32.

[7] Much of my previous article (above, n. 1) is devoted to this subject.

[8] Ibn Ezra's remarks here apparently allude to Targum Onkelos on Deut. 3:11, where the words "four cubits wide by the standard cubit" are rendered "four cubits wide by the king's cubit." In other words, Og's height should apparently be measured by the "king's cubit," perhaps referring to the forearm of Og himself; see *Targum Yonatan* on this verse. See also Shinan, ibid., p. 144 and n. 224. Rashi comments on Deut. 3:11: "'By a person's forearm' – by Og's forearm." See also the discussion in the various supercommentaries on Rashi (*Mizrahi, Siftei Hakhamim,* and *Gur Aryeh*), and in Nahmanides' commentary ad loc.

[9] Ed. Kafih (Jerusalem 1977), p. 269.

sleeps in it. It is common for the bed to be about one third longer than the person. If this bed was nine cubits long, then the person who slept in it, according to the usual proportion for beds, would have been about six cubits or a bit taller in height. The Torah says "by a person's forearm," referring to the forearm of an average person, that is to say, of the rest of mankind and not Og's forearm. For a person's limbs tend to be proportional, and the Torah says that Og was twice the height of other people, or a bit more. This is undoubtedly rare in the human race, but by no means impossible.[10]

In short, these commentators emphasize that the Talmud's explanation should not be accepted at face value, as the literal sense of the Torah indicates differently. Og was approximately twice the size of an average person, and this exceptional height is noted in Deuteronomy rather emphatically. Evidence of his extraordinary size was preserved in his iron bedstead which survived in Rabbat Ammon.

How, then, are we to understand the fantastic story in the Talmud about Og's vast size? Among the important landmarks in the medieval interpretative tradition of symbolic interpretation, two major interpretative schools that influenced the approaches of later authorities (*aharonim*) should be noted. One is the mystical, kabbalistic approach, and the other is the allegorical approach. An allegorical interpretation of the legend sees in the legend symbols of highly significant spiritual matters.[11] Here it assumes that Og's superhuman might and gigantic size should be viewed as symbolizing a special kind of might, not necessarily physical, in contrast to the plain

---

[10] Cf. Chaim Rabin, "Og," *Eretz Israel* 8 (1967), p. 254, n. 44, citing Wright's finding that the height of the average prehistoric man in the land of Israel was approximately 1.5 meters (=4.92 feet).

[11] On the symbolic interpretation of the aggadah, which began in the geonic period, see Yonah Frankel, *Darkhei ha-Aggadah ve-ha-Midrash* (Givatayim 1991), pp. 501–531. Maimonides maintained that interpreting the *aggadah* literally when it does not meet the test of rationality is foolish, and brings disgrace on the rabbis and the Torah (see Maimonides' commentary on the Mishnah, introduction to *Perek Helek* [ed. Kafih, p. 200]).

sense of the Torah.[12] Thus, according to in these commentaries (even if this is not stated explicitly and is only implied), the war on Og is transformed from a national-historical war, as presented in the Torah, to a mythical war taking place in worlds not visible to the human eye.

The kabbalistic interpretation of the story of Og, which had an impact on later exegesis, is found in *Sefer ha-Bahir, Hukkat* 3.184a:

> "But the Lord said to Moses, 'Do not fear him [*oto*]'" (Num. 21:34). The word *oto* is written twice with full orthography in the Torah, once here and the other time "until your fellow claims it [*oto*]" (Deut. 22:2).[13] What does this mean? That both were actually signs [*ot*]. In the case of "until your fellow claims it," this means that the claimant must identify the sign of the item he lost. Here, too, *oto* refers to Og, a follower of Abraham, one of the people in his household, who was forced to live with him. [Therefore Og] took upon himself the sign of sanctity [=circumcision].[14] When Og saw the Israelites approaching him, he said, "Surely I can overcome the merit they have, and with this I shall confront them." At that very moment, Moses was seized with fear: How could he obliterate the sign that Abraham had

---

[12] A notable and relatively late exception is the interpretation by Maharal of Prague in his *Hiddushei Aggadot* on *Niddah* 24b. He interprets the Talmudic legend about Og symbolically, but stresses repeatedly that Og's strength "was entirely physical, but the might of the people Israel is not physical, for they adhere to the Lord Almighty. Therefore Og was distinguished by entirely physical traits, such as his great height." Yet elsewhere, even Maharal adopted the position usually accepted by commentators; see his commentary on Num. 21:35. For other interpretations of this legend, see the list of commentaries in *Ein Ya'akov* on *Berakhot* 54b, and the detailed list in R. Zechariah Porto, *Asaf ha-Mazkir* (Venice 1680), pp. 38a and 299b. (I am indebted to Prof. Yaakov Spiegel for drawing my attention to this work.)

[13] This verse refers to someone who found a lost object. In both of these passages, the word *oto* is not spelled with a *vav* in the middle. However, the Kennicott Bible (Numbers, p. 322; Deuteronomy, p. 409) cites at least one manuscript in which each of these words is spelled a *vav* in the middle.

[14] This is clear from the reference earlier in this passage to Gen. 17:27: "And all his household, his home-born slaves and those that had been bought from outsiders were circumcised with him."

made? God said to him, "Surely his right hand[15] is dead," for a right hand is needed to vanquish him. Immediately God said, "Do not fear him [oto]" – do not fear the sign that he bears, and you will not even need your right hand. "For I shall deliver him...into your hand" – your left hand will remove him from this world, for he defaced his sign, and whoever defaces this sign deserves to be removed from the face of the earth. All the more so your left hand, which is "your hand," will remove him from this world.

According to this interpretation, Moses feared that Og had spiritual merit related to the sign made in his flesh when he was one of Abraham's servants – the sign of circumcision.[16]

Another commentary in a similar vein was written by R. Solomon ben Aderet of Barcelona (Rashba) in the thirteenth century.[17] Presumably, Rashba was greatly troubled by the bizarre nature of this legend, which was brought up repeatedly by the Christians in their attacks on the irrationality of Talmudic stories. Rashba addressed the challenge of these attacks, attempting to resolve these difficult passages in a way that would be acceptable to the intellectuals of his times. Some scholars even believe that he debated Raymond Martini face to face,[18] one of the main adversaries of the Talmud during that time.

This legend about Og was one of the most well-known examples used by Christian polemicists to discredit the Talmud. Evidence of this has

---

[15] R. Judah Ashlag, *Ha-Sulam la-Zohar* (vol. 16, *Parashat Hukkat*, p. 29), suggests that the Zohar was referring here to Aaron, Moses' brother.

[16] The kernel of the idea that Og accumulated "merit points" for good deeds that he had performed in the past is found in *Genesis Rabbah* 41.13 (ed. Theodor-Albeck, pp. 413–414), which states that God promised to reward Og for the meritorious act of informing Abraham of Lot's capture: "By your life, you shall receive reward for your steps – you will live long in this world."

[17] See *Ein Ya'akov* on *Berakhot* 54b, s.v. *'akar torah*. On Rashba as an interpreter of *aggadah*, see Carmi Horowitz, "'Al Perush ha-Aggadot Shel Rashba: Bein Kabbalah Le-Philosophiah," *Da'at* 18 (1987), pp. 15–25; Aryeh L. Feldman, ed., *Hiddushei ha-Rashba, Perushei ha-Haggadot* (Jerusalem 1991), pp. 5–17; Yonah Frankel, *Midrash ve-Aggadah*, 3 (Tel Aviv 1997), pp. 868–870.

[18] Cf. Jeremy Cohen, "The Polemical Adversary of Solomon ibn Aderet," *JQR* n.s. 71 (1980), pp. 48–55.

survived in the arguments by Nicholas Donin in his disputation with R Yehiel of Paris.[19] This story was also cited as evidence of the Talmud's total lack of rationality by Petrus Alfonsi[20] in his arguments against the Talmud, and was similarly attacked by Peter the Venerable of Cluny.[21]

Alfonsi reckoned as follows: According to this story, Og's head measured approximately ten cubits, and therefore a grasshopper would have had to make a ten-cubit hole in the mountain in order for the mountain to descend around Og's neck. How could this have been possible?

Accordingly, Rashba prefaced his interpretation of this legend with a lengthy discussion of the difficulties of interpreting legends of the Talmud generally, "which for many reasons are phrased in obscure language." That this legend greatly troubled Rashba is also evident from the fact that he flatly rejected any literal interpretation of *Berakhot* 54b. Flat rejection of the plain sense of the text was an approach that he rarely took except for certain special cases where he felt that these legends served as a target for Christian attacks.[22]

In interpreting this story, Rashba used an intriguing method. On the one hand, he was not ready to entirely abandon the description of Og as a conventional human being, albeit one of exceedingly tall and huge dimensions. On the other hand, he did not consider the legends of the Talmud mere unfounded exaggerations. The solution he suggested was to distinguish between the two texts: the *baraita* (*Berakhot* 54a), which assumes that one could still find the rock which Og sought to throw on the Israelites, and the wondrous story that follows about Og uprooting a

---

[19] *Vikkuah Rabbenu Yehiel mi-Paris*, ed. Reuven Margaliyot (Lwow 1928), p. 24. Donin was an apostate from Judaism (according to some, a Karaite), who apparently joined the Franciscan order. Following the disputation with R. Yehiel of Paris, the Talmud was seized and burned, apparently in 1242. See H. Merhavyah, *Ha-Talmud bi-Re'i ha-Natzrut* (Jerusalem 1970), pp. 227–248. See also Jeremy Cohen, *The Friars and the Jews* (Ithaca and London 1982), p. 61, n. 19.

[20] See Merhavyah, ibid., pp. 105–106. Petrus Alfonsi was born Moshe the Sephardi, and converted to Christianity in 1106; see further Merhavyah, ibid., p. 93 ff., and the studies cited there on p. 94, n. 4.

[21] See Merhavyah, ibid., pp. 139–140, and p. 128 ff.

[22] See Horowitz (above n. 17), p. 25.

mountain (ibid. 54b). Rashba viewed the rock in the first text as quite real, and this certainly fits the description of Og as a person of exceptional size. In contrast, he believed that the story about the mountain should be interpreted allegorically.

According to Rashba, the "mountain" that was to have served as Og's weapon alludes to the merits of the patriarchs, who were associated by various homilies with mountains.[23] Thus, Og relied on the same merit given to Abraham, who was one of the patriarchs and was considered like a "mountain." This was why Moses feared him. The grasshoppers, an allusion to the prayers of the Israelites ("their might being in their tongues"), caused the merits of this "mountain" to disintegrate. Later Moses also joined in the fray, countering the merits of Og with three other types of merit: that of the patriarchs, alluded to by the ten-cubit leap which Moses took into the past, as it were, to take the merits of the patriarchs to assist the Israelites; Moses' own personal merits, alluded to by the fact that he was ten cubits tall; and the merits of the people of Israel as a whole, alluded to by the ax in Moses' hand ("comparing them to an instrument placed in his hands that he would use"), which was ten cubits long. All these formed the weapon that Moses wielded against the merits of Og, and through them Og was ultimately vanquished.

In conclusion, we can say that in medieval Jewish exegesis, Og was restored to realistic dimensions as a powerful giant of a man, rather than as a fantastic creature of incredible size, as he is depicted in Talmudic legend.

---

[23] Rashba cites such a homily on Mic. 6:1: "Come, present [My] case before the mountains." The only explicit homily to this effect, to the best of my knowledge, is found in a late midrash called *Alpha Betot*, published by Solomon Aaron Wertheimer in his *Batei Midrashot* (Jerusalem 1973), 2.443: "'Come, present [My] case before the mountains, and let the hills hear you pleading' – the mountains are the fathers of the world [=the patriarchs]...and the hills, the matriarchs" (see Wertheimer, ibid., n. 41). The idea behind this homily, however, appears in the Talmud; see *Rosh Ha-Shanah* 11a: "'Hark! My beloved! There he comes, leaping over mountains, bounding over hills' – Leaping over mountains – by the merits of the patriarchs; bounding over hills – by the merits of the matriarchs." See also *Tanhuma Balak*, 12: "[Balaam] began by saying, 'I was among the lofty, keeping company with the patriarchs.'"

Parashat Balak

"A HOUSEFUL OF MONEY"

Prof. Yaakov Spiegel

Naftal-Yaffe Department of Talmud

THIS WEEK'S READING recounts how King Balak of Moab sent the elders of Moab and Midian to Balaam, requesting that he curse the Israelites. Balaam did not answer immediately; instead, he invited the elders to spend the night in his house so that he could receive instructions from God as to how to respond. Indeed, that night God revealed Himself to Balaam and said: "Do not go with them. You must not curse that people, for they are blessed" (Num. 22:12). Accordingly, Balaam told them the next morning, "Go back to your own country, for God will not let me go with you" (v. 13). Balak, however, did not give up; he sent Balaam a second delegation, this one comprised of "dignitaries more numerous and distinguished than the first." They appealed to Balaam: "Thus says Balak son of Zippor: Please do not refuse to come to me. I will reward you richly and will do anything you ask of me" (vv. 16–17). To this entreaty Balaam answered, "Though Balak give me his house full of silver and gold, I could not do anything, big or small, contrary to the command of the Lord my God" (v. 18).

Balaam's response recalls what we read in Song of Songs 8:7: "If a man offered all his wealth for love, he would be laughed to scorn." The plain meaning of this verse is that one cannot buy love, and anyone that tries to do so will be scorned and his love rejected. In other words, here as in the case of Balaam, the expression "to give all of one's wealth" expresses hyperbole.

To this we may add the passage in I Kings 13:1–9, which records a dialogue between King Jeroboam and the man of God. This text states, "The king said to the man of God, 'Come with me to my house and have some refreshment, and I shall give you a gift.' But the man of God replied to the king, 'Even if you give me half your wealth, I will not go in with you, nor will I eat bread or drink water in this place, for so I was commanded by the word of the Lord: You shall eat no bread.'" Here, too, the expression "half your wealth" serves as a form of hyperbole.

Thus, our initial impression is that Balaam's response was proper. Knowing that God had forbidden him to curse Israel and unwilling defy God's word, he flatly refused Balak's emissaries: God's word is not to be transgressed, even for vast riches.

The Sages, however, understood this passage differently. In Mishnah *Avot* 5.19 we read:

> Whoever has these three qualities is of the disciples of our father Abraham, but those with three other attributes are of the disciples of the wicked Balaam. Those with a generous eye, a modest spirit and a humble soul are of the disciples of Abraham; those with a jealous eye, a haughty mind and a vainglorious soul are of the disciples of the wicked Balaam.

Avot De-Rabbi Natan (version B, ch. 48) explains these three traits in light of the verses in our Torah reading. We quote the relevant parts here: "What is a 'vainglorious soul'? As it is written, 'Though Balak were to give me his house full of silver and gold.'" *Midrash Tanhuma*, ibid. (=*Numbers Rabbah* 20.10) is more explicit:

> "A vainglorious soul," as it is written, "Though Balak were to give me." Balaam thought: If the king hired mercenaries to fight the Israelites, the soldiers might be victorious or they might fall in battle. So it is only fair that he pay that much to me in order to win. From this we deduce that this is what he asked for.

Based on this, Rashi commented on Balaam's response as follows:

> "His house full of silver and gold" – This tells us that he was vainglorious and covetous of other people's wealth. He said: It is

appropriate that he give me the equivalent in silver and gold that it would cost him to hire many mercenaries without being certain of victory, while I could assure him victory.

How did the Sages deduce from the words "Though Balak were to give me" that Balaam was avaricious? Balaam's answer appears to be a rejection of the offer, using conventional exaggeration to do so.

Many commentators on Rashi have addressed this question. Here we present answers given by two such commentators. First, R. Elijah Mizrahi (Re'em), who wrote: "Were this not so, why did he make the possibility of contravening God's word contingent on money? He should have said, 'Though they were to kill me, I could not do anything contrary to the word of the Lord.'"

In response to this explanation, R. David Pardo[1] noted that Balaam's response to Balak mentioned money since Balak had made an offer of money. After all, the emissaries that the king had sent said, "I will reward you richly," meaning, as Rashi interpreted, "I shall give you even more than your accustomed fee in the past."[2] In other words, Balak promised Balaam a substantial financial reward. Hence Balaam could not have responded to Balak's emissaries, "I shall not come even if you kill me," since a person generally responds in kind, using the same words used to address him. This is why Balaam mentioned money, so our verse does not necessarily prove that he was avaricious.

R. Jacob Kneizel[3] explained the rabbinic claim differently, relying on a linguistic analysis of Num. 22:18. The second half of Balaam's response, "I could not do anything...contrary," can be interpreted in two ways: (1) I am incapable of doing anything contrary to God's will; (2) I am not permitted

---

[1] *Maskil le-David* (Venice 1761).

[2] The first printed edition of Rashi's commentary (Reggio de Calabria 1475), does not include these words, although they did appear in the edition used by R. Elijah Mizrahi, who cites them.

[3] His work was first printed in Constantinople, 1524, and was published in a new edition based on manuscripts by R. Moshe Phillip (Petah Tikva 1998). Not much is known about him, except that he was a contemporary of R. Elijah Mizrahi, although the two scholars do not refer to each other's works.

to act contrary to God's will (cf. Onkelos).[4] R. Kneizel explained why this claim was not logical according to either interpretation, by drawing on examples from a completely different realm.

According to the first interpretation of "I could not do anything," it would make no sense for a person to make a statement such as "Though you were to give me your house full of silver and gold, I could not fly up to heaven." Such a statement is clearly illogical, since it is obviously impossible for a person to fly up to heaven. According to the second interpretation of "I could not," the appropriate statement should have been: "Though you give me...I am not permitted to fly up to heaven." This statement does not make sense either, since permission does not depend on the silver and gold that a person is given, and receiving money does not affect the prohibition that applies to him. The only sensible reading of Balaam's words is as follows: Even if you give me silver and gold, I shall not act contrary to God's words. Such a statement expresses a person's free choice – that if he chooses to act contrary to God's word for the sake of financial gain, he is capable of doing so.

However, as R. Kneizel points out, since this is not what Balaam actually said and what he did say was a non sequitur, the rabbis concluded that Balaam's response consisted of two clauses: (1) if Balak were to give me his house full of silver and gold; and (2) I cannot act contrary to the words of the Lord. The first clause was in response to Balak's words, "I will reward you richly," and refers to money, as Rashi interpreted. Balaam's answer to this was that he deserved to be richly rewarded, since, as Rashi explained, if the king were to send an army against the Israelites, the battle could go either way, whereas Balaam could assure him of victory. The second clause, which Rashi himself presented as a separate statement, means: I am incapable of acting contrary to God's word. As Rashi wrote: "He reluctantly acknowledged that he is controlled by others, and prophesied here that he was unable to undo the blessings that the patriarchs had received from God."

---

[4] The difference between "I could not" and "I shall not" is also discussed by R. Jacob Toledano, *Ohel Ya'akov* (Jerusalem 1997), and R. Hisdai Almosnino, *Mishmeret ha-Kodesh* (Leghorn 1824).

This explanation also resolves the difficulty in the words of the man of God appearing in the book of Kings. Recall that there he had said: "Even if you give me...I will not go in with you, nor will I eat bread." Neither ability nor permission is mentioned here, for performing or not performing the action was a matter of free choice, entirely dependent on the person himself.

Parashat Pinchas

"LIGHTING A CANDLE OR FILLING A VESSEL"?

Prof. Shaul Regev
General Jewish Studies Program

"LET THE LORD...APPOINT SOMEONE" (Num. 27:16). Why did Moses see fit to make this request after the passage on inheritance? Seeing that the daughters of Zelofehad been given their father's inheritance, Moses said, "The time has come for me to petition for my own needs. If these daughters inherit, it is only proper that my sons inherit my majesty." God said to him: "He who tends a fig tree will enjoy its fruit" (Prov. 27:18). Your sons did not busy themselves with the Torah. Joshua served you well and gave you much honor, working from early morning to late at night in your council. He arranged the seats and laid out the mats. Since he served you with all his might, he is worthy of ministering to Israel. Single out Joshua son of Nun in fulfillment of the words, "He who tends a fig tree will enjoy its fruit" (*Numbers Rabbah* 21.14).

After all his attempts to persuade God to allow him to enter the land were rejected, Moses finally accepted His verdict and sought to transfer the mantle of leadership to whomever God chose to be his successor. While the above homily associates the previous passage, about the daughters of Zelofehad, with the next passage, which deals with the change of leadership, it also teaches us that spiritual leadership in not inherited; it is conferred on those who make the necessary efforts to deserve to receive it. It appears that Moses wished to pass the mantle of leadership on to his own sons, but God told him to pass it to Joshua, for whom no task was too difficult or demeaning, as long as he could be close to Moses in order to learn the Torah from him. Rather than boast of being Moses' servant, he was prepared to perform even the most menial tasks, such as arranging seats and laying out mats.

The transfer of authority and leadership was carried out through two actions which Moses was commanded to perform publicly: laying his hands on Joshua's head before Elazar the Priest and all the people, and conferring some of his majesty on Joshua. While the act of laying hands is one that can be performed publicly before the entire people and certainly before the leaders, it is difficult to explain the second act in physical terms. How was Moses to confer some of his majesty, which was seemingly related to Moses' inner essence and nature, on Joshua? Beauty and majesty are not qualities that can be transferred from one person to another. In any event, Joshua did not emerge from either of these actions with any external indications of either the authority or leadership that had been conferred on him.

The Midrash, however, says: "Lay your hand upon him, like one who kindles one candle from another. Give him majesty, like one who pours from one vessel to another" (*Numbers Rabbah* 21.15). This Midrash appears to contradict itself, since in the first act the light of the first candle is not diminished, implying that Moses himself loses nothing by laying his hands on Joshua's head. The second act, however, "pouring from one vessel to another," describes a situation in which the first vessel loses some of its contents.

Rabbi Shem Tov Melamed, in his exegetical work *Keter Shem Tov* (Venice 1601), offered two ways of resolving this contradiction, both of which teach us about the transfer of leadership. According to the first approach, the transfer of leadership from Moses to Joshua had two aspects. One was spiritual leadership, represented by prophecy, and the other was social-political leadership of the nation, represented by sovereignty and dominion. Prophecy was transferred to Joshua in the same way that one candle is lit by another: The conferring of prophetic ability on Joshua through Moses' laying his hands in no way detracted from Moses' own level of prophecy. In fact, this happened earlier with the seventy elders upon whom Moses conferred prophetic spirit, without losing anything of his prophetic powers. Joshua apparently did not understand this duality in leadership and thought that every prophet was necessarily also a political leader. Therefore, when he saw Eldad and Meidad prophesying in the camp, he assumed that this was an uprising against Moses' political leadership and suggested that they be arrested. Moses, however, distinguished between political and spiritual leadership and responded, "Would that all the Lord's people were prophets" (Num. 11:29).

On the other hand, where political leadership is concerned, two kings cannot wear the same crown. Political leadership cannot be divided among several parties, but must be kept entirely in the hands of a single body. This sovereignty – political leadership – Moses transferred like "pouring from one vessel to another." With Joshua's inauguration as leader, Moses could no longer continue to lead the people, and he had to pass the mantle of leadership on to Joshua.

As R. Melamed put it:

> Moses bequeathed to Joshua two things: prophecy and sovereignty. Therefore, regarding prophecy [the Midrash] says, "Like lighting one candle from another," since Moses lost nothing at all. Concerning this [the Torah] says, "Lay your hand upon him." Regarding the sovereignty that [Moses] had, [the Torah] said, "Invest him with some of your majesty"; this is the majesty of kingship. Regarding this [the Midrash] says "like pouring from one vessel to another," since two kings cannot wear the same crown (*Keter Shem Tov*, 190a).

R. Melamed's explanation reflects the different perspectives of the person who gives and the person who receives. In terms of the giver, the appropriate metaphor is that of lighting one candle with another, since the giver loses what he had beforehand. Conferring prophecy on Joshua did not detract in any way from Moses. On the other hand, from the vantage point of the receiver, the correct metaphor is that of pouring from one vessel to another, since Joshua's previously empty vessel was now filled. The metaphor of lighting one candle from another was inadequate to demonstrate how much Joshua was receiving. Hence the second metaphor, of pouring from one vessel to another, was necessary, as if what had been in the first vessel now passed into the second one, filling it.

R. Tuvia Halevi of Safed, in his commentary *Hen Tov* (Venice 1605), suggested that all the commandments given to Moses concerning Joshua were aimed not only at establishing Joshua's position, but also at advancing him to a status higher than he had enjoyed previously. So far, we did not encounter Joshua as a spiritual leader. The daughters of Zelofehad had appealed to Moses and Eleazar, but Joshua was not mentioned. There was also a hierarchy of instruction when Moses taught the people: first Moses taught Eleazar, who taught the princes, and then all the people, of which Joshua too was a member. Now Moses was told to position Joshua before Eleazar, but not in the physical sense; rather, he was instructed confer on Joshua a rank higher than that of Eleazar. In other words, the order of instruction would now be as follows: Moses would instruct Joshua and with that Moses' role would end; Joshua would instruct Eleazar, Eleazar the princes, and the princes all the people. Thus, from now on Joshua would rank second to Moses, in contrast to his previous position.

However, we find a discrepancy between the instructions given to Moses and their implementation. Moses was commanded to lay his *hand* on Joshua's head, and thereby to transfer part of his prophetic ability to Joshua. According to R. Tuvia Halevi's understanding, Joshua was not a member of the seventy elders on whom Moses had conferred his spirit. He remained, as the Midrash portrays him, one who "set up seats in the Beit Midrash," and was not yet ready for prophecy. Therefore, Moses was instructed to lay only one hand on Joshua, symbolizing a limited transfer of prophetic ability. Henceforth Joshua would supplement what he was lacking by inquiring of the *urim ve-tummim*. Joshua would not be a perfect leader, as he would have to consult Eleazar and the *urim ve-tummim* for assistance in leadership.

Moses, however, wanted to demonstrate that he was not jealous of Joshua's leadership, and he prepared Joshua more fully for prophecy than he had originally been instructed. Hence Moses laid both hands on Joshua, conferring a double portion of prophetic ability on him. Henceforth Joshua became a consummate leader, ranking above Eleazar; he no longer needed Eleazar's assistance or that of the *urim ve-tummim*. Indeed, we do not find Joshua constantly consulting the *urim ve-tummim* in his subsequent years as leader.

Parashat Mattot

"IN HIS NAME, AFTER HIS NAME"

Prof. Yaakov Spiegel

Naftal-Yaffe Department of Talmud

R. JUDAH HE-HASID, a noted medieval rabbi (ca. 1150–1217), wrote many works, including one called the Testament of R. Judah he-Hasid (*Tzava'at R. Judah he-Hasid*). This work contains teachings that are not found in rabbinic literature, some of which seem to contradict the Talmud. This work was studied extensively by later rabbis. Although an in-depth discussion of this book is beyond the scope of this article, we will consider one item from the Testament and show how later scholars attempted to find the source for it in the Torah.

In his Testament he wrote:[1] "A man should not marry a woman whose name is the same as his mother's, or whose prospective father-in-law's name is the same as his own. And if he married such a woman, one of them should change his name, and then there might be hope."

The generally accepted explanation of this ruling is that if the bride and her mother-in-law or the husband and his father-in-law share the same name, it will be impossible to properly fulfill the commandment of honoring one's parents. How so? When the groom calls his bride by her name, one might mistakenly think he is calling his mother by her name, which is forbidden according to the *halakhah*. Others suggest that this

---

[1] I used the edition of R. Judah Hasid's Testament printed in *Sefer Hasidim*, ed. R. Margaliyot (Jerusalem 1957), p. 17. For textual variants of the Testament in the manuscripts and printed editions, see Ari Y. Shevat, "Tzava'at R. Judah he-Hasid," *Talelei Orot* 10 (1992), pp. 82–152. The instruction discussed here appears on p. 127 (the variants there are not significant).

ruling was issued for reasons of modesty, lest he call his bride and cause his mother to think that he was calling her.

Later rabbinic authorities agreed that R. Judah he-Hasid's instruction did not apply when a person's name was changed before marriage, and that his comment that "then there might be hope" applied only to name changes after marriage. This raises the question of whether taking an additional name constitutes a name change for purposes of R. Judah's instruction. For example, if the bride and the groom's mother both shared the name Rachel, the couple may not marry, according to the Testament. Suppose that henceforth the bride would be called Rachel Leah, or Leah Rachel. Would that constitute a change in her name, permitting the couple to marry? Or is the addition of another name meaningless, so the prohibition still applies, according to R. Judah?

Our Torah reading provides an answer to this question. For we read: "Yair son of Menasheh went and captured their villages, which he renamed Havvot Yair. And Novah went and captured Kenat and its dependencies, renaming it Novah after himself" (*bi-shemo*; Num. 32:41–42).

Both Yair and Novah named the places they captured after themselves. But the Torah emphasizes this only with respect to Novah, saying, "renaming it Novah after himself," whereas the Torah does not mention in connection with Havvot Yair that this place was named "after himself." Basing themselves on this distnction, some scholars inferred from these verses that the name Havvot Yair was not viewed as identical to Yair. Hence they concluded that any addition to a person's name – in this case, the word Havvot – constitutes a new name which is distinct from the person's original name.[2]

Returning to the question raised above, a bride who is now called Rachel Leah is considered to have a completely new name, totally unrelated

---

[2] The same applies to toponyms. Joshua's oath, "Cursed by the Lord be the man who undertakes to fortify this city, Jericho" (Josh. 6:26), was interpreted in *Sanhedrin* 113a as a prohibition, inter alia, against building a different city by the name of Jericho. There is currently a settlement called Vered Yericho ("Rose of Jericho"); according to the thesis advanced here, this name poses no problem (even if we assume that Joshua's prohibition still applies today, an issue which requires further discussion). Cf. the ruling of R. Yoel Schwartz, *Tiferet Jericho* (Jerusalem 1994), p. 72, who, however, presents no arguments in support of this ruling.

to her former name, Rachel. This also accounts for the custom of some people to call people who have more than one name by all of their names. For example, if a person is named Reuven Shimon, they will always call him Reuven Shimon, and not simply Reuven or Shimon. We may also infer from this line of reasoning that the name Reuven Shimon is not the same as Shimon Reuven; rather, these are two entirely different names.[3]

It is interesting to note that three rabbis presented this argument: R. Baruch Epstein, author of *Torah Temimah*, in his commentary on the Torah, *Tosefet Berakhah*; R. Reuven Margaliyot, in his edition of the Testament of R. Judah he-Hasid; and R. Eliezer Silver, in the wake of the following incident.[4] When the first son of R. Yitzhak Ausband, head of the Telshe Yeshiva of Cleveland, was born, R. Yitzhak wanted to name him after his late father-in-law, R. Yitzhak Bloch, the rabbi of Telz. He was not sure, however, whether this would be proper, since he too was called Yitzhak Isaac, and according to Ashkenazic custom, a son should not share his father's name if the father is alive. R. Eliezer Silver ruled that it was permitted to name the son Avraham Yitzhak, since this name is totally different from the father's name (Yitzhak Isaac), and he adduced the above argumentation to support this ruling.

R. Baruch Epstein and R. Eliever Silver cited Deut. 3:14: "Yair son of Manasseh received the whole Argov district, that is, Bashan, as far as the boundary of the Geshurites and the Maakhathites, and he named it after himself (Heb. *'al shemo*) Havvot Yair, as is still the case." Note that the Torah is precise in its choice of words, saying *'al shemo*, which might be rendered literally as "*after* his name," as opposed to *bi-shemo*, which would be literally calling it by his name. This indicates that Havvot Yair was named after Yair, but was not his actual name. Interestingly, I have not found this linguistic distinction noted in lexica or grammars of Hebrew.

---

[3] See Margaliyot's notes, ibid.

[4] R. David Eliach, *Peninim mi-Shulhan Gavoah* (Jerusalem 1995) on the end of *Parashat Mattot*, who notes that he heard this from R. Avraham Ausband (I am indebted to my son Boaz, who referred me to this source). R. Eliach adds that he heard such a view attributed to R. Joseph Rozin, the Rogatchover Gaon, and to the Hazon Ish. Indeed, a similar ruling is cited by R. Shlomo Cohen, ed., *Sefer Pe'er ha-Dor*, 4 (Bnai Brak 1973), p. 200, albeit without any explicit proof from the Torah.

Further support for this distinction may be adduced from other texts:

1. "Now Absalom, in his lifetime, had taken the pillar in the Valley of the King and set it up for himself, for he said, 'I have no son to keep my name alive.' He had named the pillar after himself (*'al shemo*), and it has been called Absalom's Monument to this day" (II Sam. 18:18). In other words, since the site is called Absalom's Monument (*yad Avshalom*), this name is distinct from the name Absalom. Therefore the Torah says *'al shemo*, i.e., "after his name" = recalling his name.

2. Sometimes a name change is carried out by adding a few letters rather than an extra name. In such cases, too, the Torah uses the phrase *'al shemo*. For example, "Then he bought the hill of Samaria from Shemer for two talents of silver. He built [a town] on the hill and named the town which he built Samaria, after (*'al shem*) Shemer, the owner of the hill" (I Kings 16:24). Similar we read in Est. 9:26, "For that reason these days were named Purim, after (*'al shem*) the lot (*ha-pur*)." Here the difference between the two forms is a difference between singular and plural (*pur / purim*).

A seeming objection to this idea may be raised from Ex. 39:6: "They bordered the lazuli stones with frames of gold, engraved with seal engravings of the names (*'al shemot*) of the sons of Israel" (Ex. 39:6), and similarly from a later verse: "The stones corresponded to the names (*'al shemot*) of the sons of Israel: twelve, corresponding to their names; engraved like seals, each with its name, for the twelve tribes" (Ex. 39:14). These texts concern writing the names of the tribes on stone, with no change in the names, so why is the expression *'al shem* used here?

The answer is clear. The stones did not bear the names of the tribes, nor were they named after the tribes. What the Torah meant is that the names of the sons of Israel were engraved on these stones, as we see from the verses where the Jews were commanded to engrave these names: "Take two lazuli stones and engrave on them the names of the sons of Israel, six of their names on the one stone, and the names of the remaining six on the other stone, in the order of their birth" (Ex. 28:19).

Another seeming difficulty can be resolved in similar fashion. We read in Ezek. 48:31: "The gates of the city shall be three gates on the north, named for (*'al shemot*) the tribes of Israel: the Reuven Gate, one; the Judah Gate, one; the Levi Gate, one" (Ezek. 48:31). Here too the prophet meant that the names of the tribes should be written on the city gates; note that the structure of this verse is the same as we saw above.

The last verse which remains to be discussed deals with levirate marriage: "The first son that she bears shall be accounted to the dead brother ('al shem), that his name may not be blotted out in Israel" (Deut. 25:6). According to what we have seen so far, this verse might suggest that the newborn son should not be given the same name as the deceased brother, but rather a name that demonstrates some relationship to the name of the deceased.

The sages, however, interpreted this verse differently, as we read in *Yevamot* 24a:

> The rabbis taught: "Shall be accounted to the dead brother" – as regards inheritance. You might ask whether this regards inheritance, or perhaps only name? [In other words, if the deceased was called] Joseph, then [the newborn] is called Joseph; [if he was called] Yohanan, then [the newborn] is called Yohanan. Therefore the Torah says: "Shall be accounted to his brother," and elsewhere it says, "They shall be recorded [lit. "called"] instead of ('al shem) their brothers in their inheritance" (Gen. 48:6). Just as inheritance is meant there, so too inheritance is meant here.

In other words, it might be thought that the Torah requires the newborn son to be named after the deceased. However, the rabbis explained that this commandment has nothing to do with the child's name; rather, it means that the newborn should receive the inheritance of the deceased.[5] Hence it is appropriate to use the expression 'al shem here, rather than be-shem.

We conclude with a comment about another, related expression, found elsewhere in the Bible. Gen. 4:17 states: "Cain knew his wife, and

---

[5] Nahmanides ad loc. proves this interpretation on the basis of Boaz's words in Ruth 4:10: "I am also acquiring Ruth the Moabite, the wife of Mahlon, as my wife, so as to perpetuate the name of the deceased upon his estate, that the name of the deceased may not disappear from among his kinsmen"; note that the son born to them was named Oved, not Mahlon.

she conceived and bore Hanokh. And he then founded a city, and named the city like the name (*ke-shem*) of his son Hanokh." What is the difference between *ke-shem* (lit. "like the name") and *be-shem* ("by the name")? The answer is found in the following verse: "And they changed the name of Leshem to Dan, after (*ke-shem*) their ancestor Dan" (Josh. 19:47). The same subject is discussed in Judges, but there the Bible says: "And they named the town Dan, after (*be-shem*) their ancestor Dan" (Jud. 18:29). This clearly indicates that there is no difference between the words *be-shem* and *ke-shem*. Indeed, in both of these verses, the name was left unchanged, and therefore the term *be-shem* was certainly appropriate.

Parashat Mas'ei

GO'EL HA-DAM – THE BLOOD-AVENGER

Dr. Yair Barkai
Jerusalem

"THE BLOOD-AVENGER himself shall put the murderer to death; it is he who shall put him to death upon encounter" (Num. 35:19). *Parashat Mas'ei* mentions the blood-avenger several times in contexts dealing with premeditated murder and manslaughter. The concept of blood vengeance is not foreign to modern society; however, it is universally considered to be against the law. How are to we understand the Torah's attitude towards the avenger?[1]

Let us begin with basic definitions of the term. R. David Zvi Hoffmann's commentary on Deut. 19:6 explains the concept of the blood-avenger (Heb. *go'el ha-dam*) as follows: the primary meaning of the root *g-a-l* is to demand restitution of something one possessed before it was lost. The Bible uses this expression to refer to a claim on someone's life (cf. *doresh damim*, Ps. 9:13), i.e., to avenge. Thus, *go'el ha-dam* is a relative who avenges the blood of a family member.

Revenge, or *nekamah*, the act committed by the avenger, is defined as exacting punishment by grieving someone for having caused harm or insult. Revenge stems from an inner drive to get back at someone for an evil deed.

---

[1] For a discussion of the halakhic aspects of this law, see *Encyclopedia Talmudit*, s.v. *goel dam*; Aharon Shemesh, "'Al 'Arei ha-Miklat," *Mahanayim* 13 (1996), and "Mi Goleh le-'Arei Miklat," *Perot ha-Ilan* (Ramat-Gan 1998), p. 505; Menahem ben-Yashar, "Al Ta'am 'Arei Miklat," ibid., p. 506; Itamar Wahrhaftig, *Tehumin* 11 (1990), p. 326 ff., and idem, in *Ha-Zofeh*, 14 Tishre 5746 (1986). See also Moshe Reiss, *Hamodia*, 6 Av 5752 (1992).

Indeed, a parallel passage on this subject in *Parashat Shofetim* indicates the motive: "lest the avenger of blood pursue the slayer while his heart is hot with anger" (Deut. 19:6).

The roots of the commandment to take blood vengeance go back to Gen. 9:6: "Whoever sheds man's blood, by man shall his blood be shed." The symmetry of this verse suggests that blood vengeance contains an element of atonement for the moral wrong committed against the murdered person. This need for atonement is emphasized in the Bible several times, the first being after Abel's murder: "Your brother's blood cries out to Me from the earth" (Gen. 4:10); hence the oft-repeated phrase, "his blood shall be upon his own head" (e.g., Lev. 20:9, Josh. 2:19). If human beings fail to perform the responsibility that has been imposed on them, God will avenge the blood (e.g., Gen. 9:5; Deut. 32:43; II Kings 9:7; Ezek. 33:6).[2]

Following this earliest appearance in Scripture, however, the notion of blood vengeance is viewed with reservation. In his commentary on Genesis, M. D. Cassuto noted that "these passages convey an important message. Their seminal and innovative idea: *protest against the practice of blood vengeance*" (emphasis in the original, Y. B.)[3]...The laws of the Torah show a tendency to limit this practice...In cases of manslaughter, the law provides for cities of refuge to prevent acts of blood vengeance." Cassuto interpreted the words "if anyone kills Cain" (Gen. 4:15) in this spirit:

> Blood vengeance is forbidden. Here the Torah voices its opposition to the practice of blood vengeance common in the ancient Near East. The Lord alone is Judge of the entire earth. The right to pass sentence on murderers belongs to the human

---

[2] Several tales based on this commandment appear in rabbinic literature, e.g., the story about the blood of the prophet Zechariah in *Sanhedrin* 96b. On this story and its parallels, see Joseph Heinemann, *Aggadot ve-Toldoteihen* (Jerusalem 1974), p. 31 ff. There Heinemann cites the following story from *Deuteronomy Rabbah* 2.25: "Once there were two brothers, one of whom one killed the other. What did their mother do? She took a cup and filled it with his blood and placed it in the tower. Every day she came in and saw that the blood was bubbling. One day she came to look and found that the blood was still. At that moment she knew that her other son had been killed."

[3] *Commentary on Genesis* I (Jerusalem 1961), pp. 184–185.

judges who judge in His name, not to the relatives of a murderer acting in hot anger (ibid., p. 225).

Similarly, on Ex. 21:13, "If he did not do it by design, but it came about by an act of God, I will assign you a place to which he can flee," Cassuto writes:

> The Torah wishes to amend the ancient practice of blood vengeance and to express its opposition to the system reflected in the Code of Hammurabi (§229) that whoever causes the death of another person, even unintentionally, must be put to death (ibid., p. 188).

But if the Torah does not view the practice of blood vengeance positively, why did it establish such a commandment? What motivates this question, of course, is our discomfort with the "institution" of the blood-avenger itself. In effect, it is the responsibility of judicial bodies to exact judgment; if, after proper legal proceedings, the offense is proven to be premeditated murder, the court is authorized to execute the murderer. Why then does Torah law grant the blood-avenger the opportunity to carry out the sentence passed by the court? Is he given rein to shed blood solely under the assumption that he is in "hot anger"?

Shadal,[4] in his commentary on Num. 35:12, addresses this question:

> In early generations, before people accepted the jurisdiction of kings, officers, judges and magistrates, each family avenged its losses from other families; it was the role of the victim's closest relative to avenge his death. The Torah established judges and magistrates, thereby transferring revenge from the hands of individuals to the entire community. In case of premeditated murder, the avenger could be appeased with the assurance that the judges will handle the matter. They will investigate, and if [the

---

[4] Samuel David Luzzato, 1800–1865, biblical exegete, historian, philosopher, literary scholar, educator, and poet, one of the founders of the *Wissenschaft* movement.

suspect] deserves to die, they shall put him to death. In cases of manslaughter, however, the potential avenger could not be assuaged. To see his father's or brother's murderer go unpunished was unbearable. It would appear, in his own eyes and in the eyes of all who knew him, that he did not love his father or brother, since he was not avenging their death. This sort of view could be eradicated only gradually. And indeed, Divine Wisdom perceived that even if blood vengeance was punishable by death, that would not deter all blood-avengers, or even the majority of them, from avenging their relatives' murder. As a result, many people would be killed pointlessly. The measure the Torah took was, on the one hand, to permit the blood-avenger to avenge the death of a relative but, on the other hand, to establish a place of refuge to which the manslayer could flee, where he would be protected from the blood-avenger.

Shadal's remarks suggest that the Torah recognized the difficulty human beings have in breaking habits of long standing, and thus initiated a process of gradual education to alter their behavior in stages. First, people had to become accustomed to the existence of legal institutions and to accept their jurisdiction and authority to carry out sentences. One who committed manslaughter was not to be harmed unless, after having been exiled to a city of refuge, he failed to fulfill the Torah's command not to leave that city until the death of the current High Priest. The High Priest's death would atone for all sins committed unintentionally.

The restrictions the Torah placed on the commandment of blood vengeance thus appear to be didactic stages intended to free human beings from the primitive form of this practice. The allowance made for the blood-avenger would be temporary, until human beings reached a stage where they could be weaned of their desire to kill as a need for revenge.

Clearly, the ancient practice stemmed from natural human sentiments. The Torah permitted people to translate their feelings from theory to practice, but placed restrictions on them to engender more profound understanding of this issue. Ultimately, the Torah taught that one must strive to free oneself from the drive to express extreme anger in a destructive manner.

The same tendency can be seen in commandments regarding the "beautiful woman" (Deut. 21:10 ff.), the Hebrew slave (Ex. 21:1 ff.), the "urge to eat meat" (Deut. 12:20 ff.),[5] and, in Maimonides' view, the commandments regarding sacrifices (see *Guide for the Perplexed*, 3.32). All these are examples of "concessions" made by the Torah in a gradual process of education towards goals. Nechama Leibowitz, in *Studies in Devarim* (pp. 138–139), puts it as follows:

> It will perhaps sound odd to the reader to learn that the commandments of the Torah are not absolute. Surely it is one of the fundamental principles of the Torah that it will never be changed!...These dispensations, concessions to human frailty that they are, so long as man has not yet achieved the ideal of "all of them shall know Me," constitute the greatness of the Torah.

She quotes Rabbi Kook, *Talelei Orot*, chapter 8:

> In this lies the virtue of a morality anchored to its Divine source, in that it knows the correct timing for every design. Sometimes it withholds its impetus in order to husband its strength for a later period. But this the impatience of a morality divorced from its source cannot abide (p. 139).

In Nechama Leibowitz's understanding,[6] this means that "an autonomous ethic (divorced from religion) cannot feel its way gradually and cautiously and even sometimes make concessions. It does not possess the authority to make concessions. It knows only the categorical imperative, whereas the Torah knows graduated rules."

---

[5] See Rav Kook's famous remarks in *Talelei Orot*, chapter 8.

[6] Ibid., p. 130. See Leibowitz's comments on p. 187 ff., which provide the underlying ideas for this article.

In other words, the Torah restricted the practice of blood vengeance to the most narrow circumstances possible: the avenger was empowered to carry out the court's sentence, both in cases of deliberate homicide and unintentional manslaughter, *only* when the manslayer left the city of refuge. This served as a deterrent against the manslayer's leaving the place to which he had been sent by the court. The Sages restricted the biblical formulation even further. Mishnah *Makkot* 2.1 does not even mention the need to flee to a city of refuge, replacing the act of flight with punishment by exile: "These are they who go into exile." This led Nechama Leibowitz to conclude that "the cities of refuge were no longer needed as a protection against the angry pursuer since the blood-avenger no longer pursued his victim. This instinct of personal vendetta had been blunted" (ibid., p. 193).

A similar development[7] can be noted regarding the other commandments mentioned above. For example, the numerous restrictions placed on the owner of a Hebrew slave led the Talmud in *Kiddushin* 20a to conclude: "To buy a slave is like buying oneself a master." We can perceive this trend towards minimalization in two other contexts as well: Regarding a city that had been seduced to commit idolatry (Deut. 13:13–19) and a defiant son (Deut. 21:18–22), the Talmud says (*Sanhedrin* 71a): "Such a thing never happened and never will happen."

To conclude, we recall Rashi's comment on the verse, "When...you see among the captives a beautiful woman and you desire her and would take her to wife..." (Deut. 21:11). Based on the Talmud in *Kiddushin* 21b and *Tanhuma, Ki Tetze*, Rashi explains why the Torah allowed a man who had gone to war to marry a woman he desired:

> The Torah took the evil inclination into consideration, for if it were not permissible for him to [marry her], he would take her in violation of the law. Even if he marries her, though, in the end he will hate her. And thus the following verse says, "If a man has [two wives, one loved and the other unloved]" – she will bear him "a wayward and defiant son" (v. 15).

---

[7] On this trend and its moral implications, see my article, "Hebetim Musariyim be-Parshiyot Hilkhatiyot ba-Torah," *Mayim mi-Dalyav* (Jerusalem 2000), p. 7 ff.

The Torah, as teaching for life, was given to human beings, with all their shortcomings and weaknesses. Taking into consideration humankind's limited ability to control fundamental desires, the Torah accepted some of them while delimiting them with constraints and restrictions.[8] Its goal was to educate, step by step, toward ultimately achieving the ideal of moral perfection.

---

[8] Some want to rationalize the Torah's attitude towards all the above cases by citing the Sages' saying, "Scripture speaks of what is prevalent (*dibber hakatuv bahoveh*)." In my opinion this is incorrect for two reasons. First, this is a halakhic term which Bacher, *Erkhei Midrash*, defines thus: "Scripture spoke of one, usual circumstance, but actually refers to all cases which fall into that category." It seems to me that the cases discussed in this article do not suit such a definition. Second, we sought to group all the different cases together, representing a category for which the Torah establishes restrictions out of its displeasure at the practice. Thus the aforementioned term is not appropriate in these cases.

Sefer Devarim – The Book of Deuteronomy

Parashat Devarim

THE PEOPLE'S RESPONSIBILITY FOR THEIR LEADERS' ACTIONS

Dr. Itamar Wahrhaftig
Faculty of Law

MOSES' LENGTHY ORATION in the book of Deuteronomy contains numerous references to events from the past. The Sages viewed these as words of reproof.[1] Nahmanides wrote in his introduction to Deuteronomy: "Before beginning his explication of the Law, [Moses] sought to reproach them, reminding them of their sins – of how they had tried Him in the desert and of how the Lord had dealt mercifully with them – so that his words might prevent them from returning to their sinful ways." In light of these remarks, let us examine the first two stories in *Parashat Devarim*: the appointment of judges (1:9-18) and the incident of the spies (1:19-46). The appearance of these two stories at the beginning of Deuteronomy raises a number of questions:

1. Where is there an element of reproach in the appointment of judges? The original account of the incident in *Parashat Yitro* focuses on the issue of giving wise counsel, not on wrongdoing. If so, why is the matter recalled here?[2]

---

[1] See Rashi's quote of *Sifre* on Deut. 1:1.

[2] Rashi explains that the words "How can I myself alone bear your care, your burden and your strife" (v. 12) indicate that the Jews were burdensome and even heretical, distrusting Moses and filled with complaints. This would suggest that Moses' goal was indeed reproach.

2. Verse 14 reads: "You answered me and said, 'What you propose to do is good.'" The original account in *Parashat Yitro* contains not the slightest hint that the people participated in making these appointments.

3. In *Parashat Yitro*, Yitro himself takes the initiative; here we find no mention of him.[3]

4. Verse 16 presents commandments dealing with judicial procedure: "Hear out your fellow men.." What connection is there between the details of these commandments and the appointment of magistrates in the context of reproaching the people?

5. The appointment of magistrates is mentioned along with the story of the spies. Is there some relation between the two?

6. In this narrative, the initiative for sending the spies came from the people: "Then all of you came to me and said." In the original account in *Parashat Shelah*, no mention is made of the people either initiating the idea or sending the spies.[4]

7. Verse 25 reads: "And they gave us this report: 'It is a good land.'" In *Parashat Shelah*, in contrast, the spies are said to have calumniated the land.[5]

8. According to verse 29, Moses told the people not to fear the Canaanites; in *Parashat Shelah* there is no parallel to this encouragement.

In resolving these issues, we must recognize that the Torah may offer two disparate accounts of the same event, each account serving a separate function. These will differ in accordance with the specific context, including time, place and circumstances, in which it is recounted. What one story emphasizes might be omitted or glossed over in the other.

Silence as Consent

Let us begin by considering the appointment of judges. Here the primary objective was not reproach, but to teach the people the meaning of responsibility. Essentially, Moses' message was: Do not assume that all your

---

[3] See Nahmanides' commentary on v. 18.

[4] See Rashi's comments on the beginning of *Parashat Shelah*.

[5] Rashi explains that the people who gave the report in v. 25 ("they") were only Joshua and Caleb.

actions, for better or for worse, are the responsibility of your leaders rather than your own. It is wrong and undesirable to think that way. For if you have willingly accepted the initiative as a whole, you are party to it and must bear responsibility for it.

It is true that the original guiding force in appointing the magistrates was Yitro, but the people gave their consent. We can assume the people were consulted, as the second account suggests – "You answered me and said, 'What you propose to do is good.'" In *Parashat Yitro*, this detail was apparently not important; here it is stressed that the appointments were made with the people's consent, albeit not on their own initiative. This would explain the first three points we raised.

Before proceeding with the next points, let us consider the last questions regarding the spies. In both accounts, the spies convince the people that they are no match for the Canaanites; here, though, the people agree, accepting the spies' words. Thus they share the responsibility. Moses' reproof, then, was that they cannot claim the spies alone are to blame. For that reason, their story is not even presented here. We find only the first part of their report, that "it is a good land." The rest of the spies' report, including the calumnies they spread about the land, is not relevant here; it does nothing to mitigate the sin committed by the people.

Similarly, the initiative to send spies is presented differently here than in Numbers. Whether the initiative came from the people (Deuteronomy) or from God (Numbers), responsibility for the results of the mission lies with the people. The people could not evade the issue by claiming they were not the sole initiators. This answers points six and seven. Now we return to points four and five.

A Fair Hearing as the Response to the Spies

The relation between the account of appointing judges and the story of the spies seems to be that the first story prefaces the second. The Torah states that the magistrates must hear out both sides impartially and adjudicate between them (Deut. 1:16). Thus, when the spies returned in two opposing groups – two against ten – the people should have heard out "the small as well as the great," rather than considering the minority as lowly and unworthy of consideration. They should have ruled justly "between any man and a fellow Israelite or a stranger [*ger*]." Rashi explains that the stranger mentioned here is "one's opponent in the lawsuit who merely heaps [*oger*] words against him." If the spies wished to amass new arguments against the accepted view that the land is a good one and can be conquered by the Israelites, the burden of proof rested on them. And thus the commandment to "fear no man" follows immediately (v. 17), indicating that the people should not have been discouraged by the spies' contentions.

Moses continues by recognizing that the people may nevertheless be uncertain. In that case, he tells them, "Any matter that is too difficult for you you shall bring to me" (Deut. 1:17). In other words, they should have approached Moses with their misgivings in the expectation of receiving words of encouragement from Moses in the name of God, "for judgment is to the Lord." This explains the relationship between the two pericopes at the beginning of Deuteronomy, as well as the need for commanding the people regarding fair judicial procedure. Proper judgement, we learn, is the key to successfully meeting challenges, such as the challenge the spies posed to the people. In connection with our last point, we note that Moses indeed appealed to the people not to be swayed by the spies.[6] Here, too, his words about appointing judges must be understood as being equally relevant to the spies: their internal disagreement should have been perceived by the people as something "that is too difficult for you," so they should have appealed to Moses for a resolution of it.

This message is timeless. When a nation consents to decisions taken by their leaders, they bear common responsibility for actions taken and their results. Responsibility cannot be evaded by claiming that one was not an initiator or active agent. Silent consent or abstention from opposition makes the people party to an act or to the failure to act. The spies cannot shoulder the people's blame, nor does Yitro's appointment of the judges

---

[6] Why this was not mentioned in *Parashat Shelah* remains unclear. Nahmanides (on Num. 14:5) explains that the words "Then Moses and Aaron fell on their faces" mean that Moses and Aaron tried to persuade the people not to be swayed by the spies. Here, in contrast (Deut. 1:25), Nahmanides says that the words "Have no dread or fear of them" (v. 29) do not refer to past events. Rather, they are Moses' words at that moment, in the course of delivering his reproach.

detract from the people's credit. This message holds true for the ancient Israelites and for any nation or public body, past and present, as well.

Parashat Va-Ethanan

"A WISE AND DISCERNING PEOPLE"[1]

Rabbi Professor Carmi Horowitz
Midrashah for Women

OBSERVE THEM FAITHFULLY, for this will be proof of your wisdom and discernment to other peoples, who on hearing all these laws will say, "Surely, that great nation is a wise and discerning people." For what great nation is there that has a god so close at hand as is the Lord our God whenever we call upon Him? (Deut. 4:6–7).

What is the antecedent of "this" in the first verse cited above? Is the antecedent "observe them faithfully"? In other words, does the nations' admiration of the wisdom and discernment of Israel stem from their observing the commandments? This seems to be the idea behind the rabbinic homily in *'Avodah Zarah* (4b):

> Rabbi Joshua ben Levi said: All the commandments that Israel observe in this world will be a blow in the face of idolaters in the World to Come, as it is written: "Observe them faithfully, for that will be proof to other peoples of your wisdom and discernment" (Deut. 4:6). It does not say "before the peoples" (*neged ha-'ammim*), but "in the eyes of the peoples" (*le-'einei ha-'ammim*). This means

---

[1] This article is based on remarks by my teacher, Rabbi Professor Isadore Twersky of blessed memory. See his *Introduction to the Code of Maimonides* (New Haven 1980), pp. 380–387.

that they will strike the idolaters in their faces[2] in the World to Come.

The advantage Israel has over the other nations results from their adherence to the Torah and keeping of its commandments. Not the theory of Judaism but its practice, the actual performance of its precepts, is proof of Israel's wisdom and discernment: "Observe them faithfully."

This verse has a second and better-known interpretation, according to which the antecedent of "this" is not "observe them faithfully," but rather something not explicitly mentioned in the verse. The absence of this element compels the homilist to seek something that would appear "in the sight of the other peoples," in other words, something of universal value, even for those who have not studied the Torah. R. Johanan identified one such element: calculation of the calendar (lit. "seasons and the zodiac"), the so-called "secret of intercalation," or the principles of astronomy that underlie the Jewish calendar. In *Shabbat* 75a we read:

> Rabbi Samuel bar Nahmani said in the name of Rabbi Johanan: Whence do we know that men are commanded to calculate the seasons and the zodiac? As it is written, "Observe them faithfully, for that will be proof of your wisdom and discernment to other peoples" – this refers to calculating the seasons and the zodiac.

Maimonides cited Deut. 4:6 in two different contexts in his writings, thereby illustrating his views about two central themes in Jewish intellectual history.[3] The first context is Maimonides' introduction to *Perek Helek*, his extensive and important preface to his commentary on the last chapter of Mishnah *Sanhedrin*:

---

[2] Twersky (ibid., p. 382) explains that the expression "in their faces" suggests direct and unmediated confrontation.

[3] For a list of main themes in Jewish intellectual history, see Isadore Twersky, "Joseph ibn Kaspi – Portrait of a Medieval Jewish Intellectual," in *Studies in Medieval Jewish History and Literature* (Cambridge 1979), pp. 233–234.

All Israel have a share in the World to Come, as it is written,
"And your people, all of them righteous, shall possess the land for
all time; they are the shoot that I planted, My handiwork in which
I glory" (Is. 60:21). But those who have no share in the World to
Come include all who contend that the resurrection of the dead is
not taught in the Torah and all heretics.

Two ideas troubled Maimonides: defining the World to Come, and defining
the term *apikoros* (heretic). Let us begin by considering the first of these
ideas.

To understand what the Sages meant by the World to Come, we must
first clarify how their homilies should be read and interpreted. The Sages'
attitude towards *aggadah*, or legend, is a central theme in Jewish intellectual
history. The status of *aggadah*, its authority, the methods of interpreting it
and defending it against attack – all these issues have been a part of Torah
scholarship from the earliest days to the present. A central theme of the
utmost importance for Maimonides was the correct reading and
appreciation of aggadic homilies, many of which are obscure and difficult
to understand based on a superficial, simplistic reading. He addressed this
subject in various contexts.[4]

In his introduction to *Perek Helek*, Maimonides categorized readers
according to their attitude towards aggadic midrash. The first group was
described as follows:

In my observation, this group comprises the majority. Their
works and what I have heard of them suggests that they accept
[aggadic midrash] at face value, with no glance at hidden
meanings; they view everything, however unlikely, as necessarily
true. Indeed, their folly and ignorance leads them to this. They are
unable to become aware of their failings, and no one has yet been
found to awaken them. They believe that the Sages, in all their
upright and proper words, meant nothing more than what they

---

[4] See the introduction to his *Commentary on the Mishnah, Guide to the Perplexed*, and his
Iggerot.

themselves are capable of understanding through their own superficial reading. Indeed, some of the Sages' words may well sound outrageous and even senseless were they recounted to common folk, not to mention to the wise. With a bit of reflection, they themselves might wonder how anyone could possibly say such things or presume them to be correct beliefs. This class of the intellectually weak is to be lamented for their foolishness. In so considering the Sages with their limited resources, they actually degrade them without realizing what they are doing. Such people obscure the Torah's glory and tarnish its radiance; God's teaching is reversed, its meaning confounded. For God, in His perfect Torah, promised that if they observe all these laws, everyone will recognize that that great nation is a wise and discerning people. But when this group presents the Sages' teachings, the peoples of the world listen and respond: How foolish and stupid is this little nation. These preachers teach the masses, interpreting things they do not grasp. Better they should be silent, as they have neither knowledge nor understanding, as it is said: "If you would be quiet, it would be considered wisdom on your part" (Job 13:5). Alternately, they should admit: We do not understand what the Sages meant by these words, or how to interpret them. But they presume to understand them and attempt to teach the people as well, misrepresenting the Sages' words. And they preach from Tractate *Berakhot*, *Perek Helek* and the like according to their plain sense, word for word.

We note that in making the verse which speaks of the Jews being a "wise and discerning people" a pivotal part of his text, Maimonides ascribed a crucial role to the interpretation of *aggadah*. In the Sages' search for an area of universal significance in interpreting this verse, they cited the calculation of the calendar; Maimonides ascribed a similar critical role to understanding *aggadah* correctly. Profound and philosophical interpretation centered on uncovering the abstract principles concealed in the *aggadah* leads to a revelation of the universal aspect of the Torah. It is this aspect that will cause other nations to realize the depth of meaning concealed in rabbinic thought and to respond, "Surely, that great nation is a wise and discerning people." A rational or philosophical reading of *aggadot* that cannot be understood literally is a sanctification of God and His Torah.[4] Simplistic literal interpretation engenders a converse reaction and a profanation of all that is holy. This preface empowered Maimonides to deal with those rabbinic *aggadot* that seem to describe the World to Come in physical terms.

Reasons for the Commandments

The second context in which Maimonides quoted our verse is *Guide for the Perplexed*, 3.31:[5]

> Some people consider it grievous that reasons should be given for any law; what would please them most is that the intellect would not find a meaning for the commandments and prohibitions. What compels them to feel thus is a sickness in their souls, a sickness to which they are unable to give utterance and of which they cannot furnish a satisfactory account. For they think that if those laws were useful in this existence and had been given to us for this or that reason, it would be as if they stemmed from the reflection and the understanding of some intelligent being. If, however, there is a thing for which the intellect could not find any meaning at all and that does not lead to something useful, it indubitably derives from God; for the reflection of man would not lead to such a thing. It is as if, according to these people of weak intellects, man were more perfect than his Maker. For man speaks and acts in a manner that leads to some intended end, whereas the Deity does not act thus, but commands us to do things that are not useful to us and forbids us to do things that

---

[4] On different medieval approaches to interpreting *aggadah*, see Isadore (Yitzhak) Twersky, "Rabbi Yedaiah ha-Penini and his Commentary on the Aggadah," in *Studies in Jewish Religious and Intellectual History Presented to Alexander Altmann*, edited by Raphael Loewe and Siegfried Stein (Alabama 1980), pp. 63–82. For a helpful survey of attitudes towards rabbinic *aggadot*, see Jacob Elboim, *Le-Havin Divrei Hakhamim: Mivhar Divrei Mavo la-Aggadah ve-la-Midrash mi-Shel Hakhmei Yemei ha-Beinayim* (Jerusalem 2001), and the literature cited there. See also my review of this book in the *Jewish Quarterly Review*.

[5] Cited in I. Twersky, *A Maimonides Reader* (New York 1972), pp. 326–327.

are not harmful to us. But He is far exalted above this...the whole purpose consists in what is useful for us, as we have explained on the basis of what is written: "For our lasting good and for our survival, as is now the case" (Deut. 6:24). And it is written: "Who on hearing of all these laws [*hukkim*] will say, Surely that great nation is a wise and discerning people." Thus it is stated explicitly that even all the statutes [*hukkim*] will show all the nations that they have been given with wisdom and understanding. Now if there is a thing for which no reason is known and which does not either procure something useful or ward off something harmful, why should one say of one who believes in it or practices it that he is wise and understanding and of great worth?[6] Rather things are indubitably as we have mentioned.

This passage from *Guide for the Perplexed* follows several chapters about the reasons for the commandments. Chapter 31, cited here, ostensibly adds nothing to clarify Maimonides' position in the previous chapters. There he argues that it is inconceivable that God, the source of wisdom, would command actions not based on wisdom. The innovation in this chapter would thus be in Maimonides' use of the verse under discussion, specifically in its reference to *hukkim*, i.e., religious statutes that have no evident explanation in terms of human reason. In citing our verse, Maimonides suggests that discovering the reasons for the commandments guides us to uncovering the universal foundations underlying them. As a result, other nations come to appreciate the wisdom of the Torah, and the Name of God is sanctified in the world. When we show that not only the laws (*mishpatim*) but also the statutes (*hukkim*) have rational significance, we

---

[6] As Twersky noted, this was already suggested by Ibn Ezra in his *Yesod Mora*, chapter 8 (see the new edition edited by Joseph Cohen and Uriel Simon: *R. Abraham Ibn Ezra, Yesod Mora ve-Sod ha-Torah* [Ramat-Gan 2002], p. 150: "Thus a wise person may know many reasons for laws in the Torah, some of them evident and others clear only to one person in a thousand. Our master Moses, of blessed memory, said of all the commandments, 'Surely, that great nation is a wise and discerning people,' and if the precepts did not have discernible reasons, how would other peoples recognize them as righteous laws and those who observe them as wise?"

cause the Name of God to be sanctified and cause the entire world to appreciate our Torah.[7]

In Maimonides' view, our verse is to be interpreted as evidence for the philosophical substructure of *aggadah* or for the rationale behind the commandments. Our status in the eyes of the nations is based on wisdom and reason. Maimonides thus followed the approach of the Sages in seeking the universal elements of the Torah, those aspects that spur acknowledgement and admiration – "Surely, that great nation is a wise and discerning people."

---

[7] Cf. Twersky (above n. 1), ch. 6, for an exhaustive discussion of the reasons for the commandments in Maimonides' thought. See also his "Berur Divrei ha-Rambam Hilkhot Me'ilah Perek 8, Halakhah 8 – le-Parashat Ta'amei ha-Mitzvot la-Rambam," in *Perakim be-Toledot ha-Hevrah ha-Yehudit bi-Yemei ha-Beinayim u-va-'Et ha-Hadashah Mukdashim le-Professor Ya'akov Katz*, ed. Emanuel Etkes and Joseph Salmon (Jerusalem 1980), pp. 24–33.

Parashat Ekev

How Many Arks Were There?

Dr. Itamar Wahrhaftig
Faculty of Law

Deut. 10:1–5, which discusses the second set of tablets, raises numerous questions. Here we shall deal with questions relating to the ark of the Torah.

Why is the ark mentioned four times in such a short passage? Why is it emphasized that the ark is made of wood? In verse 3 we are told that Moses made an ark of acacia wood. Was this the same ark that was in the Tabernacle?

Several solutions have been offered to these questions. Nahmanides, in his commentary on these verses, maintains that this ark is the same one mentioned in the commandment to build the Tabernacle, and that God commanded the Jews to build the Tabernacle before the episode of the golden calf took place. The primary reason for the Tabernacle's construction was for the sake of the ark it housed. Moses was commanded to prepare the ark before he received the first set of tablets, and he was commanded to prepare the same ark again for the second tablets. This repetition led Moses to infer that the commandment regarding the Tabernacle remained in force. According to this interpretation, the ark mentioned here is the same ark of acacia wood mentioned in the passage on the Tabernacle (*Parashat Terumah*).

One difficulty with this interpretation is that if this commandment is simply a repetition of the commandment to build the ark of the Tabernacle, this repetition was performed in a rather indirect manner. Moreover, verse 4 states that Moses placed the tablets in the ark, but in fact he first placed them in the Tent of Meeting, where they would have lain until the ark was constructed. Another difficulty is that Moses is claimed here to be the builder of the ark, while according to *Parashat Vayakhel* (Ex. 27:1) the person who built the ark was Betzalel.

Rashi claims that this ark had no connection with the Tabernacle, which the Jews had not yet been commanded to build. Rather, this was a temporary ark intended to serve until the ark of the Tabernacle was completed. Why, then, was its existence recorded if it was only temporary? Rashi explains that this ark had to be taken out when the Israelites went out to battle. Nahmanides, however, maintains that this is a minority view, followed only by Rabbi Judah ben Lakish, as cited in the Jerusalem Talmud (*Sotah* 8.3 and *Shekalim* 6.1). The fragments of the first tablets were said to rest within the ark.[1]

Rashi's interpretation indicates that the ark was taken out to war. This view is supported by other sources as well, but we cannot go into further detail about this here.[2]

Nahmanides explains that according to the view of the Sages in the Jerusalem Talmud (ibid.), there was only one ark. It contained both the second tablets and fragments of the first tablets. That ark was not generally removed from the Tabernacle or the Temple to be taken out to battle. It was taken out to battle once, in the days of Eli, and was captured (I Sam. 4).[3]

---

[1] Nahmanides asked where this ark was kept, for the Torah speaks of only one ark that was kept in the Tabernacle and the Temple. One possibility is that the fragments of the first tablets were always kept in the ark in the Tabernacle. Only in time of war were they taken out and a wooden ark built to hold them and to take them out to battle. *Tosafot 'Eruvin* 63b and Rabbenu Bahya's commentary here (*Parashat 'Ekev*) explain that Moses' ark as described here was put away when the Temple was built, and from then on the fragments of the tablets were kept in the ark made by Betzalel that was kept in the Temple.

[2] See Num. 10:33 and Rashi ad loc.; Num. 14:44; Deut. 20:4 and Rashi ad loc.; Josh. 6:2; I Sam. Ch. 4; I Sam. 14:18; II Sam 11:11; and Mishnah *Sotah* 8.1.

[3] Several of the sources are explained in the Jerusalem Talmud, *Sotah* (ibid.): "A verse from Scripture supports the Sages' argument: 'Woe to us! Who will save us from the power of this mighty God?' (I Sam. 4:8) – they had never seen such a thing in their lives." In other words, the ark was not generally taken out of the camp to battle.

In his critique of Maimonides' *Sefer ha-Mitzvot* (§3) Nahmanides remarks that the ark may be carried forth in "future battles before King Messiah, as Phinehas did in the battle against Midian, for it is written that he was 'equipped with the sacred utensils' (Num. 31:6). This was interpreted in *Sifre* as referring to the ark."

If so, the wooden ark mentioned in this week's reading was a temporary ark that served until it was stored away, when the Tabernacle and its ark were built. Hence the Torah's emphasis that this was a wooden ark, not covered with gold. In other words, it was not the ark built by Betzalel. In this view, the ark was not ordinarily taken out to battle, and any evidence to the contrary requires further analysis.

This dispute might have ideological underpinnings. According to Rashi, all the battles fought by Israel were sacred, so they were all won with the aid of the ark. As he explains in his commentary on Deut. 20:4: "'For it is the Lord your God who marches with you to do battle for you' – this refers to the camp of the ark." Compare Rashi's comment on *Sanhedrin* 20b that Israel's demand for a king to lead them in battle had been made by the common folk. This led to their downfall, as all battles belonged to God.

According to Nahmanides, however, battles are governed by natural law. Thus the request of the Israelites to dispatch scouts was not a sin (so Nahmanides on the beginning of *Parashat Shelah*). Only in specific battles was the ark necessary.[4]

Maimonides' approach on this issue and the views of other *Rishonim* require further consideration. We will leave them for another occasion.

---

[4] This explanation is more appropriate according to the view that the ark was not always taken out to war.

Parashat Re'eh

FORBIDDEN FOODS

Yaron Seri
Department of Arabic

AMONG THE SUBJECTS discussed in this week's reading are the forbidden foods, mentioned earlier in *Parashat Shemini*. Among the forbidden animals is the swine (Deut. 14:8). This animal bears a similar name in various Semitic languages: *hazir* in Hebrew, *hazira* in Aramaic, and *hanzir* in Arabic. *Sus Scrofa* is the current scientific identification of the animal.[1] The Torah mentions the swine specifically because it is the only creature in the entire animal kingdom that has a cloven hoof but does not chew its cud.[2] As the Sages put it, "He who rules His world knows that nothing else has a cloven hoof and is unclean; therefore the Bible names it explicitly" (*Hullin* 59a).

The swine symbolizes all that is ugly and repulsive: "Like a gold ring in the snout of a pig" (Prov. 11:22). This impression is transmitted in R. Saadiah Gaon's translation of Isaiah, which makes the pig a metaphor of ugliness: "Who eat the flesh of swine" (Is. 65:4) = "Who eat what resembles the flesh of swine"; "who present as oblation the blood of swine" (Is. 66:3) = "and whose oblations are like the blood of swine." So

---

[1] For further information on swine and archaeological findings in Israel from various periods, see *Encyclopedia Mikra'it*, 3.90–94, s.v. *hazir*. On pig farming in the land of Israel after the Roman period, see B. Rosen, "Gidul Hazir be-Eretz Israel le-Ahar ha-Tekufah ha-Romit," *Cathedra* 78 (1996), pp. 25–42.

[2] Amru ibn al-Bahar al-Jahth, *Kitab al-Hayuan*, 4 (Beirut 1955), p. 52, cites Aristotle as saying that some pigs do not have cloven hoofs.

base is the pig's image that many fastidious Jews refrain from calling it by name, using instead the euphemism *davar aher*, "another thing."[3]

The Sages compared the Roman regime to swine: "'Also the swine' – this refers to the wicked nation of Edom."[4] And the Koran speaks of people whom God cursed, turning them in His wrath into monkeys and swine.[5]

Like the swine, the dog is also considered to be a most despicable creature. The two are sometimes mentioned together to express disgust. For example, "Who immolate dogs, who present as oblation the blood of swine" (Is. 66:3); "one who raises dogs is like one who raises swine" (*Bava Kama* 83a); "likewise a proselyte who received dogs and swine in his inheritance" (*Bava Kama* 80a); "there is nothing poorer than a dog, and nothing richer than a pig" (*Shabbat* 155b). The New Testament makes similar associations: "For them the proverb has proved true: 'The dog returns to its vomit,' and 'The sow, after a wash, rolls in the mud again'" (II Peter 2:22); "'Don't give dogs what is holy; don't throw pearls before swine'" (Matthew 7:6).

In Jewish tradition, the pig symbolizes forbidden foods in general. This is true in Islam as well: the proscription against eating swine flesh appears in the Koran four times.[6] Al-Jahth believed that this proscription stems from the fact that before the spread of Islam, many Arabs used to eat swine because of the excellence of its flesh. Thus swine were mentioned explicitly in the Koran, unlike other animals such as the dog and the monkey; these were not singled out, presumably because they were not commonly eaten due to their repulsive nature.[7] Al-Antakhi cites a different reason for the proscription: in the period before Islam it was customary to sell the flesh of human corpses, passing it off as pork.

---

[3] For the origins of this custom, see *Berakhot* 43b.

[4] *Leviticus Rabbah* 13.5. Compare *Tanhuma, Shemini* 14.

[5] *Sura al-Maida*, v. 60. Commentators explain that the souls of these people were reincarnated in the bodies of monkeys and pigs.

[6] *Sura al-Bikra*, v. 173; *Sura al-Maida*, v. 3; *Sura al-Anaam*, v. 145; *Sura al-Nahal*, v. 115.

[7] Al-Jahth, 4, p. 41.

Concerning the Torah's proscription, Maimonides cited medical and hygienic reasons:

> Let me say that the foods which the Torah forbade us are, all of them, very bad in terms of nutrition. Do not think that all the forbidden foods are harmful save for the swine and the fatty parts. This is not so, for the swine is overly moist and extremely fatty. Moreover, the Torah found it disgusting because of its excessive filth, as it feeds itself on garbage. We know full well how strict the Torah was about the sight of filth, even in the encampment in the wilderness, and all the more so in urban places. Were we to raise swine for food, our markets and even our homes would become filthier than a latrine, as can be observed in certain lands even now. As we know, the Sages have said: "The mouth of the swine is like feces on the move" (*Berakhot* 25a).[8]

According to Maimonides, swine and animal fat are the only things the Torah forbids that one could mistakenly assume to have no negative effects. And yet these foods are actually harmful to the body, despite their widespread popularity as delicacies. Eating swine is forbidden for hygienic reasons as well,[9] although Maimonides remarks more than once in his medical works that pork was widely thought to be the best meat of any animal.

Loewinger noted this seeming contradiction in Maimonides' writings and attempted to resolve it.[10] Al-Antakhi's medical treatise remarks that the finest meat is that of the "black pig" (i.e., wild boar), with its thick, hairy

---

[8] *Guide for the Perplexed*, 3.48.

[9] Cf. *Kiddushin* 49b: "Ten measures of plagues descended to the world; nine of them went to swine, and the tenth went to the rest of the world."

[10] Y. Loewinger, "Ha-Ma'akhalot ha-Asurot ve-Ta'ameihem lefi ha-Rambam," *Mehkerei Yerushalayim be-Mahashevet Yisrael* 2 (1983), pp. 515–528. Loewinger suggests that Maimonides' statements about the virtues of pork refer solely to its medicinal value. Use of pork as a medication was permitted. Indeed, a pregnant woman who has a craving for pork may eat it until she feels satisfied (*Yoma* 82a).

coat, when it is no more than two years old.[11] He claims that pork has a certain sweetness and that the flesh of swine is preferable to its fat. Unlike Maimonides, Al-Antakhi believed that pork had medicinal value "in that it generates blood and balances the humors, opening blockages and removing leanness; when digested, its nutritional value is maximal, as it is the animal most similar to the human humor."[12] Nevertheless, Al-Antakhi noted that when pork is not eaten together with wine, it can cause chronic headaches, "elephant's disease,"[13] arthritis, exhaustion, or abdominal distress.[14] Medieval medicine made use of most parts of the pig: its liver, gall, fat, heel, blood, and even its feces and urine.

Although the pig [*hazir*] is the most disdained and repulsive of creatures, midrashic tradition says: "The Holy One, blessed be He, will ultimately restore it to us" [*le-hahaziro*].[15] Variants of this Midrash state that God will "restore its former glory" [*le-hahazir atarah le-yoshnah*],[16] or that He "will restore it to us" or "will restore it to Israel."

Interestingly, this Midrash does not appear in the Babylonian Talmud or the Jerusalem Talmud. It is not found in early midrashic sources, and there is no trace of it in early rabbinic sources. How, then, did it find its way into the works of important exegetes such as Rabbenu Bahya, Ritba, Abarbanel, Recanati, *Or Ha-Hayyim* and others? Many suggestions have been made.[17] In one view, the flesh of the swine will become permitted only after God gives that animal its missing indicator of *kashrut* – chewing its cud. In another view, pork would be permitted only temporarily, as an

---

[11] Al-Antakhi, p. 132.

[12] Cf. *Ta'anit* 21b: "Swine is different, since its intestines are similar to those of human beings."

[13] A disease that causes inflammation of the calf and foot due to abscesses. Medieval Arab medical literature mentions a skin disease called *hanazir* ("pigs"), apparently characterized by large abscesses that developed around the back of the neck.

[14] Al-Antakhi, p. 132.

[15] *Midrash ha-Gadol* on Lev. 11.7 (ed. Steinsaltz, p. 249).

[16] *Midrash Tanhuma, Shemini* 12.

[17] For a comprehensive discussion of the views on this issue, see H. Karlinsky, "He-Hazir ve-'Hetero' le-'Atid Lavo," *Shanah be-Shanah* (1972), pp. 243–254.

emergency measure, just as it had been permitted in the time of the conquest of the land of Israel (*Hullin* 17a).

Most scholars today doubt the authenticity of the latter statement, seeing it as a falsification or distortion of the text, which echoes Christian bias.[18] Steinsaltz, however, holds that this statement is authentic.[19] He bases his opinion on a similar passage from *Kohelet Rabbah* (on Eccl. 1:9), where the phrase is missing. Its absence creates a missing link, and the sense of the following text is thus distorted. Steinsaltz surmises that these words disappeared from the text of other midrashim due to internal censorship, to prevent heretics from denying the eternal validity of the Torah.

---

[18] Thus, the Christians argued that the Torah was no longer valid, and hence claimed that the prohibition against eating pork no longer applied. As proof of this argument, they cited the rabbinic statement that "the Holy One, blessed be He, will ultimately restore it to us."

[19] A. Steinsaltz, "'Atid ha-Kadosh Barukh Hu le-Hahaziro," *Tarbiz* 36 (1967), pp. 297–298.

Parashat Re'eh

"MIKKETZ" – BEGINNING OR END?

Rabbi Judah Zoldan
Midrashah for Women

THE EXACT MEANING of the Torah's words concerning remission of debts during the sabbatical year – "every seventh year you shall practice remission of debts" (Deut. 15:1) – is disputed. The Hebrew expression used here, *mikketz sheva' shanim*, could be rendered literally as "at the end of seven years." The question is which year "end" is meant – the beginning of the seventh year, or the end of the seventh year? *Sifre* Deuteronomy 111 states:

> "Every seventh year" – does that mean the beginning of the year or the end? We could argue as follows: the word *ketz* (end) here also appears further on (Deut. 31:10). In the latter instance, *ketz* means at the end and not the beginning; thus, here too, *ketz* means at the end and not the beginning.

Similarly, the Talmud states: "The sabbatical begins at the end of the year, as it is written, 'At the end of seven years you shall have a remission'" (*'Arakhin* 28b). But the *Tosefta* says: "When is the *prosbul* written? On the eve of the New Year of the seventh year" (*Tosefta Shevi'it* 8.10). A variant text, however, reads: "the eve *after* the New Year at the end of the seventh year."[1]

---

[1] S. Lieberman, *Tosefta ki-Fshutah*, 2 (New York 1945), pp. 592–593, notes that several manuscripts and Rishonim cite an alternate version of the Tosefta, which reads "on

Ibn Ezra notes in several places in his commentary on the Bible that the word *mikketz* can be interpreted either as beginning or end. Thus, he writes about Num. 13:25, which states that "At the end of [*mikketz*] forty days [the spies] returned from scouting the land": "Sometimes *mikketz* denotes the beginning, and sometimes *mikketz* is the end." Similarly, regarding Moses' descent from Mt. Sinai, where the Torah states: "At the end [*mikketz*] of those forty days and forty nights, the Lord gave me the two tablets of stone, the Tablets of the Covenant" (Deut. 9:11), Ibn Ezra comments: "At the end or at the beginning of the forty days."

Elsewhere, however, Ibn Ezra is more decisive, interpreting *ketz* as the beginning. For example, in this week's reading, Ibn Ezra writes regarding the commandment to take tithes out of one's house at the "end" (*miktzeh*) of three years (14:28): "At the end [*miktzeh*] – at the beginning." Similarly with regard to our verse about debt remission, Ibn Ezra comments: "At the beginning of the year, as I have explained. And the proof is the verse: 'Gather the people'" (Deut. 31:12). Ibn Ezra's prooftext here is based on the law of *hakhel*, when the people were assembled for a festive Torah reading once every seven years; here too the Torah uses the expression *mikketz sheva' shanim* ("at the end of seven years," Deut. 31:10). This presumably means every seven years (JPS) at the *beginning* of the year, in light of the reference here to reading the Torah "on Sukkot," which is only two weeks after the New Year (Rosh Hashanah). Ibn Ezra reiterates this interpretation in his commentary on Deut. 31:11, where the law of *hakhel* appears: "'Every seventh year, the year set for remission, on the Sukkot holiday' – at the beginning of the year."[2]

Elsewhere, Ibn Ezra proves his point from the verse, "In the seventh year [*mikketz sheva' shanim*] each of you must release any fellow Hebrew who may be sold to you; when he has served you six years, you shall set him free" (Jer. 34:14). According to the Torah, a Hebrew servant is released after six years, at the beginning of the seventh year. Here Ibn Ezra explains: "He shall work for six years and no more, and at the beginning of the

---

the eve of the New Year of the seventh year." Other manuscripts attest another variant, "at the close of the seventh year."

[2] A similar interpretation is given by Ibn Ezra on Ex. 31:13 and in the commentaries attributed to him on Ps. 119:96 and Est. 2:12.

seventh year from the time he was sold he shall go free, no matter which year it is. And do not be puzzled by the wording in Jeremiah, which speaks of 'the end [*mikketz*] of seven years,' for everything has two ends or extremes. Sometimes the meaning is the beginning, and elsewhere the end" (Ibn Ezra on Ex. 21:2).[3] In practice, remission of debts is generally agreed to take place at the end of the seventh year, and therefore a *prosbul* is customarily written just before the beginning of the eighth year of the sabbatical year cycle.[4]

Ibn Ezra's view that remission of debts should take place at the beginning of the seventh year accords with his comments elsewhere. Nehemiah 5:1–5 tells of popular complaints against Jews who exploited their fellow Jews because of their debts. The commentary attributed to Ibn Ezra[5] (on Neh. 5:9) states: "This happened during the year of remission (=the sabbatical year), and therefore the people cried out." The masses apparently understood that the wealthy Jews who had given loans had no intention of remitting the debts, as the Torah demands, and this caused an outcry. This outcry erupted during the construction of the wall around Jerusalem, which commenced on the third of Av and concluded on 25 Elul

---

[3] Certain commentators have challenged Ibn Ezra's view, especially concerning remission of debts. See e.g. R. Meir Leibush Malbim, *Ha-Torah ve-ha-Mitzvah* on Deut. 15:1, but see R. Barukh Halevi Epstein, *Torah Temimah* on Deut. 15:1. Rabbi Jonathan Eybeschutz, *Sefer Urim ve-Tumim*, 67.26, interpreted Ibn Ezra as meaning that beginning with the onset of the seventh year, the lender cannot demand repayment of a debt, but if the borrower wishes to repay him, the lender is not obliged to forgo the debt. This follows the approach of Rabbenu Asher (Rosh), *Gittin*, 4.18: "Heaven forbid that we attribute even a suspicion of heresy to [Ibn Ezra], as if he opposed the Sages, who held that remission of debts takes place at the end of the sabbatical year." R. Israel of Shklov, *Pe'at ha-Shulhan*, *Beit Yisrael*, in his discussion of the laws of *prosbul* (§96) wrote: "The saintly Ibn Ezra's reputation is unstained. He explained the plain sense of Scripture." Others, however, suspected Ibn Ezra of taking a position similar to that of the Karaites, who held that *mikketz* meant "from the beginning." See D. Henshke, "Eimatai Hu Zemano Shel Hakhel?" *Sefer Hakhel* (Kefar Darom 2001), p. 454. For further discussion of Ibn Ezra's position, see R. Yeshayahu Hadari, *Shabbat u-Mo'ed ha-Shevi'it* (Jerusalem 1986), pp. 71–79.

[4] So Maimonides, *Hilkhot Shemitah ve-Yovel*, 9.4; *Shulhan Arukh, Hoshen Mishpat* 67.30. For a survey of the sources, see R. Ovadiah Yosef, *Yehaveh Da'at*, 4.62. Some people today are especially stringent and make a *prosbul* before the beginning of the seventh year.

[5] Some scholars attribute this commentary to R. Moses Kimhi. See A. Weiser, *Perushei ha-Torah le-R. Abraham Ibn Ezra* (Jerusalem 1977), p. 15.

(Neh. 6:15). This shows that this event took place towards the end of the year.

Now, computing the years and the events that took place according to rabbinic sources, we discover that this took place towards the end of the sixth year, on the eve of the sabbatical year, in accordance with Ibn Ezra's view that the remission of debts takes place at the beginning of the sabbatical year. Specifically, construction of the wall commenced with Nehemiah's arrival in Israel, in the twentieth year of the reign of Artaxerxes (Neh. 2:1, 5:14). Earlier, in the seventh year of the king's reign, in the month of Av, Ezra had returned to Israel (Ezra 7:7–9). According to Rav Ashi, the Jews began calculating the sabbatical year anew upon Ezra's return ('Arakhin 13a), and the reckoning of the sabbatical year commenced on the new year after Ezra's arrival.[6] The eighth year of the king's reign was the first year in the reckoning of the sabbatical year. Thus the fourteenth year of the king's reign was the first sabbatical year during the Second Temple period, and the twenty-first year of his reign was the second sabbatical year of the Second Temple period. We may therefore conclude that the twentieth year, when Nehemiah returned to Israel and the people cried out against exploitation and usury, was the sixth year of the cycle, on the eve of the sabbatical year. Bearing in mind Ibn Ezra's contention that remission of debts took place at the beginning of the sabbatical year, when the people realized there would be no remittance of debts, the reason for the popular outcry becomes clear.

---

[6] The following discussion follows Rashi on 'Arakhin, ibid. For the computation of the years according to the views of Rashi, Rabbenu Gershom, and Maimonides, see E. Shulman, Seder Shemitot ve-Yovelot (Kol Mevasser 2001), pp. 53–60.

Parashat Shofetim

"YOU MUST NOT DEVIATE"

Prof. Hannah Kasher
Department of Philosophy

IF A CASE IS TOO BAFFLING for you to decide, you shall appear before the levitical priests or the magistrate in charge at the time. You shall act in accordance with the instructions given you and the ruling handed down to you. You must not deviate from the verdict they announce to you either to the right or to the left (Deut. 17:8–11).

What sort of "deviating" was prohibited here?[1] Maimonides and Nahmanides disagreed about this. Based on the context of this passage, Maimonides identified three principal elements to this prohibition (*Hilkhot Mamrim* 1.2; see also *Sefer ha-Mitzvot*, positive commandment 174):

"In accordance with the instructions given you" – (A) these are the regulations, decrees, and practices that the rabbis instructed the masses in order to strengthen their faith and improve the world. "And the ruling handed down to you" – (B) these are

---

1   See especially H. Henokh, *Ha-Ramban ke-Hoker u-khe-Mekubbal* (Jerusalem 1978), pp. 355–360; M. Idel, "R. Moshe ben Nahman – Kabbalah, Halakhah u-Manhigut Ruhanit," *Tarbiz* 64 (1995), pp. 535–580; S. Rosenberg, *Lo Ba-Shamayim Hi* (Alon Shevut 1997); Y. D. Silman, *Kol Gadol ve-Lo Yasaf* (Jerusalem 1999); Y. Blidstein, *Samkhut u-Meri be-Hilkhot ha-Rambam* (Tel Aviv 2002); Havivah Pedayah, *Ha-Ramban – Hit'alut, Zeman Mahzori ve-Text Kadosh* (Tel Aviv 2003); E. Wolfson, "By the Way of Truth: Aspects of Nahmanides' Kabbalistic Hermeneutic," *AJS Review* 14 (1989), pp. 103–178.

things inferred through one of the thirteen rules by which the Torah is interpreted. "That they announce to you" – (C) these are the received traditions passed from one individual to another.

Nahmanides' list is quite different (*Hasagot ha-Ramban*, 1):

This prohibition "do not deviate" refers only to what the rabbis said when interpreting the Torah. It includes those things inferred from the Torah through *Midrash Halakhah* using any of the thirteen hermeneutic principles (B1), or interpretations derived from the [plain] meaning of the biblical verse itself (B2), or what was handed down from Sinai (*halakha le-Moshe mi-Sinai*, C).

The focus of the dispute between Maimonides and Nahmanides is which laws should be included in the prohibition against "deviating." The category of "rabbinic regulations, decrees, and practices" (A), according to Maimonides, is part of the corpus from which we are warned "not to deviate"; it is absent from Nahmanides' list. Nahmanides based his position, *inter alia*, on the following argument:

The verse says, "If a case is too baffling for you to decide, be it a controversy over homicide, civil law" – i.e., when something is not clearly revealed to them, and the rabbis or judges disagree about the laws of the Torah, its proscriptions and punishments. This prohibition cannot include rabbinic regulations, e.g., lighting Hanukkah lights. That is not the intent of the verse, "If a case is too baffling for you to decide"; such regulations are derived from another verse: "Ask your father and he will inform you, your elders and they will tell you" (Deut. 32:7, and cf. *Shabbat* 23a).

In light of his tendency to attribute critical importance to the plain sense of the biblical text, Nahmanides infers from the words "If a case is too baffling" that the prohibition "do not deviate" pertains to halakhic rules that are not completely clear to begin with. Since our prohibition deals exclusively with such a situation, it does not include regulations, decrees and practices that were established independently by the Sages (A).

The second difference between Maimonides and Nahmanides here concerns their approach to halakhic rules that are derived from the plain sense of the biblical text (B2). According to Maimonides, the prohibition "not to deviate" refers only to rabbinic statutes (*de-rabbanan*). However, according to Nahmanides, the commandment "not to deviate" applies to "everything that the Sages said about the laws of the Torah, including the plain sense of Scripture." Thus, Nahmanides also disagreed with Maimonides' understanding of the rabbinic dictum that "Scripture never leaves its plain sense" (*ein mikra yotze midei peshuto*). According to Maimonides, this statement means that we must always take the plain sense of the biblical text into account, and hence we may not consider as Torah law (*de-oraita*) an obligation to perform or refrain from particular acts which is inferred through halakhic midrash (*Sefer ha-Mitzvot*, 2). By contrast, Nahmanides argues in his glosses to Maimonides' *Sefer ha-Mitzvot* that only where the laws inferred through halakhic midrash "completely uproot the plain sense of the Torah" may we argue that "Scripture never leaves its plain meaning." This interpretation reflects Nahmanides' mystical view of the written Torah, which he held could be read in a variety of ways: "We have [a verse's] homiletic meaning along with its plain sense, and neither is disregarded; the Bible bears multiple meanings and they are all true." This dispute of opinion has led some to assume that Maimonides rejected the notion that the biblical text can be interpreted in many ways, but this is incorrect.

The two remaining categories – rules of *halakhah* that are derived from halakhic midrash (B1) and rules of *halakhah* that have been handed down by tradition (C) – appear in both Maimonides' and Nahmanides' lists. Nevertheless, they differ about these two categories. In Maimonides' view, category C, "things received by tradition," are never a subject of controversy (*Hilkhot Mamrim* 1.3). Controversy (*mahloket*) arises over category B1, "when many things are examined, since each person draws inferences from them according to his intellectual abilities, but the people did not err concerning a received tradition" (Introduction to Maimonides' *Commentary on the Mishnah*). As a result, the Great Sanhedrin could make mistakes: "For the Torah allows no erroneous decisions regarding points of *halakhah*, except in the case of the Great Sanhedrin" (*Guide for the Perplexed* 3.41). Even so, this does not mitigate the importance of centralized authority, for without such an authority, "human beings would have perished due to the multiplicity of differences of opinion and the subdivisions of doctrines" (ibid.). Thus, Maimonides was willing to assume that in declaring the beginning of a new month (*kiddush ha-hodesh*), the Sages might have "inadvertently erred" (*Sefer ha-Mitzvot*, positive commandment 153). Nevertheless, their calendrical determinations remain valid, and to contest the dates they set would be a violation of the prohibition "You shall not deviate."

In contrast, Nahmanides, as a mystic, held that the court-set times of the Jewish holidays were sacred and correct. In his opinion, the new month was always sanctified at precisely the correct time. This holds true whether or not it was sanctified "properly by the authorized court in the Chosen Land" (Nahmanides' glosses on *Sefer ha-Mitzvot*, positive commandment 153). Nahmanides, like R. Judah Halevi (*Kuzari* 3.41), maintained that God is involved in decisions made by the Great Court of Law. "This is intimated by the verse 'God stands in the divine assembly; among the divine beings He pronounces judgment' (Ps. 82:1), for the Divine Presence is among them and agrees with them" (commentary on Num. 11:16). Thus Nahmanides believed that God would never allow a judge to sentence the innocent to death (ibid. 19:18), nor would He let the members of the Great Sanhedrin reach a fundamentally erroneous decision. "The Divine Spirit accompanies those who sanctify Him, and He will not abandon his followers, but will forever protect them from errors and stumbling blocks" (commentary on Deut. 17:1). According to Nahmanides, "The Sages prophesy through ways of wisdom. They know the truth through the spirit of holiness within them" (*Hiddushei ha-Ramban* on *Bava Batra* 12a). In attributing prophecy to the Sages, Nahmanides takes sharp issue with Maimonides' distinction between sages and prophets regarding matters of *halakhah* (see Maimonides' introduction to his *Commentary on the Mishnah*).

Thus, Nahmanides' interpretation of the prohibition "not to deviate" must be understood in the context of his mystic approach. Nahmanides was aware that someone who dissents from the ruling of the Great

Sanhedrin is likely to be absolutely convinced of the justice of his position. Such a person is likely to find himself in a difficult dilemma when forced to do something he finds traumatic: "How can I eat this, which in my opinion is forbidden fat, or how can I kill this innocent person?" (see Nahmanides' commentary on Deut. 17:11). To assuage such concern, Nahmanides suggests that even if one is not completely convinced of the truth of the Sages' words, he must realize that "God gave us the Torah according to the understanding of the Sages, even if they are completely wrong." Of course, this statement reflects Nahmanides' response to the questioner's mistaken assumption; for Nahmanides himself, the Sages cannot be wrong, since they are saved from error through Divine guidance.

It should be stressed that there is no connection between Nahmanides' view here and his aforecited approach about the multi-layered character of biblical meaning, according to which both the plain sense of the text (*peshat*) and halakhic midrash are "true." For here we are dealing with a case where "one of the views is unquestionably mistaken" (*Hasagot ha-Ramban*, 6), although this erroneous view was rejected by the Sages. Nahmanides effectively extended the prohibition against "deviating" so that it included not just an obligation to obey the Sages, but also an obligation to believe that what they said is true: "For you must believe that what they call right is right" (commentary on Deut. 17:1). Similarly, "One must put aside one's own opinion and believe what they said, based on this prohibition, for it obligates us to believe in the Torah according to the interpretation that [the rabbis] give" (*Hasagot le-Sefer ha-Mitzvot*, 1). Thus, cognizance of the fact that God would not let the Sages of the Great Sanhedrin err should encourage people to reject incorrect views, even if they had previously been convinced that these views were true.

Parashat Ki Tetze

THE LAW OF THE BEAUTIFUL CAPTIVE WOMAN

Dr. Israel Zvi Gilat
School of Education

THE COMMANDMENT OF *yefat to'ar* found in our Torah reading (Deut. 21:12) differs from the commandment regarding the stubborn and rebellious son, "who never was and never will be, and was written only to reward those who expound it" (*Tosefta Sanhedrin* 13.6). It also differs from the commandment regarding the rebellious city (*'ir ha-nidahat*), which also "never was and never will be" (ibid.). The law of the beautiful captive woman was already in force, according to the Talmudic rabbis, during the time of the biblical kingdom of Israel, and will apparently remain in force forever.

Moreover, according to talmudic tradition, King David's family troubles began because of the commandment of *yefat to'ar*. According to one rabbinic opinion, Tamar was David's daughter from Ma'akhah, the daughter of King Talmi of Geshur, whom he had captured in battle. Tamar told her half-brother Amnon (David's son from a different wife) to "speak to the king; he will not refuse me to you" (II Sam. 13:13). As the daughter of a *yefat to'ar* born to David during her mother's captivity, she was not concerned about incest. Therefore, despite Tamar's later conversion, she was not considered David's daughter, halakhically speaking.

Leaving aside contemporary debates about the appropriate treatment of prisoners of war, we find numerous halakhic authorities, from the Talmudic period to the early twentieth century, who analyzed the laws of the captive woman. Is having sexual relations with the captive woman a right, or might it be unworthy and even contemptible? *Midrash Tanhuma, Ki*

Tetze, 1, infers from the hermeneutic principle of juxtaposition (*semikhut*) that whoever takes a beautiful captive will eventually bear a rebellious son. We see this in the case of David. His desire for Ma'akhah, the daughter of King Talmi of Geshur, when he went to battle led to the birth of Absalom, who rose to kill him, slept with his wives in the presence of all Israel and in broad daylight, and was responsible for the deaths of tens of thousands of Israelites.

This would suggest that although the Torah might permit *yefat to'ar*, it certainly frowns upon the practice. On the other hand, we read in *Hullin* 109b:

> Yalta (R. Nahman's wife) once said to R. Nahman, Note that for everything that the Torah has forbidden us, it has permitted us an equivalent. It has forbidden us to eat blood, but it permitted liver. It forbids intercourse during menstruation, but permits us the blood of purification...It has forbidden us gentile women, but it permits us the beautiful captive woman.

Yalta's remarks imply that the Torah permits *yefat to'ar ab initio*: just as a Jew has no need to abstain from permitted relations, eating liver, and the like, so too this commandment need not be feared or avoided.

Most sources take an intermediate position: cohabitation with a *yefat to'ar* in wartime is undesirable. Nevertheless, this law was included in the Torah to prevent even worse behavior. This view is expressed clearly in the Talmud (*Kiddushin* 22a and parallels): "Our Rabbis taught: 'If you see among the captives' – when taking her captive; 'a woman' – even married; 'of beautiful appearance' – it is better for Israel to eat the flesh of dying animals that were ritually slaughtered rather than downright carrion." Hence we see that the numerous restrictions on cohabitation with a *yefat to'ar* in the Torah and rabbinic literature were meant to minimize or even eliminate the objectionable aspects of the action.

Let return for a moment to the rabbinic metaphor about "dying animals that were ritually slaughtered," which is clearly analogous to the law of the beautiful captive woman. If the commandment of *yefat to'ar* is comparable to the commandment of ritual slaughter, an act which permits what would otherwise be forbidden, who or what are the "dying animals" in this analogy? The proper analogy, it would seem, should be to the slaughter of healthy animals.

Recall the well-known rabbinic comment that "in the *mitzvah* of *yefat to'ar*, the Torah sought to counteract the evil impulse" (*Midrash Tannaim* 2.9). At first glance, that might be interpreted as meaning that the very act of taking a beautiful captive woman is unethical and undesirable. In that sense, the beautiful captive is analogous to "an animal about to die," and hence she should be prohibited. Closer analysis, however, reveals that the rabbis' aim was to *expand* the sphere of action: cohabitation is permitted not only with a beautiful captive, literally *yefat to'ar*, but also with an "ugly captive woman." The rabbis did not criticize people who implement the permission granted to them by the Torah.

Thus, we see that the commandment of *yefat to'ar* does not entail inherently inappropriate behavior, and it enables us to disregard various prohibitions, both Torah and rabbinic proscriptions, which would ordinarily apply. Therefore, even the slightest deviation from the exact parameters of these laws can transform "kosher animals" to "carrion" (to use the expression in the Midrash), rendering what might seem a permissible action outright sin.

What, then, is the "carrion" (to use the words of the Midrash) which the Torah seeks here to permit? In other words, what potential prohibitions might the commandment of *yefat to'ar* render permissible?

1. The Talmud (*Kiddushin* 21b) asks, "Is a *kohen* allowed take a captive woman?" This question is based on the fact that *kohanim* are not allowed to marry converts. According to Rav, who maintains that a *yefat to'ar* is permitted to a *kohen*, this commandment is an exception to the halakhic rule that a *kohen* is forbidden to marry a convert.

2. The war discussed here is an "optional war" (so *Sifre* ad loc.), not an obligatory war to take possession of the land of Israel. The *yefat to'ar* may be a member of one of the seven Canaanite nations whom it is prohibited to spare in times of war (Deut. 21:10). Thus, the law of the *yefat to'ar* here demonstrates that the prohibition "you shall not let a soul remain alive" (20:16) is not ethnic but territorial, and hence there is no obligation to

destroy members of the seven nations found in conquered territory outside of the land of Israel.

3. Similarly, the prohibition "You shall not intermarry with them" (Deut. 7:3), which applies to members of the seven Canaanite nations even after they convert, does not apply to a *yefat to'ar*. Likewise, the prohibition (ibid.) "Do not give your daughters to their sons or take their daughters for your sons" does not apply to a *yefat to'ar*.

4. Even if the *yefat to'ar* was married to a gentile when taken into captivity, her Jewish captor may marry her, and he does not violate the prohibition of adultery by so doing. Thus, we see that the laws of *yefat to'ar* permit numerous actions which would be prohibited under normal circumstances.

Parashat Ki Tetze

ECOLOGY IN THE TORAH

Dr. Yael Shemesh
Department of Bible

TOWARDS THE END of *Parashat Shofetim*, whose language and content resemble that of *Parashat Ki Tetze*, the Torah prohibits chopping down fruit trees in time of war when laying siege to an enemy city (Deut. 20:19). This commandment strongly influenced post-biblical Jewish thought about ecology, as we shall see below.

During the last three decades, great interest has been shown in ecology, especially the branch of ecology known as environmental ethics or eco-ethics, primarily due to the irreversible damage that human beings have been causing the earth. Motivated by short-term profit, people have been destroying the world in which they live, destroying rain forests, polluting the water and air, depleting natural resources, and causing global warming and the extinction of various species of animals and plants. This process of destruction began to accelerate relatively recently, beginning with the industrial revolution in the eighteenth century. It is therefore quite surprising to discover the great interest in ecology shown by our ancient sources – the Bible itself, and even more so in the Oral Torah, the writings of the Sages.

Anthropocentric vs. Biocentric Ecology
Two opposing approaches can be identified among environmental activists regarding the place of human beings in the world: the anthropocentric approach, which revolves around human beings, and the biocentric approach, which revolves around nature. In the anthropocentric approach,

human beings are responsible for the world's resources, which must be managed wisely, sparingly, lovingly and responsibly, especially for man's own sake. Hence the term "stewardship." In contrast, the biocentric approach, termed "deep ecology," rejects placing human beings at the center of the world, and instead views them as simply another species, of no greater importance than the others. Deep ecology emphasizes that the right of rivers, trees, pandas, etc., to exist does not stem from the benefit that they bring human beings, but from their very existence.

The Two Approaches in Judaism

When we ask ourselves about Judaism's view of the place of human beings in the world, our most likely response might be that it adopts the anthropocentric approach. In the story of Creation, man alone was created "in the image of God" (Gen. 1:27), and the task assigned the first human beings in the Garden of Eden was "to till it and tend it" (Gen. 2:15). And yet, an instructive article by Fink shows that along with the anthropocentric approach Judaism also adopts a biocentric approach.[1]

A prime example of the Bible rejecting the anthropocentric approach can be found in the book of Job, where the presumptuousness of men thinking themselves to be the center of the universe is scorned. God's first response out of the tempest describes the miracles of creation. These find expression, *inter alia*, in the fact that God sends clouds and thunderstorms "to rain down on uninhabited land, on the wilderness where no man is, to saturate the desolate wasteland and make the crop of grass sprout forth" (Job 38:26–27). God's concern for places that are not settled by men is not consonant with a view of man as the primary objective of creation. Further on, God describes a vast variety of animals over which His providence extends, animals which provide no benefit to human beings: the wild ass or the wild ox (39:5–12) and the *behemoth* and the *leviathan* described in God's second speech (40:15–32). The text emphasizes that all of these are animals that man cannot subdue and domesticate to serve his purposes. In other

---

[1] Dan Fink, "Between Dust and Divinity: Maimonides and Jewish Environmental Ethics," in *Ecology and the Jewish Spirit*, ed. Ellen Bernstein (Woodstock 1998), pp. 230–239.

words, they have an autonomous reason for existence, which bears no relationship to human existence. How radically this differs from the views so deeply rooted in our psyches about man's place in the universe!

Fink illustrates the tension between the two ecological schools by citing *Sanhedrin* 38a, which explains why men were created at the end of creation. According to one opinion, it was "so that he could join the banquet immediately. It is like a king of flesh and blood who builds a hall, decorates it, prepares a banquet, and then allows his guests to enter." In other words, mankind is the pinnacle of creation, the guest of honor in God's world, which was created for the pleasure and use of the human race.

This view, however, is contrasted with the opposite stance: "Should man become haughty, God would say to him: The mosquito was created before you." Fink concludes that the tension between faith in our ability to influence Creation (stewardship) and recognition of our own insignificance (deep ecology) – a tension which finds expression in classical Jewish sources – creates a balance between the call to action and the need to maintain a measure of humility.[2]

Biblical Commandments with an Ecological Purpose

Several commandments in the Bible aside from the prohibition against chopping down fruit trees apparently have an ecological purpose which is central or incidental to the commandment. For example, one of the reasons given by Maimonides for the commandment to let the land lie fallow in the sabbatical year (Lev. 25:1-5) is "so that the yield of the land should improve from not having been planted."[3] In other words, the land will renew its strength and be improved by the temporary rest given it.

R. Samson Raphael Hirsch offers an interesting ecological explanation for the commandment to rest on the Sabbath. He suggests that the Sabbath has didactic importance: after six days of activity, during which men act as "stewards of the universe," using the land, plants and animals to satisfy their wishes, the Sabbath arrives, a day intended to remind us that what

---

[2] Ibid., pp. 237–239.

[3] *Guide to the Perplexed*, 3.39.

surrounds us does not belong to us, but to God. Therefore, "Every Sabbath, return to God His universe, acknowledge the Lord your God, and remind yourself yet again that this universe is borrowed from God. Remember who is its Master, that this borrowed universe belongs to the Lord, and that He, not you, rules everything."[4]

Parashat Ki Tetze also contains several commandments which have ecological purposes, or at least ecological outcomes:

> • The commandment to chase away the mother bird (Deut. 22:6–7), for which Nahmanides suggests, aside from its educational purpose (shunning cruelty), an ecological explanation: "The Torah did not permit destructiveness, wiping out a species."
> • The prohibition against certain hybrids (Deut. 22:9; Lev. 19:19), which serves to warn us "to safeguard each variety, so that one variety will not become mixed with another" (Ibn Ezra on Lev. 19:19). This is because "a person who combines two varieties introduces change and alters an aspect of primordial creation. It is as if he believes that the Holy One, blessed be He, had not sufficiently perfected His world; he wishes to assist in the creation of the world by adding new creations" (Nahmanides on Lev. 19:19).
> • The instructions (with specific directions) about maintaining proper hygiene in army camps (Deut. 23:13-14).
> • The obligation to bury the dead immediately (Deut. 21:22-23), which was intended to prevent pollution of the air, according to Ralbag: "'You shall not defile the land' – by the putrefaction that will be there if the corpse remains unburied."

Ecological-Halakhic Aspects of Rabbinic Thought

1. The prohibition against chopping down fruit trees

The biblical prohibition against chopping down fruit trees is discussed extensively in rabbinic and post-rabbinic sources. The Talmud states that

---

[4] R. Samson Raphael Hirsch, *Sefer Horev* (New York 1953), pp. 69–70.

one who chops down goodly trees "never sees blessing in this world" (*Pesahim* 50b). Rabbi Hanina explained that his son died an untimely death because he chopped down a fig-tree before its time (*Bava Kama* 91b). People who chop down goodly trees are responsible for others being "stricken by curses" (*Tosefta Sukkah* 2.5). According to *Pirkei de-Rabbi Eliezer*, ch. 33 (ed. Higger, p. 202), "When a fruit tree is chopped down, the sound resounds around the world, but is not heard."

2. Wanton destruction

The Sages extended the biblical proscription against destroying fruit trees, developing it into a broad prohibition against destroying anything that is useful or beneficial to mankind (*bal tashhit*, "you shall not destroy"). Maimonides summarized the idea as follows: "[This applies] not only to trees. It includes any act of breaking vessels, tearing clothing, demolishing a building, blocking a spring, or wasting food by spoiling it. All of these violate the prohibition against destroying, and the punishment is lashes by rabbinic injunction" (*Hilkhot Melakhim* 6.10).

3. Industries that cause pollution

The Sages warned us to remove industries from inhabited areas, in order to minimize harm to people. For example, the Mishnah (*Bava Batra* 2.8) rules that threshing floors must be kept far from the city because of the chaff, and that the leather industry, which causes pollution, must be kept at least fifty cubits from the city (*Bava Batra* 2.9). The Tosefta cites Rabbi Nathan's ruling: "Kilns [i.e., lime kilns for firing pottery] are to be kept fifty cubits away from a city" (*Tosefta Bava Batra* 1.10).[5]

4. Water pollution

The Sages also emphasized the importance of keeping water sources fresh and clean. We see this in the following ruling: "When dens are made to serve the public for washing the face, hands, and feet, if a person's hands and feet are soiled with mire or feces, it is forbidden [to wash there];

---

[5] See further Nahum Rakover, *Eikhut ha-Sevivah* (Jerusalem 1993); Barry Freundel, "Judaism's Environmental Laws," in *Ecology and the Jewish Spirit*, pp. 214–224.

whether a well or a pit, in any case it is forbidden" (*Tosefta Bava Metzia* 11.31).[6]

Poetry and *Belles Lettres* on Nature – From the Bible to Rav Kook

The beauty of nature has a tremendous effect on human beings. Esthetic enjoyment of God's world is often accompanied by religious experience. For example, contemplating creation brought the author of Psalms to a recognition of God's might and wisdom: "O Lord, how manifold are your works! You have made them all in wisdom; the earth is full of Your creatures" (Ps. 104:24). According to *Pirkei Shirah*,[7] all of creation, including all the plants and animals, sings God's praises.[8]

This idea was eloquently expressed by R. Nahman of Bratslav (*Likkutei Moharan*, 29b): "Know that every single shepherd has a unique tune according to the grass growing in the place where he pastures his sheep. For every single animal has a special grass that it needs to eat...and according to the grass and the place where he pastures, so too he has a tune. For every blade of grass has a song that it sings which is like a passage of poetry. And the tune of the shepherd is composed from the song of the blades of grass." R. Nahman recommended praying in nature "among the blades of grass and trees," because "when a person prays and meditates in the field, the blades of grass and shrubs of the field all enter his prayer, helping him and giving him strength in his prayer and meditation."

Rav Kook believed that when people live their lives in harmony with nature, they are able to restore the sense of natural bliss, fine character and the experience of spiritual elation that was lost when man grew away from nature.[9] Rav Kook himself was extremely careful not to destroy God's works unnecessarily. In his memoirs, R. Aryeh Levine recounts how he

---

[6] See further Rakover, ibid., pp. 73–76.

[7] *Pirkei Shirah* (Mantua 1681), written between the fifth and seventh century C.E.

[8] For example, the snake is said to sing: "The Lord supports all who stumble, and makes all who are bent stand straight" (Ps. 145:14); the mouse sings: "I extol you, O Lord, for You have lifted me up and not let my enemies rejoice over me" (Ps. 30:2); the cat sings: "I pursued my enemies and overtook them" (Ps. 18:38).

[9] R. Abraham Isaac Hakohen Kook, *Ein Ayah, Berakhot*, vol. 2 (Jerusalem 1990), p. 297.

learned compassion from Rav Kook when accompanying him to meditate in the field:

> On the way I picked a plant or flower. Rav Kook was shocked, and said to me quietly, "Believe me, all my life I have taken care not to vainly pick any grass or flower that could grow and flourish, for there is not a blade of grass in the lower realms that has no corresponding one in the upper realms telling it: Grow! Every blade of grass says something, every stone whispers some secret, every creation sings some song." These words, emanating from a pure and holy heart, became deeply engrained in my being, and since then I have begun to have more compassion for everything.[10]

Rav Kook's admiration for every blade of grass or flower, for every animal and person, stemmed from his realization that they are all God's creatures and hence important, bearing a unique place in the world that He created. This approach recalls the eloquent words of R. Samson Raphael Hirsch:[11]

> The earth does not belong to you; rather, you belong to it. You must respect it as holy ground and view every creature as a creation of God and as a brother to you, loving it and helping it fulfill its destiny according to God's design. Thus, every creature should be reflected in your soul, and your heart should resonate with each cry of distress and every shout of glee in the world. Your heart should rejoice when buds appear in the land, and it should mourn over every flower that wilts...They have all been given to you on loan, and they will all appear some day before God's throne to testify either for you or against you, if you ignored them or used them, whether for blessing or for curse.

---

[10] Simhah Raz, *Ish Tzaddik Hayah* (Jerusalem 1973), p. 74.

[11] R. Samson Raphael Hirsch, *Iggerot Tzafon* (Benei Brak 1967), pp. 46–48.

I conclude with the edifying remarks of the Midrash on the consequences of damaging the world, and its warning to mankind, so relevant to us today:

> "Consider God's works! Who can straighten what He has twisted?" (Eccl. 7:13). When God created Adam, He took him and showed him all the trees of the Garden of Eden and said to him: Behold how fine and excellent are all the things that I have made! And everything that I created, I created for your sake. Take care not to spoil and destroy My world, for if you spoil it there will be no one to follow you and repair it (*Kohelet Rabbah* 7.1 [13]).

Parashat Ki Tavo

TRADITIONS OF TORAH READING FOR THE *TOKHEHAH* PASSAGES

Rabbi Dr. Hayyim Talbi
Department of Talmud

THE *TOKHEHAH*, or "admonition," refers to the passages in the Torah containing curses which Moses uttered to admonish the Jews, providing them with moral instruction. Two such passages appear in the Torah, one in *Parashat Behukkotai* (Lev. 16:14-46) and the other in *Parashat Ki Tavo* (Deut. 28:15-69). The Mishnah (*Megillah* 3.6) states: "One should not pause during the curses; rather, the same person should read them all." In other words, the verses of the *Tokhehah* should not be divided into two *aliyot*, and the entire passage should be read as one *aliyah*. Two reasons for this are given in the Talmud (*Megillah* 31b): "R. Hiyya bar Gamda said in the name of R. Asi: Scripture says (Prov. 3:11), 'Do not reject the discipline of the Lord, my son.' Resh Lakish said: One does not say a blessing over divine retribution."

According to the first reason, if the reading of *Tokhehah* would be interrupted in the middle, it would seem as if the reader had rejected the Torah's admonition, consequently requiring another person to replace him. According to the second reason, stopping in the middle of the *Tokhehah* would require blessings to be recited over the next *aliyah*, and this would be tantamount to reciting a blessing over divine retribution. Hence one person is called to the Torah for the *Tokhehah*, and he begins reading several verses before the *Tokhehah* and concludes several verses after it.

The Babylonian Talmud does not explain why a blessing is not recited over divine retribution, but the Jerusalem Talmud does (*Megillah* 3.7): "R.

Levi taught, The Holy One, blessed be He said: It is not right that my children be cursed while I am blessed, as it is written, 'I will be with him in distress'" (Ps. 91:15). According to Abbaye in the Babylonian Talmud (ibid.), however, this applies only to the *Tokhehah* in Leviticus, which is formulated in the plural and is directed at all of Israel: Moses transmitted these words directly from the Almighty, and they are particularly harsh and severe. The *Tokhehah* in Deuteronomy, however, was formulated in the singular, by Moses, and is addressed to each individual. Therefore, the reader may pause in the middle, and the next person called to the Torah can finish reading it.

The Jerusalem Talmud apparently did not accept the view that the admonition in *Parashat Ki Tavo* is less severe than that in *Parashat Behukkotai*. No distinction is made there between the curses in Deuteronomy and those in Leviticus. Perhaps the rabbis of the Jerusalem Talmud held that there should be no interruption in the middle of the curses because "the reader must begin on a positive note and conclude on a positive note," and curses are never good.

The accepted view is that reading the *Tokhehah* in Leviticus should not be interrupted. These verses should be read as a single unit, with something positive included before them and after them. According to the Babylonian Talmud, a break may be made in reading the curses in Deuteronomy. However, Maimonides wrote that "It has become customary not to stop in the middle, but to have a single person read them,"[1] which seems to reflect the view of the Jerusalem Talmud.

A different approach was taken by other medieval halakhic authorities. They hold that the curses in Deuteronomy are more severe precisely because they are formulated in the singular. These verses seem to threaten the person called up to read this passage. Hence various authorities begin to express concern about calling someone up for this *'aliyah*, lest the curses

---

[1] Maimonides, *Hilkhot Tefilah* 13.7; *Derashot R. Yehoshua ibn Shu'ib*, ed. Z. Metzger, 2 (Jerusalem 1992), p. 481; *Orhot Hayyim, Hilkhot Keri'at Sefer Torah*, p. 52, *Tur* and *Shulhan Arukh, Orah Hayyim* 428.6.

there seem to be directed against him. Thus, Maharil (R. Jacob Moellin, 1365–1427) writes:[2]

> For the *Tokhehah* in *Behukotai*, the *gabbai* called out, "May whoever wishes come up to the Torah." Maharil reproved him and told him to call a specific person, as was customary for the rest of the Torah. Only in Deuteronomy is the summons [to read the Torah] addressed to "whoever wishes," because [the curses] are in the singular...In Mainz it was customary to instruct the *shamash* of the synagogue when hired that if no one else could be found to read the *Tokhehah* portion, he must come up and read it himself. Since this was part of his duty, it was considered less severe.

Nevertheless, Maharil was not always pleased by people who "volunteered" to accept *aliyot* to the Torah for the *Tokhehah*. Consider the following story (ibid.): "Once I saw an impoverished person come up to the Torah to read the *Tokhehah* in Deuteronomy, and Maharil said to him, 'Why are you so doleful? After all, you have already been smitten by the curses of the *Tokhehah* on account of your many sins.' And [Maharil] was angry at him for coming up."

The tradition Maharil records had become accepted practice by the time of R. Isaac of Vienna, the author of *Or Zarua*, who wrote:

> The great *hasid*, my teacher R. Judah he-Hasid, of blessed memory, told me that the *gabbai* must be well-liked by his congregation. If not, when the *Tokhehah* is read it is dangerous for whomever he does not like. [R. Judah] told me that if a person knows that the *gabbai* does not like him and he calls him to read the *Tokhehah*, he should be careful not to accept, for he might suffer if he does so.[3]

---

[2] *Sefer Maharil, Minhagim*, ed. S. Spitzer (Jerusalem 1989), pp. 454–455.

[3] *Or Zarua*, 1 (Zhitomir 1862), §114. Based on this, Rema ruled (*Orah Hayyim* 53.19): "One who despises the Torah reader [and hence is presumably despised by the Torah reader as well] should not accept an *aliyah* when the *Tokhehah* is being read." But others, including *Knesset Gedolah* (*Orah Hayyim*, §53), the Vilna Gaon (ibid. 33), and

During later times, too, we find that the public was hesitant about accepting an *aliyah* for the *Tokhehah*, and they considered the *Tokhehah* in Deuteronomy more severe than the one in *Behukkotai*.

Fear of this *aliyah* was so great and so deeply-rooted in certain communities that the Torah reading was sometimes delayed for hours until someone was found to accept this *aliyah*. During this time the Torah scroll remained open, reflecting disrespect for its holiness. The brother of Maharal of Prague, R. Hayyim b. R. Betzalel, who was one of the leading Ashkenazic scholars of the sixteenth century, related that some rabbis even ascribed the destruction of certain communities to this practice.[4] He wrote:

> People tend to avoid accepting an *aliyah* to the Torah for the *Tokhehah*. And the *Tokhehah* in Deuteronomy is avoided most of all, as it is formulated in the singular and in the second-person as if, Heaven forbid, the things described there should happen to the person who receives this *aliyah*. This is not the case with the *Tokhehah* in Leviticus, which is formulated in the plural.

In addition to the reluctance to be called up to the Torah, we find two other techniques which were used to avoid reading the *Tokhehah*:

1. Some people chose to leave the synagogue until after the reading of the *Tokhehah*. Rabbi Elijah Shapira, a preacher from Prague in the seventeenth century, recounted: "I once saw one of my ancestors, the *Gaon* of blessed memory, go outside the synagogue until after the reading of the *Tokhehah*."[5]

2. In some nineteenth-century communities, the entire Torah reading was omitted on the Sabbaths of the *Tokhehah*. R. Israel Meir Ha-Cohen of Radin testifies, "I have seen something scandalous in this regard among the

---

Sha'arei Ephraim 3.2, hold that one should accept an *aliyah* under such circumstances, because by refraining from doing so one dishonors the Torah. Besides, "one who obeys the commandments will know no evil" (Eccl. 8:5).

[4] *Sefer Ha-Hayyim* (Jerusalem 1996), p. 65.

[5] *Eliyah Rabbah* (repr. Jerusalem 1999), *Orah Hayyim*, §428, p. 536.

masses. In some places, on the Sabbaths when *Behukkotai* and *Ki Tavo* should be read, the Torah is not read at all. This is reprehensible." [6]

In other communities the Torah was read, but the person who was called up for the *Tokhehah* did not recite a blessing over the Torah reading, either before or afterwards. [7] Much opposition to this custom, which is practiced in certain places to this day (among Vishnitzer Hasidim, *inter alia*), has been voiced; it has been described as "a mistake" [8] and "totally unfounded," [9] among other things.

In contrast, the *Tokhehah* passages were perceived by certain hasidic courts as curses which concealed great blessings. [10] This idea apparently originates in the *Zohar*, [11] where it is said that all the words of warning and admonition in the Torah are blessings, even though they seem to be curses. The *Zohar* recounts that Elijah said to Rabbi Simeon:

> Arise! Rouse yourself from your slumber! How fortunate you are, for the Holy One, blessed be He, wishes to honor you. All the promises and words of consolation for Israel are written in these curses. Pay heed: a king who loves his son may curse him and beat him, yet he loves him from the depths of his heart. Thus it is with the Holy One, blessed be He. Though He cursed, His words are love. Outwardly they seem to be curses, but they are great beneficence, because these curses were uttered in love. [12]

---

[6] *Be'ur Halakhah*, §428, s.v. *ba-pesukim she-lifneihem*.

[7] Maharshak (R. Shlomo b. Joseph Aaron Kluger), *Teshuvot Ha-Elef Lekha Shlomo* (repr. Jerusalem 1968), *Orah Hayyim*, §63.

[8] R. Moshe Feinstein, *Iggerot Moshe*, *Orah Hayyim* 2.35.

[9] R. Ovadiah Yossef, *Yabbia' Omer*, 7.19

[10] R. Samuel of Sokhachov, *Shem mi-Shmuel* (Jerusalem 1957), pp. 366–367; M. Buber, *Or ha-Ganuz* (Tel Aviv 1947), p. 71.

[11] *Zohar Hadash, Parashat Ki Tavo*, p. 3.

[12] For further discussion, see my "Hishtalshelut Minhagei Keri'at ha-Torah be-Parashot ha-Tokhehah," *Kenishta* 2 (2003), pp. 31–55.

Parashat Nitzavim-Vayelekh

THE MOTIF OF RETURN

Menahem Ben-Yashar
Department of Bible.

THE FIRST TEN VERSES of chapter 30 in this week's reading are known as *parashat ha-teshuvah*, the section about repentance. In biblical Hebrew, *teshuvah* denotes double returning, both Israel's returning to God and God's returning to Israel, as Malachi said (3:7): "Return to Me and I will return to you."[1]

After the lengthy admonition in *Parashat Ki Tavo* (Deut. 28:15–68), with its depictions of catastrophic divine retribution, our passage on repentance comes as a happy ending, just as the *Tokhehah*, or passage of admonition, in Leviticus (26:14–43) is followed by a promise of redemption (Lev. 26:42, 44–45). In Deuteronomy, however, the passage about redemption does not immediately follow the admonition; first, Moses issued a warning to his own generation (Deut. 29:1–8). This warning is followed by an admonition to the people, most if not all of whom were sinners, and a warning to isolated individuals or tribes indicating that they too will be punished if they sin (Deut. 29:9–20). Next comes a description of the impact of the destruction of the land on the surrounding nations (Deut. 29:21–27). This is followed by v. 28, which limits the threat of punishment, stating that the masses will not be punished for sins covertly

---

[1] Elhanan Samet, *Iyyunim be-Parashot ha-Shavua*, 2 (Jerusalem 2002), pp. 400–416, describes this part of the Torah as "the section about repentance and redemption." I have learned much from this analysis and utilized it in this article.

committed by individuals.[2] All these appendices to the *Tokhehah* are followed by *parashat ha-teshuvah*, describing the mutual return of God and Israel.

Of the seven (or eight)[3] occurrences of the verb *shuv*, which serves as a sort of *leitmotif* in the *parashat ha-teshuvah*, two describe the beginning of Israel's repentance. The first of these, *va-hashevota el levavekha*, "you take them to heart" (Deut 30:1), indicates that Israel has not yet turned back to God; rather, they are beginning to contemplate matters. They had enjoyed Divine beneficence in the past, when they behaved appropriately, but when they fell into sin, destruction and exile followed.

Hence the next stage is *ve-shavta 'ad adonai elohekha* – "you shall return to the Lord your God." The word *'ad* ("to") refers to returning from a distance: Israel returns emotionally, spiritually, and even geographically, since returning to God renews the Jews' aspiration to return to the holy land. And while the Torah states that they now "heed His command, as I enjoin upon you this day," this does not refer to actual observance of the commandments, for the Torah continues: "and obey all His commandments" (30:8), "keeping His commandments and laws" (30:10). In the impure foreign land where Israel begins their journey of repentance, the commandments cannot be properly observed.[4] While still in exile, the people can, at best, refrain from prohibited acts, particularly idol worship.

The next stage in this reciprocal process is God's return to Israel (30:3–5). At this point the root *shuv* occurs twice (or three times). Here, too, the return is first emotional, as it were, and then real: "Then the Lord your God will restore (*shav*) your fortunes (*shevutkha*)" (so the new JPS version; the old JPS version renders, "He will turn your captivity"). The structure of

---

[2] See Rashi, Ibn Ezra, and Rashbam on this verse, Rashbam on Deut. 27:15, and Ibn Ezra on 17:14–19.

[3] If we include the noun *shevut*, which is used along with the verb *ve-shav*. The number seven traditionally symbolizes perfection, while the number eight symbolizes supreme, supernatural perfection.

[4] See *Sifre* Deuteronomy §43 (ed. Finkelstein, p. 102); *Ketubbot* 110b; Nahmanides on Lev. 18:25.

this verse indicates that God will return to you[5] after having hidden Himself from you in your exile.[6] Similarly it is written: "[He will] take you back in love," which is followed by the actual return: "He will bring you together again," to the land that was once the inheritance of Israel's ancestors, which will again become their inheritance. Moreover, "He will make you more prosperous and more numerous than your fathers" (30:5).

While the first stage was spiritual – turning back to God – the second stage is mainly practical – bringing Israel back to their land and to a state of well-being. The third stage (v. 6) returns to the theme of spiritual return: God will open up (literally "circumcise") Israel's hearts to enable them to love Him and worship Him wholeheartedly. Two questions arise here. First, why was this necessary after the first stage of return, when Israel returned to God "with all [their] heart and soul" (10:2)? Second, doesn't "circumcising" Israel's hearts seem to contradict the principle of free choice?[7] I would suggest that "circumcising" the heart does not entail intervention in people's actual decisions. Rather, this refers to the removal of whatever might prevent people from receiving correct impressions. The era of corruption and idolatry that preceded the exile and the period of exile itself, with its travails and foreign environment, all envelop the heart with negative thoughts and feelings that are difficult to overcome. God will assist Israel to struggle with these forces and begin anew. To leave the impure land of exile and enter the land of Israel requires purity of heart. Such purity is essential, for once the nation resettles, multiplies, and becomes prosperous, as it had in the past, the danger exists that once again "Jeshurun would grow fat and kick" (cf. Deut. 32:15). Sin and exile would follow, and the cycle would repeat itself. Circumcising the heart is thus a preventative measure. This is intimated at the end of v. 6, which states "that you may live," i.e., that you may live in tranquility from now on.

---

[5] So R. Sa'adiah Gaon. Cf. Menahem Ben-Yashar, "Shuv Shevut," *Sefer ha-Yovel le-Rav Mordechai Breuer* (Jerusalem 1992), pp. 639–656.

[6] Cf. Deut 31:17–18.

[7] Samet (above, n. 1) discusses this problem and suggests a different answer. The classic answer, of course, is that God is the primary cause of all human actions and emotions.

The next verse (30:7) also describes divine intervention, but this time towards the other nations: the curses mentioned in the *Tokhehah* in connection with Israel will now apply to the nations that sinned against Israel. The world is founded on truth, justice and peace (*Avot* 1:18); truth and justice demand that the sinner be punished, so that justice and peace may prevail. When Abraham, the father of the Jewish people, heard the decree of bondage, he also heard, "But I will execute judgment on the nation they shall serve" (Gen. 15:14). Here, too, his descendants are promised that their persecutors will be punished.

The passage recounting the future punishment of Israel's persecutors is preceded and followed by passages dealing solely with Israel. In each of the last three verses in our passage on repentance, the verb *shuv* appears: *tashuv* – "will again heed" (30:8); *yashuv* – "will again delight" (30:9); and again *tashuv* – "once you return" (30:10). As in the first three units, here, too, there is an element of reciprocity: Israel returns, then God turns back to them, and finally Israel returns to their Creator.

As indicated above, the description of Israel's return in v. 8 refers to the Jews obeying all the commandments in the Holy Land. God's response to such conduct is exalted: "For the Lord will again delight in your well-being, as He did in that of your fathers" (30:9). The cause, or perhaps the necessary precondition for this, is specified in the last unit of the *parashat ha-teshuvah*, which deals, once again, with Israel's conduct: "Because you heeded the Lord your God and kept His commandments and laws." Here, sounding the final chord, as it were, the Torah is mentioned: "[the commandments] that are recorded in this book of the Torah" (30:10). This section and the entire passage on repentance conclude with the familiar *leitmotif* of return: "Once you return to the Lord your God with all your heart and soul." Thus Israel's return to God, "with all your heart and soul," is the motif that introduces and concludes the passage on repentance. This teaches us that Israel's return to God, with them mending their ways after they violated the covenant, is a necessary precondition for God's return to Israel.

Parashat Ha'azinu

HAKHEL AFTER THE DESTRUCTION OF THE TEMPLE

Rabbi Judah Zoldan
Midrashah for Women

THE SONG OF *HA'AZINU* was recited in the presence of the entire congregation, as we read: "Then Moses recited the words of this poem to the very end, as the entire congregation of Israel listened" (Deut. 31:30). In a sense, this song concludes the process of re-acceptance of the Torah in the plains of Moab, just before the Jews entered the promised land, forty years after they had received the Torah at Sinai – the theme of Deuteronomy. At the conclusion of this process, we are commanded in *Parashat Vayelekh* to re-enact the act of receiving the Torah through the *hakhel* ceremony, which is held every seven years, at the close of the sabbatical year, during Sukkot (31:10-13).

The giving of the Torah at Mount Sinai is called *yom ha-kahal*, "the day of the Assembly" (Deut. 9:10; 10:4; 18:16), while the ceremony described here, which is held every seven years to re-enact what happened at Mount Sinai, is called *hakhel*. Aside from the linguistic connection, Maimonides (*Hilkhot Hagigah* 3:6) notes a substantive link: The ceremony of *hakhel* aims "to prepare [the people's] hearts and to set their ears to listening, to listen in fear, awe, joy, and trembling, as on the day when [the Torah] was given at Sinai."

The Torah does not describe the *hakhel* ceremony which was held during Sukkot at the end of the sabbatical year. Other, similar ceremonies are described in the Bible, but these were held at different times. There are descriptions of gatherings of the people – men, women and children – when parts of the Torah were read to them, and the rabbis even inferred rules governing the *hakhel* from these ceremonies. Such gatherings were organized by Joshua (Josh. 8:35; 23–24), Solomon (I Kings 8; II Chr. 6–7), Josiah (II Kings 23:1–3; II Chron. 34:29–32), and Ezra and Nehemiah (Ezra 10:1; Neh. 8:3).

The rabbis note that the *hakhel* ceremony was observed in the First Temple period during the reign of Rehoboam (Yerushalmi *'Avodah Zarah* 1.5; Bavli *Sanhedrin* 101b), and near the end of the Second Temple period when King Agrippa led the ceremony (*Mishnah Sotah* 7.8). In another description of the ceremony, we are told that R. Tarfon participated (Yerushalmi *Megillah* 1.10 and *Horayot* 3.2).

With the destruction of the Temple, the *hakhel* ceremony ceased to be observed. Without a national framework in the land of Israel, no point remained in holding this ceremony. Indeed, no *hakhel* ceremony was held throughout the long generations of exile, and the rabbis did not even establish any ceremonies "in memory of *hakhel*" in the way that they established certain practices "in memory of the Temple." Nevertheless, during the period immediately after the destruction of the Second Temple, a ceremony was held that might have been intended to commemorate the original *hakhel* ceremony. Thus we read in *Tosefta Sotah* 7.9:

> Once R. Johanan b. Beroka and R. Eleazar Hisma came from Yavneh to Lod and went to welcome R. Joshua in Peqi'in. R. Joshua asked them: What new teaching was there in the *beit midrash* today? They replied, We are your disciples and we drink your waters. He replied: Even so, there is no *beit midrash* without some novel teaching. Whose Sabbath was it? [They replied:] It was the Sabbath of R. Eleazar b. Azariah. "And what was the theme of his discourse?" "Assemble the people, men, women, and children" (Deut. 31:12). He said to them, What did [R. Eleazar] teach about this? They answered, he taught thus: If the men came to learn, the women came to hear, but why did the children come? In order to grant reward to the people who bring them.

According to *Massekhet Soferim* (18:8), this sermon or a similar one was delivered on the day that R. Eleazar b. Azariah was appointed head of the academy. R. Eleazar began by saying: "You are standing here today, all of you, your children and your women. The men have come to hear, the women to be rewarded for coming. Why were the children brought? To reward those who bring them."[1]

These sources describe the period when the patriarchate was shared by Rabban Gamaliel and R. Eleazar ben Azariah, with Rabban Gamaliel delivering the sermon on three Sabbaths and R. Eleazar b. Azariah on the fourth Sabbath. Hence the question, "Whose Sabbath was it?" (see *Berakhot* 28a).

The wording of the question "Whose Sabbath was it *today*," and similarly the following question: "What was the theme of his discourse *today*" (for the word "today," see *Bamidbar Rabbah* 14.4), as well as the reading in *Hagigah* 3a, "What new teachings were heard in the *beit midrash* today," imply that this incident took place on the Sabbath. But if so, how did the rabbis travel such long distances on the Sabbath? The distance between Lod and Yavneh or even Peqi'in[2] is far greater than may be traversed on the Sabbath. Indeed, it is not permitted to violate the laws of the "sabbath boundaries" (*tehum Shabbat*) even to greet one's teacher (*'Eruvin* 36b).

Likewise, it is strange that R. Eleazar ben Azariah's sermon seems to address several themes. The students tell R. Joshua that R. Eleazar ben Azariah delivered his sermon about *Parashat Hakhel* (verses in *Parashat Vayelekh*) and verses from *Ki Tavo* and *Kohelet*. (In some versions, it was R. Joshua who delivered the sermon on the verses of *Kohelet*; see *Hagigah* 3a.)

Accordingly, we suggest that this event took place during *Hol ha-Mo'ed Sukkot*, and that R. Eleazar ben Azariah held a sort of *hakhel* ceremony.[3]

---

[1] Cf. *Mekhilta de-Rabbi Ishmael*, Bo, Pisha, 16, s.v. *li hu*.

[2] See Lieberman, *Tosefta Ki-Fshutah* ad loc. (p. 679), for a discussion of whether this refers to Peqi'in in the Galilee or in Judea.

[3] Cf. R. Hayyim Zvi Taubes, *Sefer Hakhel* (Kefar Darom 2001), p. 12, and Shmuel Kalman Mirsky, ibid., p. 647; Shmuel Zanvil Kahana, *Be-Vo Kol Yisrael* (Jerusalem 1995), pp. 25–26; Shlomo Na'eh, "Sidrei Keri'at ha-Torah be-Erez Israel: 'Iyyun

The subject of his sermon was *Parashat Hakhel*. R. Eleazar continued by expounding verses from the Torah which were read by the king from *Parashat Ki Tavo* before the *Tokhehah*, verses that stress the nationalist aspect of *hakhel* – "Who is like your people Israel, a nation unique in all the world." The final homily delivered at this gathering deals with *Kohelet*, citing verses that were recited in the *hakhel* ceremony, as implied by the name of this book (*Kohelet* literally means "assembler"). Indeed, we read in *Kohelet Rabbah* 1.1: "Why is the book of *Kohelet* called *Kohelet*? Because its contents were recited at the *hakhel* ceremony, as it is written, 'Then Shlomo gathered (*az yakhel*).'" By expounding verses from the book of *Kohelet*, R. Eleazar ben Azariah also confirmed the sanctity of this book, in accordance with a decision he rendered on the day he was appointed patriarch (Mishnah *Yadayim* 3:5).

In the course of time, this custom to expound *Kohelet* at ceremonies held in commemoration of *hakhel* led some communities to establish the custom of reading of the Book of *Kohelet* every year at Sukkot.[4] Interestingly, R. Eleazar ben Azariah completed his exegesis of this book with a comment on the opening verse of Deuteronomy: "'These are the words' (Deut. 1:1) – 'All of them were given by one shepherd' (Eccl. 12:11). One God gave them, one leader uttered them, from the mouth of the Lord of all creation, blessed be He, as it is written: 'And God spoke all these words'" (*Hagigah* 3a). Indeed, the first verse in the book of Deuteronomy, cited here, introduced the king's Torah reading at the *hakhel* ceremony.[5]

As patriarch, R. Eleazar b. Azariah presided over the ceremony. R. Joshua's question "Whose Sabbath was it today?" need not be interpreted to mean that this happened on the Sabbath. Rather, this might mean "Who was there," or "who presided over the ceremony"? The division of responsibility between the two leaders might have taken place on a weekly

---

Mehudash," *Tarbiz* 67 (1998), pp. 184–186. I thank Dr. Aaron Ahrend for drawing my attention to this article.

[4] R. Avraham Ha-Yarhi, in his *Sefer ha-Manhig*, writes of the custom of reading Kohelet on Sukkot: "I found a pleasing explanation – King Solomon of blessed memory read it during the *hakhel* ceremony on the holiday."

[5] In other words, the verse expounded was Deut. 1:1 and not Exodus 20:1. See Na'eh (above, n. 3), n. 79.

basis. The question "whose Sabbath?" would then mean, "Whose week was it?"[6] Perhaps R. Eleazar b. Azariah's turn to deliver the sermon fell on *Hol ha-Mo'ed Sukkot*, and hence he led the ceremony in commemoration of *hakhel*.

R. Joshua's remark in *Tosefta Sotah* 7:11, "The generation in whose midst R. Eleazar dwells is not orphaned," might not refer just to R. Eleazar's biblical interpretations, but to the ceremony commemorating *hakhel*. Such a ceremony would have reinforced R. Eleazar's position as patriarch after the crisis with Rabban Gamaliel, in addition to strengthening the nation as a whole, burdened as they were with the spiritual and practical difficulties which befell them after the Temple's destruction. The very act of commemorating the Temple and the *hakhel* ceremony only a few years after the destruction of the Temple showed that "that generation was not orphaned," for it had leadership.

When we examine the parallel texts, which describe R. Eleazar b. Azariah as delivering similar homilies, whether on the day of his appointment or on other occasions, we see that R. Eleazar called upon the rabbis to open the houses of study to everyone. He encouraged the people – men, women and children – to join forces with Torah scholars in a variety of ways. Such encouragement, delivered on an occasion that represented a sort of "commemoration of *hakhel*" when people were coming to welcome him, would have strengthened Torah study among the masses after the destruction of the Temple.[7]

We know of no attempts in later generations, before the establishment of the State of Israel, to commemorate the *hakhel* ceremony. Over a hundred years ago, however, R. Eliyahu David Rabinowitz-Te'omim of Ponevitz (Aderet), who was later appointed rabbi of Jerusalem, proposed observing such a ceremony. He wrote an unsigned treatise, *Zekher le-Mikdash*,[8] in which he called for the observance of a ceremony commemorating *hakhel*. He took no practical steps to implement this

---

[6] See J. N. Epstein, *Mevo'ot le-Sifrut ha-Tanna'im* (Jerusalem 1957), p. 427.

[7] R. Meir Simhah Ha-Kohen of Dvinsk expanded on this idea in his *Meshekh Hokhmah* on Deut. 31:9 (ed. Copperman, p. 297).

[8] Reprinted in *Sefer Hakhel* (above, n. 3), p. 495.

suggestion, even at the end of the sabbatical year of 5664 (1924), when he was rabbi of Jerusalem, but he was the first scholar to make such a suggestion.

The first ceremony commemorating *hakhel*, following the call of Rabbi Rabinowitz-Teomim, took place at the end of the last sabbatical year before the establishment of the State of Israel, in Sukkot 5706 (1946). Perhaps observance of this ceremony reflected the feeling that the people of Israel were indeed on the threshold of renewed national sovereignty in their land. This initiative was supported by R. Shmuel Zanvil Kahana, who later became Director-General of the Ministry of Religions of the State of Israel, and who supported other, similar gatherings later on. Since this initial ceremony, other ceremonies commemorating *hakhel*, some modest and others extravagant, are held in Israel at the end of every sabbatical year.

Parashat Ve-Zot Ha-Berakhah

"HE SHONE UPON THEM FROM SEIR; HE APPEARED FROM MOUNT PARAN"

Prof. Hannah Kasher
Department of Philosophy

TWO BLESSINGS ARE RECITED before studying Torah: "Blessed are You...Who has chosen us from among all the nations and given us His Torah," and "Blessed are You...Who has given us a Torah of truth and planted eternal life within us." Both of these statements consist of two parts joined by the Hebrew word for "and," which is represented the Hebrew letter *vav*. However, this letter sometimes explains what precedes it (the so-called exegetical *vav*) rather than serving as a conjunction. Interpreting the *vav* this way, these blessings would mean: "Blessed are You...Who chose us from among all the nations *by* giving us His Torah," and "Blessed are You...Who has given us a Torah of truth *and in doing so* planted eternal life within us." According to this interpretation, the giving of the Torah reflects God's choice of the Jews as His people and is an intrinsically rewarding act, insofar as it confers eternal life on those who accept the Torah.

This assumption that the giving of the Torah is an intrinsically rewarding act raises the question: why were the Jews singled out for this privilege, and why was the Torah not given to any other nations?[1] Indeed,

---

[1] Cf. M. Hirshman, *Torah le-Khol Ba'ei 'Olam* (Tel Aviv 1999), especially pp. 10–95.

some gentiles have claimed that God discriminated against them by not granting them the Torah.[2]

> Why did the merciful Lord cause the nations...to be doomed because of lack of knowledge of God's ways? (Porphyry, third-century C.E. neo-Platonic philosopher)

> He left all the nations from East to West and North to South...to worship idols...except for one small nation...If He is equally the God of us all and the Creator of all, why did He estrange Himself from us? (Julian the Apostate, fourth-century C.E. Roman emperor).

This question is already addressed by various Midrashim, which answer it by citing a verse from our Torah reading, "He shone upon them from Seir; He appeared from Mount Paran (Deut. 33:2):[3]

> [The Gentiles asked God]: Lord of the Universe, did You give us the Torah, that we declined to accept it? – [The Talmud replies:] How could they say such a thing? Why, it is written: "The Lord came down from Sinai and shone upon them from Seir; He appeared from Mount Paran." And similarly it is written: "God comes from Teman" (Hab. 3:3)...and R. Johanan said: This teaches us that the Holy One blessed be He offered the Torah to every nation and to every tongue, but no one accepted it until He came to Israel, who accepted it ('Avodah Zarah 2b).

According to this Midrash, the Torah was offered to other nations before it was offered to the Jews, but the other nations refused to accept it. In other

---

[2] See D. Rokeah, *Ha-Pulmus Bein Yehudim ve-Nozrim 'al ha-Behirah*, in S. Almog and M. Heyd (editors), *Ra'ayon ha-Behirah be-Yisra'el u-va-'Ammim* (Jerusalem 1991), pp. 73–75.

[3] For additional sources and discussion, see E. E. Urbach, *Hazal, Pirkei Emunot ve-De'ot* (Jerusalem 1969), pp. 472–474, and J. Heinemann, *Aggadot ve-Toledotehen* (Jerusalem 1974), pp. 118–119.

words, it was not God who chose Israel, but it was the other nations who refused to accept the Torah that led to the Torah being given to the Jews.

The claim of the non-Jews that God acted unfairly towards them in choosing to give the Torah to only one nation prompted various responses in Jewish thought. According to one view, the revelation to the Jewish people was uniquely suited to their special qualities. R. Judah Halevi offered such an explanation in his *Kuzari*. In this book, which reports a discussion between the Kuzarite king, a converted heathen, and a rabbi, this question is raised several times. The first time (1.26–27), after the Kuzarite king objects to the rabbi that "your belief is confined to yourselves," the rabbi responds:

> Yes, but any gentile who joins us unconditionally shares our good fortune, without, however, being quite equal to us. If the Law was binding on us only because God created us, white men and black men would be equal, since God created them all. But the Law was given to us because God led us out of Egypt and He remained attached to us, since we are the pick of mankind.

The Kuzari's explanation here provides an answer to the objection of Julian the Apostate, cited earlier, according to which God unfairly estranged himself from the various peoples on earth. R. Judah Halevi explains that while all men are creatures of God, the Torah expresses a special bond between God and man that applies only to a particular elite group.

The Kuzarite king raises the question of inequality in another context as well (1.101-103). There the rabbi presents the exclusivist claim that "Moses invited only his people and those of his own tongue to accept his law." The Kuzarite king objected: "Would it not have been better or more commensurate with divine wisdom if all mankind had been guided in the true path?" To this the rabbi responded with a rhetorical question: "Would it not have been best for all animals to have been reasonable beings, or capable of speech?" This argumentation reflects one of the basic assumptions of R. Judah Halevi – that not all creatures (or men) are equal, and that the Jews are the pinnacle of creation. Accordingly, the Torah enables the Jews, who occupy the highest level of creation, to realize their innate qualities and establish a special relationship with God.

Maharal follows in R. Judah Halevi's footsteps. After quoting the familiar Midrash that God offered the Torah to all the nations, Maharal explains (*Gevurot Hashem*, 72):

> We do not find that God sent [the nations] prophets. Rather, he checked their suitability to receive the Torah. He did not find them prepared, and this is why they were rejected. For certainly an animal "rejects" intelligence because he lacks an infrastructure for intelligence, and similarly the Gentiles were not prepared to accept the Torah, but Israel was.

According to Maharal, the Midrash does not mean that God sent every nation a prophet and that He found them unwilling to receive the Torah. Rather, the "unwillingness" of the nations to receive the Torah as described by the Midrash refers to the nations' innate inability to accept the Torah. Maharal's explanation of this Midrash is thus reminiscent of R. Judah Halevi's notion of the various levels of creation: Just as animals are unable to attain a human level of intelligence, so too the Gentiles lack the qualities which would enable them to accept the Torah. In similar vein, Rav Kook wrote that "only a prepared vessel in the form of a holy nation, in whose soul the Divine light is inscribed, can receive this hidden prize" (*'Olat Re'iyah*, in the commentary on Yigdal).

Another answer was provided by Maimonides in his *Guide to the Perplexed* (2.25). In the course of discussing our question Maimonides explains: "The answer is...that this was God's will. So decreed His divine wisdom...We cannot fathom His will or the ways of His Wisdom."

To be sure, this suggestion is evasive, as already noted by the fourteenth-century commentator on Maimonides, R. Moses of Narbonne, who proposed an alternative explanation as being more in line with Maimonides' teachings (see *Sheloshah Kadmonei Mefarshei ha-Torah*, 36b):

> Why did God give His Torah to a particular nation and not another? Because the prophet arose from among this people, and

we accepted our roots from our first ancestor [Abraham]...When we were borne on eagles' wings and God brought us close to Him...He showed us the Great Teacher [Moses], and we declared "we will observe" [the commandments] before "we will listen" [to them].

According to this explanation, the Jews were given the Torah because the person who was fit to serve as the agent for this – Moses – was born to the Jews. Thus, for R. Moses of Narbonne, a combination of natural and historical circumstances was responsible for the Jews being chosen to receive the Torah.

Hundreds of years later, in the eighteenth century, Moses Mendelssohn also discussed this question. He claimed that "according to the true tenets of Judaism, all the world's inhabitants are invited to share in a life of contentment," for they were all granted "the powers of reason." To think that only a specific religious revelation could facilitate such a life was to limit God's power and goodness. In the nineteenth century, Rabbi Ezriel Hildesheimer wrote in one of his responsa that God's initial inclination was universal: "All the inhabitants of the world are the handiwork of the Creator, blessed be He: one God created us all. When He appeared in His goodness to crown Israel with the Torah, He intended to give it to all the people of the world, as the Rabbis said in *Avodah Zarah* 2b." Nevertheless, like Maharal, R. Hildesheimer suggests that the Gentiles could not receive the Torah because of their unsuitability: "When he saw meanness of spirit in them, He gave [the Torah] to Israel alone." Nevertheless, R. Hildesheimer maintains that God wanted to improve the Gentiles' character, and so He chose Israel as "priests of Light":

And so it is written: "Indeed, all the earth is Mine, but you shall be to Me a kingdom of priests" (Ex. 19:5-6). For all the earth is Mine, and I want everyone to have merit. But since there is no light shining among them, you shall be priests for all the peoples: when you draw close to Me, they too will see the light.